Advance Praise for *The Soul of Civility*

"I need this book. And you do too."

—Joel Stein, author of *In Defense of Elitism*

"*The Soul of Civility* offers pearls of philosophical wisdom and engaging historical anecdotes all woven into a compelling argument for rediscovering the virtue of civility. Her exploration of the distinction between mere politeness and genuine civility, and the centrality of civility to human flourishing couldn't be more timely or needed."   —Donald Robertson, author of *How to Think Like a Roman Emperor*

"This book should be at the top of the reading list for anyone who is eager to reconnect with a vital part of our heritage, and to rediscover a proven path to renewing America's social institutions."   —Don Eberly, author of *Restoring the Good Society* and *America's Promise*

"*The Soul of Civility* is a book that needed to be written, at a moment in American history marked by deepening rancor and polarization, and by growing challenges to traditional norms of decency and civility."   —George H. Nash, PhD, author of *The Conservative Intellectual Movement in America Since 1945*

"While most commentators are seeking to sow division during this time of cultural crisis, Hudson provides a hopeful vision for America's future rooted in solidarity, neighborliness, and faith in our best traditions."   —John A. Burtka, president and CEO, Intercollegiate Studies Institute

"We live in a divided moment where reasonable and clear thinking is urgently needed. Knowing that Alexandra Hudson is a leading voice in our public discourse and of her generation, I have hope for the future of our country."

—Lee Hamilton, former Democratic congressman from Indiana and founding board member of the National Institute for Civil Discourse

"Alexandra Hudson is a force of nature. Graceful in her prose and gracious in her spirit, she is the perfect author to tackle the topic of manners and civil society in our frequently ill-mannered and uncivil moment."

—Jim Antle, editor, *Washington Examiner*

"An insightful and inspiring call to civility in our private and public lives, and an amazing tour of what the great thinkers of history have said on the topic. This history of civility is both cautionary and comforting—as is this powerful book!"

—William J. Doherty, PhD, professor of family social science at the University of Minnesota, and cofounder of Braver Angels

The SOUL *of* CIVILITY

Also from the Author

Storytelling and the Human Condition,
a televisual series and forthcoming book produced
in partnership with Wondrium, formerly
"The Great Courses"

The SOUL *of*
CIVILITY

Timeless Principles to Heal
Society and Ourselves

ALEXANDRA HUDSON

ST. MARTIN'S
PRESS
NEW YORK

First published in the United States by St. Martin's Press,
an imprint of St. Martin's Publishing Group

THE SOUL OF CIVILITY. Copyright © 2023 by Alexandra Hudson. All rights
reserved. Printed in the United States of America. For information, address
St. Martin's Publishing Group, 120 Broadway, New York, NY 10271.

www.stmartins.com

Designed by Steven Seighman

Painting by Alicia Zanoni Lawrence, by commission of
The Sagamore Institute

Library of Congress Cataloging-in-Publication Data

Names: Hudson, Alexandra, author.
Title: The soul of civility : timeless principles to heal society and
    ourselves / Alexandra Hudson.
Description: First edition. | New York : St. Martin's Press, [2023] |
    Includes bibliographical references and index.
Identifiers: LCCN 2023016824 | ISBN 9781250277787 (hardcover) |
    ISBN 9781250277794 (ebook)
Subjects: LCSH: Civil society. | Conduct of life.
Classification: LCC JC337 .H8 2023 | DDC 306.2—
    dc23/eng/20230531
LC record available at https://lccn.loc.gov/2023016824

Our books may be purchased in bulk for promotional, educational, or business use. Please contact your local bookseller or the Macmillan Corporate
and Premium Sales Department at 1-800-221-7945, extension 5442, or by
email at MacmillanSpecialMarkets@macmillan.com.

First Edition: 2023

10   9   8   7   6   5   4   3   2   1

To Percival James and Sophia Margaux: You made us parents while I wrote this book, and grant us more joy each day than I ever imagined possible. Thank you for giving me the reason and motivation to finish this book. I hope that it helps to make our world a brighter place for you both to grow up in.

And to Grandma Margaret: You never had the opportunity to meet my children, but thank you for showing me that one person— one magnanimous soul—could create with their life a mellifluous echo that would make the world a more joy-filled place, one interaction at a time.

Contents

PART I: An Enduring Dilemma

PART II: Why Civility?

PART III: Civility in Practice

Part I

AN ENDURING DILEMMA

Introduction:
Why This Book Exists

Did you know there are at least four women named Judith who are internationally renowned experts on manners? There is Judith Ré of the Judith Ré Academie, Judith Bowman of the National Civility Foundation and Protocol Consultants International, and Judith Martin—perhaps the foremost Judith in the manners industry—who has for nearly half a century written a syndicated advice column as "Miss Manners."

Then, there is Judith Johnston Vankevich, also known as Judi the Manners Lady, to whom I am particularly partial. She is my personal favorite of these Judiths of the courtesy biz for many reasons, the most salient being the fact that she is also my mother.[1] Her life—defined by selflessness, by hospitality to the stranger, and by embracing the richness inherent in life with others—was a powerful example to my brothers and me growing up. Informed by their Christian faith, my parents raised us with beneficence, a lovely old word for "active goodness." Beyond the "do no harm" principle that life with others requires, we were taught to seek opportunities to brighten the lives of those around us.

My mother also instructed us in politeness: the techniques of mores, manners, and etiquette. Manners mattered to my mother because, she was fond of saying, they are an outward expression of our inward character. I remember I once surprised her when I divulged that I'd learned, over the course of writing this book, that this sentiment was also expressed by etiquette expert Emily Post a century prior. "Great minds can come to the same ideas independently," she quipped, a sentiment that, as we'll discover in Chapter 2, held more wisdom than I realized at the time.

Being constitutionally allergic to authority, I sometimes questioned arbitrary, capricious, and superficial niceties. When I was asked to set the table with forks of different sizes on the left and spoons and knives on the right, I questioned why we set the table as we do—or why we use forks and knives at all! I had difficulty accepting that we should continue to do things just because we've always done them, or because someone, some-where, sometime had once decided that we should. In our egal-itarian, informal moment, what purpose do stuffy norms serve, and should we have norms that show preference to people of certain ages or genders over others? I was also willing—and maybe a little too eager—to dispense with propriety and the rules of politeness if they affronted my sense of justice.

Despite my mistrust of rules of etiquette, I found that my mother's promise—that they would smooth over our interactions with others and lead to friendships, success, and happiness—came true. Politeness's polish, I found, gave me a slight advan-tage in school, work, and life in general.

Politeness and Its Discontents

The rules worked well for me.

Until they didn't.

When I moved to Washington, DC, and took a job in pol-itics, my confidence in politeness was shaken. I discovered that those who survived and succeeded in Washington often did so using two tactics: punishing ruthlessness or extreme politesse. At first, I thought these two modes were opposites, two poles on the spectrum.

I learned that instead they were two sides of the same coin: both originated from a dark place in the human spirit—a place where people are willing to instrumentalize and use others as means to their own selfish ends.

While some—usually the younger, greener politicos—chose to be overly aggressive and hostile, the seasoned political operators were cleverer. They knew that overt aggression would only take them so far. They instead used *politeness* as their weapon of choice. This allowed them to shroud their opportunism in the *appearance* of altruism, disguising their true aims while disarming their opponents. When I first met these people, I thought that I had finally found a contingent who, like me, had faith enough in social pleasantries to gloss over differences and enable working relationships. But I soon came to realize that, for them, the rules were merely a tool of self-aggrandizement. They sabotaged anyone who threatened their goals. I was confused. I heard my mother's words echo in my ears: "Manners reflect our inner character." And yet I was surrounded by people who were polished and well-mannered enough, but also ruthless and cruel.

One day, a colleague approached to ask for help with a project, a request made with an earnest smile and in saccharine, honeyed tones while telling me how particularly radiant I looked that day. His polish smoothed the path to making his request, and I agreed to assist—not realizing that he expected me to do the entire project for him. Once I sent him the completed project, gone were the pleasantries. He passed my work off as his own, and even presented my ideas at a meeting, without so much as an acknowledgment of the help I had lent him.

He had gotten what he wanted from me, and because I was no longer useful, he no longer bothered with trivialities such as compliments and courtesy.

One may smile, and smile, and be a villain.

—William Shakespeare

At least with those who chose bellicosity in their interactions with others, I knew what to expect. With the polite contingent I worked alongside, the subterfuge threw me. It felt like guerrilla warfare: I would receive their praise one moment, and then prepare for attack the next. I didn't know what to make of this mismatch between manners and morals that surrounded me, but I was determined to weather this new terrain. In this survival-of-the-fittest environment, I tacked hard in the direction that seemed most suited to success: extreme *politeness*. I did not use politeness as a ruse to actively undermine others, as I saw others do.

But I now realize that my pleasantness toward others was a coping mechanism, and masked my foundational fear: I saw people callously cast aside and fired at a moment's notice, and lived for a year of my life knowing that any day, at any time, and for any reason, I could be next. My hope was that if enough people saw me as agreeable and polite, I might be spared. Growing up, politeness had helped me advance. Now it helped me survive.

I brought in cupcakes to celebrate birthdays, handed out Christmas and Easter cards, invited coworkers to cocktail parties and dinner at my home, and took them out to coffee. My mother modeled kindness and hospitality for us, and these practices were enmeshed in our lives growing up, so doing these things had long been second nature to me. To this day, our family still sends Christmas and Easter cards, and hosting dinners and parties remains a regular practice in our home. I continue to have faith in the transformative power of friendship and hospitality—themes we'll explore throughout this book.

But looking back, when I practiced these things in government, I realize I had a second, subliminal hope for them, too: that they would help me transcend the office power games and perpetual angling, and help me become someone who everyone thought was too nice to be a target of sabotage or sacking. I may have performed kind actions in inviting my colleagues to our home—but they were at times for the wrong reasons. The pressure of being externally pleasant and agreeable, while internally fearing for my professional survival, weighed on me. Beneath these acts was fear. This strained my soul, exhausting me emotionally and physically. Though I felt stuck in a toxic environment, I knew my soul could not tolerate the burden of this strained and synthetic way of being much longer.

Lessons on Civility from Dr. King

In fall 2017, I joined a group of congressional staffers, civil servants, and political appointees from across the political spectrum on a weekend retreat along Maryland's Wye River at the invitation of the Aspen Institute, a DC-based think tank. The majestic trees, the crisp air, the ripples of the river, and the whispers of the clouds elevated our minds from the mire of Washington, and provided an ideal backdrop to our exploration of the weekend's theme: challenges to civil discourse in America, past and present. Our country was *founded* on protest and revolution. Could these modes ever be civil? Is civility always good—or are there times when departing from civility is justified? And what *is* civility anyway? The disagreement was honest, fierce, and respectful. Our conversations about big and important ideas were a soul-refreshing reprieve from the survivalism and animosity that defined my day-to-day experience in government. For the first time in nearly a year, I felt able to voice my thoughts honestly and without fear of offending anyone and making myself a target. It was a breath of fresh air, and invigorated my soul.

That weekend led me to several realizations about the role of civility, and inspired me to write the book you're now enjoying. As our group discussed Martin Luther King, Jr.'s "Letter from Birmingham Jail," I recognized three insights about civility— the "why" behind civility and our duty to respect others that I had longed for my entire life—which I had not fully appreciated before. The letter helped me understand why I was dissatisfied with the two extremes of aggressive hostility and duplicitous politeness so pervasive during my service in government. It also reminded me that it wasn't just government that struggled with instrumentalizing others. Doing so was part of the human condition, and could happen within any vocation, in any environ, in any period of time.

Now is the time to lift our national policy from the quicksand of racial injustice to the solid rock of human dignity.

—Martin Luther King, Jr., "Letter from Birmingham Jail"

First, Dr. King's letter taught me that there is a moral foundation for civility. Treating others with decency, dignity, and respect is nonnegotiable, because they are our fellow human beings. When discussing the evils of racial segregation, Dr. King invoked Martin Buber's I-it and

I-thou distinction. It is wrong to use others, because this treats a *person*—a "thou"—as though they were a *thing*—an "it." Why? As Dr. King said, human beings share an irreducible, equal moral worth. We have *dignity*, Dr. King noted, which is why he dedicated his life to creating a world without the evils of racism, and "in which all men will respect the dignity and worth of human personality."

Dr. King's words helped me realize that the defining ethos of my time in government was instrumentalizing others—seeing them as a means to an end instead of beings with dignity and moral worth, and as ends in themselves. But this tendency is not unique to politics or DC. It can surface anywhere, anytime, because it emerges from part of the human personality that we all share. Human dignity was the moral bedrock for Dr. King's battle against racism. It is also the moral foundation for civility and any environment of human flourishing.

The two extremes of aggression and faux niceness, present during my government service and in our public life more broadly, corrode human dignity because they instrumentalize human beings—treating them as "its" and not "thous." Those who are hostile and demeaning to others see people as mere means or obstacles to their ends, to be degraded and discarded along the way. Those who weaponize politeness—putting a polished exterior over malicious intent—view human beings as pawns to be manipulated. We must recover Dr. King's view of personhood and human dignity—a way of looking at others that sees them as ends in themselves, and worthy of our respect. Dr. King's philosophy of personhood helps us recover the moral foundation of civility: the basic duty we have to all people, including those who are unlike us, who disagree with us, or who can do nothing for us in return.

Second, in the same way that there are just and unjust *formal* laws, there are just and unjust *informal* laws. Informal laws include mores, manners, and social norms. Dr. King's letter offers a litmus test for how to distinguish between just and unjust laws. A just law is one that uplifts human personality, while an unjust law degrades it. Dr. King writes, "All segregation statutes are unjust because segregation distorts the soul and damages the personality. It gives the segregator a false sense of superiority and the segregated a false sense of inferiority."

His framework also applies to norms of civility, and can help us distinguish between just and unjust informal social mores. To paraphrase Dr. King, any social norm that uplifts human personality is just, while any norm that degrades human personality is unjust. A just social norm is rooted in eternal and natural law. Social norms that divide, silence, and oppress distort the soul and damage the human personality—that of the person being oppressed, but also that of the one who does the oppressing. Our task is to continue King's work, elevating norms that affirm the dignity of the human person and the unity of the human community, and devaluing norms that degrade personhood and divide us. King knew that not all laws, formal or informal, were equal, and that even laws formed with good intent could be applied in unjust ways.

I found this to be true in government when I saw people use norms of common decency and courtesy as a means of disarming and undermining unsuspecting others. Even well-intended norms can be applied in ways that instrumentalize others and can therefore be harmful. The motivation behind our compliance with social practices matters. It can transform a just law or norm into an unjust one. Blindly following hard-and-fast social rules—like unthinkingly following the blunt instrument of law—is not enough to promote justice, and can sometimes lead to injustice. Our loyalty must be to the "bedrock of human dignity"—the moral foundation of all just formal and informal laws—first.

Third, there is a fundamental difference between civility and politeness. People tend to use these terms interchangeably when referring to all things to do with mores, manners, and etiquette, as well as to general standards of social propriety and living well together. But not all social norms are equal—or desirable. Civility—the motivation behind our conduct that sees other persons as our moral equals and worthy of basic respect—is much deeper, richer, and of greater import than politeness, or external compliance with rules of etiquette. Politeness and manners are the *form*, the *technique*, of an act, but civility is more.

King's letter helped me realize the need to identify and name the way of being that allows us to navigate life together amid deep difference. This is civility. Instead of focusing on the *form* alone, civility gets to the *motivation* of an act. Civility is a disposition that recognizes and respects the common humanity, the fundamental personhood, and the inherent dignity of other human beings. In doing so, civility sometimes *requires* that we act in ways that *appear* deeply impolite, such as telling people difficult truths or engaging in civil disobedience—the example that King used.

History is peppered with brave individuals who stood up to the authorities of their day out of commitment to a higher moral authority. King gives the examples of Shadrach, Meshach, and Abednego's rejection of the laws of King Nebuchadnezzar, the early Christians who were willing to face the lions rather than renounce their faith, and even those who participated in the Boston Tea Party—the act of disobedience that instigated America's war for independence. Protest and civil disobedience, I came to realize, epitomize the soul of civility—the disposition and conduct befitting a member of the *civitas*, or the city and political community of citizens. Life in human community requires that we have a basic respect for our fellow persons.

This fundamental respect for the personhood of others empowers us—and in fact, obligates us—to be civil, not polite. We owe others the truth when we think they're wrong. We owe our fellow citizens and community action in the face of injustice. I realized that the tradition of civil disobedience is central to reviving a more accurate understanding of civility in our own era, and to recovering a mode of interacting that can enable us to navigate profound disagreements.

Finally, I realized that when we are uncivil to others, we hurt ourselves. King wrote that racist laws gave the segregator a false sense of superiority and the segregated a false sense of inferiority. Like segregation, incivility deforms the soul of both the abuser and the abused. Also like segregation, incivility often originates from an inaccurately low view of personhood. Often, people lash out at others because of their own inaccurate view of self. This can manifest in their deriving their validation in abusing others; but harming others only makes them feel lesser. Appreciating the gift of being human—and realizing that when we hurt others with our incivility, we hurt ourselves—is central to reclaiming basic decency in our world.

[Manners are at their] most perfect [when] the requirements of inner dispositions and proper form are both completely fulfilled.

—Xunzi, third-century Chinese philosopher and student of Confucius

The Difference Between Civility and Politeness

Rereading Dr. King's "Letter from Birmingham Jail" that weekend at the Aspen Institute clarified for me the essential difference between *civility* and *politeness*. Civility is a *disposition*, a way of seeing others as beings endowed with dignity and inherently valuable. Politeness, by contrast, is a *technique:* it is decorum, mores, and etiquette. Politeness, the thing that manners and mores serve, is neither good nor bad in itself. It can be used for good or for ill depending on a person's inner motivation—depending on whether they've adopted the disposition of civility. At its best, the form of politeness can help mitigate the awkwardness, discomfort, and annoyance inherent in social life—but it will only ever apply surface-level fixes, and will never be enough to help us navigate our profound and important disagreements. At its worst, politeness makes difference and disagreement worse by fostering feelings of selfishness, pride, and superiority over others. Politeness can be and has been weaponized to penalize difference, oppress vulnerable populations and voices, and silence dissent.

Civility requires rediscovering a general regard for our fellow persons and citizens. It demands that we revive the basic respect we're all owed, and that we owe to one another, in light of our shared moral status as members of the human community. We need the disposition that comes from seeing other persons as intrinsically valuable and worthy of respect, despite deep differences. The word "respect" comes from the Latin word "*specere*," which means "to look at." Respect calls us to "re-inspect" others, to see them as they really are, as beings with innate dignity, and to treat them with the decency and civility they deserve as members of the human community.

On its own, the outer form of politeness unmarried to the

inner disposition of civility is never enough, and never will be. Recovering civility, by contrast, may be our only hope for navigating and emerging from our fraught and divided present times.

Circular Definitions of Civility and Politeness

We lack precision in how we distinguish civility from politeness. We often use the words interchangeably, and have done so for a long time. When people hear the word "civility" and recoil, it's often because they've seen the word weaponized and used to silence dissent and oppress free expression. But they've confused civility with politeness. It's common to group civility and politeness together—calling for more or less of them, part and parcel. Confusion around these words and their meanings is understandable. Even the dictionary defines these two words synonymously.

The first two entries for the definition of the word "civility" are in terms of politeness: "courtesy; politeness" and "a polite action or expression."[2] In parallel, the entry for "politeness" is defined in terms of civility: "courteous; civil."[3] Samuel Johnson's 1755 *A Dictionary of the English Language*—the first definitive dictionary of the English language—got us off to a bad start and defined civility in terms of politeness, stating that civility encompassed both "freedom from barbarity; the state of being civilized" and "politeness; complaisance; elegance of behavior."[4] Given the circular definitions of these words, it's no wonder that we conflate and fail to distinguish between them.

Dictionaries, including Johnson's, are descriptive. They work within a given era to try to capture how the people of a certain era use words in everyday language. But definitions of words are not set in stone. Showing the difference between civility and politeness is a core goal of this book. I hope to change how we use these words, which will empower us to think more clearly about the respectful, peace-promoting conduct we need in our divided times.

The Etymology of Politeness and Civility

Disentangling civility from politeness is important to healing the discord of our day, but it also honors the words' etymologies, which underscore the crucial difference between them.

The word "polite" comes from the Latin *polire,* which means "to polish, to make smooth." Politeness focuses on external appearances; it is about "smoothing over" and diminishing our differences instead of equipping us to act in light of them.

"Civility" comes from the Latin *civilis,* which relates to the status, conduct, and character befitting a citizen of the *civitas,* or city. More than conformity to particular rules of conduct, civility is a general attitude toward life with others. Understanding the difference between civility and politeness is the beginning of the solution to our civility problem, and has the potential to change for the better the trajectory of our lives, our public discourse, our society, and our world.

Why the Difference Between Politeness and Civility Matters

After realizing the distinction between these two often-conflated concepts, I saw why aiming for politeness alone was not sufficient to remedy the divisions facing modern democracies. Politeness—in focusing only on compliance with superficial rules and techniques—allows people to do and say things that can *seem* respectful but that are deeply uncivil. I learned this firsthand while serving in government. Many of the modern criticisms of civility should, in fact, be directed toward politeness. While civility, grounded in respect for the personhood and human dignity of others, is *always* good, politeness can be—and frequently is—weaponized to silence and suppress disagreement. Civility never silences or steamrolls. In putting the dignity of the other person front and center, it instead seeks to listen and learn.

In addition to suffocating dialogue about important issues, politeness can also breed feelings of superiority by giving people an excuse to look down on those unfamiliar with certain rules and norms. These classist criticisms of divisive social rituals should all be directed toward abuses of politeness, not civility.

Civility requires respect of others, but also requires respect of self. Politeness, in focusing on external compliance with manners and norms, enables us to paper over important differences instead of grappling with them head on. Civility, as noted, enables us to discuss important differences while truly respecting others, but it also helps us respect ourselves

The fact that we can survive without manners, however, does not show that human nature doesn't need them in some deeper way. After all, we can survive without love, without children, without peace or comfort or friendship. But all those things are human needs, since we need them for our happiness. Without them, we are unfulfilled. And the same is true of manners.

—Roger Scruton, twentieth-century English philosopher

by empowering us to say no to others unapologetically, maintaining healthy personal boundaries.

Setting boundaries and saying "no" to others may seem impolite, and might be difficult for those of us who have been acclimated in the ways of politeness. Often, our culture values politeness, and inclines us to stay silent or say "yes" to things and people we may not want to because we don't want to offend them. But having firm personal boundaries, and ensuring our own personal space isn't encroached by becoming fluent in declining others with grace, is what civility requires, and is a means of respecting both others and ourselves.

Civility properly understood is not the problem causing our deep divides. It is in fact an essential part of solving our painful social and cultural fractures. Civility promotes the rigorous debate that might on the surface *seem* impolite but, nevertheless, authentically respects others. Civil conduct of this nature might not find a home in a high-society banquet hall. After all, we often hear that politics and religion are topics that the polite conversationalist should *avoid*. But such civil conduct is *essential* to our democracy, to our freedom, and to human flourishing across history and culture. The disposition of universal respect for our fellow human beings helps us act in ways that enable us to survive and thrive. Once we recognize the difference between politeness and civility, we see that politeness is unequal to the task of healing our social, political, and cultural rifts. Civility, meanwhile, might offer our best hope for doing so. Politeness is easy. Civility requires effort. But the hard work of civility is, as we'll see, the glue that has bound human communities and civilization across time and place. It's a difficult project that people have struggled with—but committed and recommitted to—for a long time.

	POLITENESS	CIVILITY
ETYMOLOGY	From the Latin word *polire* or "to smooth" or "polish." Politeness focuses on appearances, form, style. It smooths and polishes over our differences.	From the Latin word *civitas* or "city." Civility focuses on the disposition and conduct appropriate to citizens and their duty to the city.
ESSENCE	Focuses on technique, or compliance with rituals and rules.	Cultivates the right motivation *behind* an act instead of focusing on the act itself.
JUSTIFICATION	Practical. Can be abused to instrumentalize others and promote self-advancement. Facilitates behavioral coordination. Minimizes social friction.	Moral. Recognizes our shared humanity and the irreducible dignity we all share as human beings.

The difference between politeness and civility. Created by Alexandra Hudson, 2023.

Consider the difference between politeness and civility in these common, everyday situations.

Situation	The Polite Response	The Civil Response
Your boss gets a new haircut that looks terrible.	Politeness often does or says the right thing for the wrong reason. Flattery is a technique of choice for the polite person, who would compliment their boss on her haircut in an attempt to "smooth" things over before their upcoming annual bonus review meeting.	Civility rejects flattery. The civil person doesn't do or say things merely to win favor with others, because doing so isn't respectful toward them. The civil person would stay silent about the haircut, or they would find something else that they could compliment honestly.
You're at a formal dinner, and the guest next to you drinks from the bowl that you know is used for washing before a meal.	Politeness embraces classist rules of etiquette that divide because it allows one to feel superior to the uninitiated. The polite person would silently judge and look down on others for not recognizing a finger bowl for what it is.	Civility realizes that perfect knowledge of the rules of etiquette is not a proxy for genuinely other-regarding behavior. The civil person would overlook and immediately forget the unintentional faux pas, and strike up a conversation with their seatmate in an attempt to earnestly get to know them. Or they would discreetly inform them of their error so they might avoid it again in the future.

Situation	The Polite Response	The Civil Response
Someone you love and respect voices a political opinion with which you disagree.	Politeness "polishes" over difference and avoids tough conversations because that is the easier—if not respectful—course. The polite person would change the subject to something less controversial, smoothing over differing opinions in order to avoid the conflict.	Civility calls for telling the truth and having tough conversations, but doing so in love, care, and kindness for the other person. The civil person would voice their disagreement in a calm, respectful manner, knowing that respecting someone means not patronizing them. The civil person would also know how to gently de-escalate a conversation, as relationships matter more than winning an argument.

The difference between politeness and civility in action. Created by Alexandra Hudson, 2023.

The Plan

This book is about the question of how to do life together. We'll discover that peaceful coexistence with our fellow human beings is something we've been working at, and achieving with varying degrees of success, for ages—from the beginning of our species, in fact. Hunter-gatherer societies, the original human arrangement, and the cosmopolitan cities of our modern day have all asked the same question: What's the secret to getting on with one another despite difference and disagreement?

This book is an extended reflection on the question of how to harmoniously coexist with our fellow human beings. Each society has set up formal and informal institutions—laws and mores alike—to support its shared vision of the good and of mutual cooperation. This book draws from across the human historical record to examine how different groups across time and place have responded to the enduring dilemma of how to do life with others. This book looks at how these historical ideas about the timeless principles of civility and human flourishing apply to our own divided moment today, and how they can help us live richer and more fulfilling lives in relationship with others.

In Chapter 1, we'll discover the relatively intractable nature of our species' civility problem. The timelessness of our problem of civility is endemic to our nature. We are a species defined by self-love and love of others. We are an inherently cooperative and social species, but frequently our self-interest inhibits our ability to cooperate. Experts debate where precisely on the spectrum between these two instincts we fall, but no one disputes that both are present and foundational to the human condition. Across time and place, excessive self-love has been the defining feature of threats to human community—including tainting how people have defined and weaponized terms such as "civilization" and "civility." The innate and outsized self-love of human beings continues to be the preeminent threat to social concord today.

Chapter 2 will show how the solution to this eternal problem of excessive human self-love is just as timeless. It is civility: tempering our self-love out of respect for others, but also so that our social natures can flourish. In surveying some of the "greatest hits" in the conduct-literature and etiquette-manual genre from across history and culture, we will discover in this chapter a remarkable continuity in the advice for living well with others—advice that many writers and thinkers came to independently of one another. This suggests a certain timelessness to particular tenets of civility. Here, we will learn why civility is, and always has been, the antidote to the problems caused personally and socially by our innate self-centeredness. We will also learn why civility has been the key to unlocking multidimensional human flourishing in past eras, and why it is also the secret to doing so in our own.

Chapters 3 through 9 will explore the "why" for civility, discovering how civility supports the seven ingredients of any thriving democratic society—integrity, freedom, civil society, equality, civil disobedience, tolerance, and civil discourse—in a digital, technological era. These chapters will also show that while politeness undermines these ingredients, civility promotes them. Civility can promote the trust and friendship that supports a democratic government, and that can help citizens and public leaders alike navigate profound cultural and political differences. Civility promotes social and political freedom by empowering us to keep the expressions of our baser, self-interested instincts in check instead of relying on external forces, such as government mandates, to do so.

Civility is also the basic building block of civil society: it is what makes people want to come together to innovate and solve pressing problems of the day. Civility is therefore the lifeline of civil society, the institution that Alexis de Tocqueville noted was the necessary buttress of a free, democratic age. Civility helps us live out equality by reclaiming respect for all our fellow citizens. It can also empower us to live tolerantly with others despite deep differences, and to rigorously protest wrongs and debate issues, even if doing so seems deeply impolite. Civility helps us see the human being on the other side of the computer screen—a necessary counterbalance in an era where ubiquitous technology enables us to cut off or abuse without consequence people with whom we disagree.

These chapters will also explore how we can rediscover a high view of personhood and human dignity—central to civility—despite new dehumanizing forces unique to our modern age.

Chapters 10 through 12 will show how civility operates in practice through hospitality, as well as how we can get more of it in our educational cultures, our public life, our communities, and our homes. I hope you'll read this book in its entirety, but each of these chapters is self-contained, written to offer new and hopefully useful reflections on the subject of each chapter—each of which is an essential condition for thriving human life, personally and socially.

The Consolation of Philosophy and Declaring My Priors

I left my role in Washington exhausted, frustrated, and confused. The people who were willing to do anything, uninhibited by the constraints of common decency, seemed to consistently win. Those who resisted the extremes of angry hostility and faux politeness—and there were those who tried to authentically respect others—seemed to lose out. I looked around me at the world of our public leaders, and saw that those willing to go low and say anything were rewarded. Disheartened, I wanted to discover whether a good and civil person could survive and succeed in this fractured world. Would civility always be a barrier to professional success, or could it help us out of our fraught and divided modern life?

I realized that the questions swirling around in my head included many of those that comprised the Great Conversation, the iterative dialogue of wise men and women across history and culture who reflect on the human condition and the life well lived. I explored the moral foundations of civility by revisiting some of the foundational questions of the Great Conversation and the human experience. What does it mean to be human? What is the bare minimum of respect we are owed, and owe to others, in light of our shared humanity and irreducible worth as persons? What does it look like to live out that respect practically amid deep differences with others—including in our divided political moment?

I wrote this book in the presence of eternal questions and ideas, and in the company of my lifelong intellectual influences, including the thought of Plato, Aristotle, St. Augustine, Hebrew and Christian scripture, Dr. Martin Luther King, Jr., Blaise Pascal, Adam Smith, and Hannah Arendt, among many others. Each has formed my thinking and will appear throughout this work.

Working my way from past to present, west to east, north to south, and back again, I explored how thoughtful people throughout time and place have answered questions about the stuff of the good life, and how their answers can help us grapple with barriers to human flourishing now. My Christian faith informs my high view of humanity and, especially, my philosophy of civility. Civility is the disposition that comes from seeing all people as they really are: beings with innate dignity. It is only by embracing this disposition that we can live a good life—as individuals, as neighborhoods, as a polity, and as a unified human species. Many wise people across history and culture have reflected deeply on the nature of man, human relationships, the sacrifices necessary for building community, and the conditions of humanity's flourishing. They offer important insights into civility. I draw from this rich intellectual well throughout this book to understand what civility is and why it's essential.

What Past Writers Miss About Civility

After reimmersing myself in foundational books, ideas, and questions—such as what it means to be human, the stuff of human dignity, and the building blocks of the good life—I moved on to explore more contemporary discussions of civility. I was surprised to learn that most of them fail to link civility to basic questions of our humanity, personhood, and human nature. They have therefore missed these important aspects of civility's soul, essence, and purpose. They also insufficiently appreciate civility's importance to civilization, civil society, citizenship, democracy, friendship, and individual human flourishing. Modern writers have tended to define civility as being 1) purely manners, 2) a network of "communicative norms," 3) a concept somehow related to democracy and civil society, 4) a "strategic tool," or 5) they've avoided defining it at all, throwing their hands up and invoking former Supreme Court associate Justice Potter Stewart's now-famous non-definition of obscenity, merely claiming, "I know it when I see it."

In the past, people have struggled to define civility. As we've learned, it's often defined synonymously with mere politeness and manners, ensuring it isn't taken seriously as a "real" virtue. It's not listed among the four classical or "cardinal" virtues of prudence, temperance, courage, and justice. Nor is it among the Christian theological virtues of faith, hope, charity, and love. It is not even included in the traditional virtues of democracy, such as the rule of law, tolerance, equality, and free expression. As we'll discover throughout this book, though, the separation of civility from the realm of ethics and philosophy is a recent development in human history, and is part of the reason we find ourselves in a particularly uncivil moment. This book relies on great thinkers, writers, and philosophers of our past to remedy this problematic modern tendency to unmoor civility from its moral and philosophical roots.

The Symbolism of this Book's Cover and Why This Book Is Different

First, I yearned to harness the healing power of beauty to help me embody the ideas of my book, and the wonderful design team at St. Martin's helped me do that with what I think is an uncommonly lovely cover. Second, I adored the symbolism of the olive branch. It is the universal symbol of peace, reconciliation, friendship, and human harmony. It also invokes connotations of antiquity and the classical world, which have influenced me and formed our world today. The olive branch represents rebirth and renewal. In the Hebrew Bible, after God has destroyed a fallen world with a flood, Noah sends a dove from the ark to see if habitable land remains. The dove returns with an olive branch, which symbolizes a fresh start and a new era for humanity. The central visual metaphor of my book is civilization as a garden—the product of concerted effort, continuous care, and cultivation. The olive tree is among the oldest cultivated crops from the ancient Mediterranean world. It symbolizes the fruitfulness that is possible when the joint project of human civilization—buttressed and nourished by our individual decisions to live with civility—thrives. Third, I wanted the cover to represent an active work of art—hence the subtle paint speckle. Civilization itself—and the human social project generally—is a work of human ingenuity and creation. Like an olive grove, it requires cultivation and continuous care. It takes the active effort of each of us to sustain it and make sure it thrives. As human beings, we are each a creation capable of creating healing and beauty in our world—a central theme in this book. I wrote this book over the course of nearly a decade, but it's also the product of ideas and questions I've been considering my whole life. The ideas within it grew and matured as I did. I changed my mind about notions in this book more times than I care to count, and I'm sure my thinking on these pressing questions will continue to evolve throughout my life.

The subject of civility in life is rather vast. I've done my best to do justice to it. As we'll discover, every culture in human history has had opinions on the best way to peacefully coexist. Throughout this book, I've given a sampling of those I think are among the best thinkers and sources from different cultures and eras. Still, I'm inevitably captive to the culture in which I was raised, as well as the education I was given. I'll invariably have overlooked and omitted many sources of wisdom on this topic. This book is not a pure history of human social relationships, although I love the study of the past and draw from it frequently. Instead, I offer an explicitly normative argument—that civility is morally rooted in and inextricable from human flourishing— more suited to our fractured moment.

While reading this book, if you think of examples that support or add to my argument, please write to me. If you have ideas or examples that contradict my argument, do keep those to yourself. My hope is that this book helps us continue a long-standing conversation about the requirements and promises of doing life well together, and I'd love to invite you to be a part of it. I plan to keep the conversation going through Civic Renaissance—a newsletter, publication, and intellectual community I founded to help heal our public discourse by reviving beauty, goodness, truth, and the wisdom of the past. I invite you to write to me anytime with your reflections on this book, and to join our dialogue there. You can contact me via my website at www.AlexandraOHudson.com, and become part of the Civic Renaissance community by visiting www.Civic-Renaissance .com.

This book deals with deep, serious issues and questions related to the human experience and the human condition. It is a humanistic manifesto. Civility is about the question of what it means to be human, which makes it a subject far richer and more serious than many realize. My case for civility is grounded in a high view of humanity. I argue that adopting the disposition of civility will enable us to fulfill our potential as individuals and as a community.

I have a high view of humanity, but I also believe that human beings are imperfect, flawed, and defined by self-love. This imperfect nature is the root cause of social malaise and perennial incivility in our world. The human condition is a paradox defined by greatness and wretchedness, as seventeenth-century French polymath Blaise Pascal once wrote.[5] My theory of civility offers a moral framework that takes personhood, our common humanity, and inherent human dignity seriously. Instead of offering a static set of rules that apply uniformly, this framework will empower us to work out the applied ethics of civility in the fluid, nuanced contexts of our daily interactions with others. This book is also practical, offering many specific suggestions for how we can bring more of the disposition of civility to our everyday lives, and by extension, into our world. It offers a road map for multidimensional human flourishing, a flourishing that encompasses not only our body, but also our heart, mind, and soul.

We are not our own. We are not islands unto ourselves, and never have been. Even more so in our globalized era, we are inextricably connected to those around us, both in our communities and, thanks to novel technologies, around the world. Historically, we are also connected to those who have come before us, because their successes and failures have built our world and formed us. We are also connected to those who will come after us. We have a duty to them to steward our resources and the natural world so that they enjoy its bounty and blessings as we currently do. We are connected to those who have come before us, to those we live with now, and to those who will come after us. This connectivity to others constrains us, preventing us from doing all that we might dream or want. The limitations and inherent interdependence of human social life is a source of endless frustration and joy. Life together requires that we endure it all. A central theme of this book is that we have more power than we realize to decide which it will more often be: frustration or joy.

This is why, at the end of every chapter in this book, I offer tips that summarize some of the main, practical takeaways that can empower you to be part of creating a more civil world. The static rules of etiquette and politeness are not sufficient to help us navigate the complex nature of social life with maturity, grace, and favor. My tips aren't meant to be hard-and-fast rules, but guidelines: timeless, practical wisdom distilled from my close study of civility manuals across history and culture. I've applied them to our modern life so that we might benefit from their insights today. These lists at the end of each chapter serve as a summary of some of the major themes and ideas in my book, including the important idea that we each have the power to make the world better and more civil if we elevate how we engage with others and the world around us.

We each lead interdependent and multidimensional lives, but often deny it. We underestimate how much our negative actions can affect people for the worse, and how positive actions can affect people for the better. I hope that my suggestions of things you can do in each sphere of influence both encourage you and help you ensure that your life leaves a mellifluous echo, and leaves you feeling empowered to create a more civil, harmonious world. With patience and persistence, we'll make our homes and communities better—and we'll make ourselves better, more fully joyful and human, for having made the effort to treat our fellow human beings with the respect and kindness they deserve.

I hope readers will be encouraged to see civility through this holistic and humanistic lens, to better understand the challenges and duties of life in community, and to claim the fullness of its joys and promise. We will leave this book with an improved appreciation of the fragility, but also the fruitfulness, of life together, and will reap the great rewards on offer as part of this joint project of society. Our freedom and flourishing are sustained through our everyday exchanges, and nourished through the decisions we make to respect our fellow citizens. Our exchanges and our decisions are small but important threads that weave and strengthen the tapestry of our civilization, civil society, and democracy—and ensure our personal flourishing. We are all aware of the many complex problems facing our society today.

This book is a product of lifetimes of thinking on the stuff of human flourishing and the good life—my lifetime, as mentioned, but also those of many, many others before me. It builds on and draws from the thinking of thoughtful people from across the human experience. This book is not the final word on this topic. I hope instead that it revives a dialogue about the nature of personhood and the good life with others that people have been engaged with for a long, long time. As we think more clearly about the complexity of, and history behind, the question of civility in human life, I am optimistic that we'll have greater humility when it comes to our own failings and those of others. I am wishful for everyone reading this book to be left with a renewed vision for the high promise of life with others, and with fortified resolve to see this joint project of human community succeed.

1

A Timeless Problem

Self-love, libido dominandi, *and the garden of civilization*

Countless times each day, our lives are made more difficult by the incivility of others. We're cut off in traffic. We're demeaned or undermined by a colleague at work. Or, as television's favorite curmudgeon Larry David might lament, someone thoughtlessly abuses their sampling privileges at the ice cream shop and holds up the line. Living in society requires that we consider others alongside ourselves. Despite this, we often don't. We miss that our seemingly trivial decisions have big consequences for the survival and fate of our species.

Incivility is a serious problem because it threatens the stability and tranquility of social life. But it's not a new one. It's a timeless human problem that manifests

What has been will be again, what has been done will be done again; there is nothing new under the sun.

—Ecclesiastes 1:9

in ways large and small, and is an ever-present danger to harmonious human community.

Understanding present challenges to civility requires us to step back in time to the cradle of civilization. The oldest story in the world, *The Epic of Gilgamesh*, offers clarity into what incivility is, and why it is such an obstinate part of human social life. It's no coincidence that the world's most ancient narrative offers insights into the fragility and promise of social relationships. Peaceful coexistence is central to the survival and happiness of our species, and is important to human communities in all times and places. Despite this, as important as civility is to the survival of the human race, we'll learn in this chapter that the challenges to civility are surprisingly timeless. As we'll discover in our next chapter, however, the solutions are equally as timeless.

Gilgamesh was part man, part god, king of the ancient Sumerian city of Uruk, and not exactly renowned for being the most civil of figures. He wreaked havoc on his city, and took grotesque delight in harming his citizens. The people of Uruk feared the caprice and whims of their ruler. Gilgamesh lived without regard for anyone else. He forced his citizens to build magnificent public buildings. He took what he wanted from whomever he wanted whenever he wanted—and was especially infamous for stealing "first night's rights," forcing himself on young women on their wedding night. The people of Uruk pled with their gods for help. The gods heard their cries, and created Enkidu—a primal, hirsute, wild man whom they fashioned out of clay to defeat Gilgamesh and free the people of Uruk from his tyrannical, impulsive rule.

> *"Gilgamesh does not leave a girl to her mother, the daughter of the warrior, the bride of the young man,"* the people of Uruk cried.
>
> —The Epic of Gilgamesh

Enkidu arrived in Uruk and challenged Gilgamesh. The battle began, taking them up and down the streets of the city for days on end. The people of Uruk looked on in wonder and anxious anticipation: Who would win?

After a long, arduous fight, Enkidu surrendered, declaring Gilgamesh a warrior who could never be beaten. And then, the unthinkable happened. Enkidu offered kindness to the tyrant, an act which in turn transformed Gilgamesh from foe to friend. Anticipating Socrates, Enkidu vanquished his enemy by converting him to the good. Enkidu's offer of friendship gave Gilgamesh the motivation to become a better person and king—and even an ideal hero. Enkidu's friendship permanently changed Gilgamesh, who never again preyed on the weak and vulnerable of Uruk.

This story at the beginning of *The Epic of Gilgamesh* illuminates several important truths about the human condition. The narrative shows us why incivility always has been, and always will be, a problem for human communities in all times and places.

First, the human condition is defined by two competing forces: our love of others, and our love of self. We are an insatiably sociable species. We yearn to be in community together, yet our self-love—and our *libido dominandi*, or lust to dominate our fellow human beings—will always threaten the human social enterprise. Gilgamesh was ruler of the greatest city of his day—and yet he was ruled by his self-love and lust to dominate, resulting in his abuse of the most vulnerable among his citizens. Sometimes, when we allow our self-love to harm others, we reveal that a little bit of Gilgamesh resides within each of us. When we allow the Gilgamesh within to rear his ugly head, we undermine the social project.

Every day, we have a choice to make. Will we ennoble those around us with our tenderness and goodwill, or debase them with our callousness and cruelty? Only one of these options supports the joint project of human society. Only one option affirms and enhances our humanity, and that of those around us. In being a salve to his self-love and in harming others on a whim for his own delight, Gilgamesh also harmed himself. In disrespecting the dignity, autonomy, and personhood of those he abused, he made himself more monstrous and less human. His cruelty debased himself and corroded his own humanity. The same happens to us—our humaneness withers—in our cruelty and ungraciousness toward others.

Yet all hope was not lost. Grotesque though his actions were, Gilgamesh was not irredeemable. Enkidu's offer of friendship converted Gilgamesh from his life of selfishness and domination to a life of self-sacrifice and heroism. Though Enkidu was defeated by Gilgamesh in battle, in the end Enkidu took his savage victor captive through harnessing the transformative power of relationship. We, too, can harness this power and bring about greater civility in our world.

Man is born in society . . . and there he remains.

—Montesquieu, eighteenth-century French philosopher, as quoted by eighteenth-century Scottish philosopher Adam Ferguson

From the beginning of our lives, we yearn for relationship with others. Our relationships give our lives richness and meaning. Our need for community motivates us to subjugate our selfishness and will to dominate others so that we may enjoy the fruits of life with them. Friendship and community are also transformative. As Enkidu's friendship motivated Gilgamesh to overcome his base nature, we can also harness and deploy the transformative power of kindness. Our conduct can be a force that motivates people to rise above their self-interest and thrive—become fully human—in relationship. There is a little bit of Gilgamesh within each of us that can undermine the social project if we let it. But there is also a bit of Enkidu within us all that can heal it.

Civility and Civilization

The Epic of Gilgamesh reveals that civilization—the enterprise of human beings coming together in cooperation, collaboration, mutual understanding, and dependence—is fragile. It relies on the daily decision we make to suppress the selfishness and lust for domination in our nature. We must make this decision again and again—each person for him or herself, and each generation for itself, each day, every day—in order for civilization to survive.

The English word "civilization" derives from the family of Latin words related to the city (*civitas*), the citizen (*civis*), and the civil conduct befitting a citizen in the city (*civilis*). Like civility, civilization is an explicitly social enterprise: neither are ideals one could achieve in isolation.

The enterprise of civilization—of the advancement of knowledge and the progress of the human species—relies on the amicable negotiation of competing interests and ideas. It depends on our willingness to sometimes sacrifice our immediate wants for the greater project of community. For this reason, it is exquisitely fragile. Civilization depends on civility—surrendering the ego for the sake of the other—which enables us to navigate the inevitable differences and disagreements of human social life.

Civilization is the result of cumulative cultural accomplishments of generations over time. Civilization is often thought of in terms of a society's level of technology, artistic or cultural achievements, system of manners, preparation and consumption of food, development of its scientific knowledge, or sophistication of its governmental institutions, education system, or religions.

But it is also much more than external achievements.

Civilization—like civility, as we'll learn—is also a frame of mind. It lives or dies in the heart of a society's citizens.

The Garden of Civility and Civilization

Civilization is like a garden, an idea I will return to throughout this book. Like a garden, both civility and civilization are not natural. They are all forms of culture, and the fruit of cultivation, in the literal sense: both "culture" and "cultivation" derive from the Latin *cultivat*, which refers to taking raw, untouched land and turning it into crops or a garden. Civility and civilization require cultivating the raw stuff of humanity and making it into something better—refining it so it might become more arable and fruitful. Both civility and civilization unlock human potential because they enable us to become the best, most creative and ingenious versions of ourselves in community.

Continuing the metaphor of a civilization as a garden, each person is born as a plot of raw and fertile soil, rich in possibility. Immediately upon birth, society begins the process of cultivation, sowing seeds in the fertile ground of one's soul. This cultivation—socialization or conditioning—includes planting seeds of ritual, language, habits, attitudes, and values. Not all of the seeds implanted within our innate [agri]cultural context are equal. We must learn to tell them apart. Some seeds become beautiful flowers that delight with their beauty, or nutrient-rich plants that replenish and nurture the other plots of land and plants and animal life that surround it. Other seeds are invasive, corrosive species, weeds that zap the life from the soil, and also begin to harm and choke out the life around them. Our job is to learn to distinguish the life-giving seeds from the pernicious ones, the flowers from the thistles. We must then nourish the former while starving the latter.

Living in society means that we each participate in an iterative, interconnected, interdependent process of cultivating our own gardens while also nourishing those of others. We each contribute to the flourishing of the garden of civilization itself.

Within the fertile ground of our own soul, we can choose to uproot the invasive, toxic, barbaric weeds, such as seeds that value some forms of human life over others. We can instead redirect our resources—the water, fertilizer, and sun that are our time, energy, and attention—to nourish the seeds, or cultural values, that support the social project, such as the value that all human life is equally, intrinsically valuable. As *The Epic of Gilgamesh* showed us, there is an ongoing battle between civility and incivility—between flowers and thistle beds—within the soul of every person. This individual-level battle between seeds of life and seeds of death, civility and incivility, predicts the outcome of the societal-level battle between civilization and barbarism. To thrive both personally and communally, we must each consciously direct our personal and collective resources—sun, fertilizer, and water—away from thistle seeds, and toward the seeds of beautiful flowers that ennoble and revere life.

True civilization isn't about the sophistication, intelligence, or complexity of a society or its people. It is about the substance, the *humanity*, of it. Gilgamesh was king of the most advanced urban center of his day in a region of the world thought of as "the cradle of civilization." Yet, before his conversion to humaneness by friendship, he acted in barbaric and inhumane ways, abusing and exploiting the people around him. Enkidu, by contrast, is

An old Cherokee was teaching his grandson about life. "A fight is going on inside me," he said to the boy. "It is a terrible fight and it is between two wolves. One is evil—he is anger, envy, sorrow, regret, greed, arrogance, self-pity, guilt, resentment, inferiority, lies, false pride, superiority, and ego." He continued, "The other is good—he is joy, peace, love, hope, serenity, humility, kindness, benevolence, empathy, generosity, truth, compassion, and faith. The same fight is going on inside you—and inside every other person, too."

The grandson thought about it for a minute and then asked his grandfather, "Which wolf will win?"

The old Cherokee simply replied, "The one you feed."

depicted as simple, primitive, and closer to nature—and yet he is the one filled with kindness and humanity. Enkidu is therefore a better representative of civilization because of his kindness. Before his conversion, and despite his sophistication, Gilgamesh, by contrast, represents barbarism because of his cruelty. Reminiscent of the reportedly old Cherokee story about the two wolves within each person's soul, or Robert Louis Stevenson's *The Strange Case of Dr. Jekyll and Mr. Hyde*, there is a duality in our nature: each of us has a little bit of Gilgamesh and Enkidu within us. As the civilized and morally upright Dr. Jekyll asserts, "Man is not truly one, but truly two." Unfortunately, he only comes to this realization after nourishing his inner, evil Mr. Hyde for too long. In the battle within his soul between "angel" and "fiend"—or civilization and barbarism—fiend and barbarism permanently win.

We must choose whether we will feed our inner Gilgamesh or our inner Enkidu. When we act with charity and humaneness, we nurture our inner Enkidu, and embody the stuff of true civilization. When we mis-treat others, when we fail to accord them the respect they are owed by virtue of their humanity, we nourish our inner Gilgamesh. We make ourselves less human, and more barbaric. Each of us has more power to support the project of civility and civilization—or detract from it—in how we live out every day. Which will we allow to win?

External forces, such as novel technology, can enable our *libido dominandi* and undermine civility. Ultimately, though, these and other challenges are not the root cause of our era's challenge with civility.

We are.

It was on the moral side, and in my own person, that I learned to recognize the thorough and primitive duality of man; I saw that, of the two natures that contended in the field of my consciousness, even if I could rightly be said to be either, it was only because I was radically both.

—Robert Louis Stevenson, nineteenth-century Scottish novelist

Self-love and the Libido Dominandi: The Perennial Threat to Civility

The human condition is a contradiction, capable of greatness and wretchedness. We are each a bundle of desires and impulses that are constantly at cross-purposes. And the central tension in our nature is between our sociability and our self-love.

We are communal beings who yearn for friendship, love, and companionship. We flourish in relationship with others, and are capable of immense generosity and altruism. On the other hand, we are plagued with an intractable self-love. Our biology drives us to meet our own needs before those of others. Civility

What a Chimera is man! What a novelty, a monster, a chaos, a contradiction, a prodigy! Judge of all things, an imbecile worm; depository of truth, and sewer of error and doubt; the glory and refuse of the universe.

—Blaise Pascal, seventeenth-century French polymath, scientist, and philosopher

calls us to overcome our self-love so that we might thrive with others. Civility helps us properly channel our self-love and cultivate our social natures by requiring us to make the sacrifices necessary for society and civilization. It demands that we treat with respect those we do not like, those who are not like us, those we do not need favors from, and those who cannot do things for us in return. Our drive for self-preservation means that we must consciously battle the perennial temptation to see the world and others exclusively through the lens of our own experiences and advancement. We instrumentalize people when it suits us—and are quick to (appear to) be kind and generous when we have something to gain.

The will to dominate is a timeless expression of the self-love inherent in human nature. An early example of it may have been Gilgamesh's abuse of women and other vulnerable people in Uruk. But it didn't end there. It finds expression in our own culture all the time and at all levels of society—from the elementary school bully to office coffee rooms and the halls of Congress. Whenever a power imbalance is exploited, and the humanity of a person is diminished, someone has allowed their will to dominate others to operate unchecked.

St. Augustine of Hippo, who lived and wrote just prior to the fall of Rome in the fifth century, was among the first to offer an explanation and a remedy for the basic human drive to dominate others. He wrote in *The City of God* that the defining impulse of humanity was the *libido dominandi*, or the lust for domination.[1] For Augustine, the *libido dominandi* was the impulse to control everyone and everything around us. He thought it was inextricably linked to *incurvatus in se*, or the "inward curve to the self" that is an indelible part of our character as human beings. Both the *libido dominandi* and the *incurvatus in se* originate from our foundational self-love. Together, they vanquish any hope we might have of a tranquil social life. They alienate us from others because they lead us to objectify them. We begin to see others as things to be controlled and used for our purposes rather than as human beings to be respected and cherished.

> *Therefore, I cannot refrain from speaking about the city of this world, a city which aims at dominion, which holds nations in enslavement, but is itself dominated by that very lust of domination.*
>
> —St. Augustine, fourth-century Roman philosopher and theologian

In *The City of God*, Augustine critiqued the dominant culture of his day—Imperial Rome—for its *libido dominandi*. He dismantled the story Romans told about themselves regarding their own civilization: instead of being the greatest imperium on earth, Augustine claims, their lust for power led to their undoing. Augustine scorned the idea of Roman exceptionalism. He critiqued their view of themselves as the epicenter of civilization, urbanity, and civility. Instead of praising Rome's glory, he retold its history as a series of calamities for those the Romans conquered and for the Romans themselves. There are no victors when violence and cruelty are exerted, Augustine claimed.

The *libido dominandi* and *incurvatus in se* alienate us from others, but also harm us. The *libido dominandi*—or the dominating lust—becomes the lust that dominates. The master is revealed to be mastered by his lusts. We saw this with Gilgamesh, as his lust to dominate others soon became a lust that dominated him. The same is true for us. Consider the vain person who is constantly surveying social contexts in order to ensure that he is close to powerful people and doesn't look like a fool. That desire becomes the thing he pursues at all costs—even at the cost of his own enjoyment of life. When we desire something—or avoid something—too much, we can become controlled by it.

> *The civility of no race can be perfect whilst another race is degraded. It is a doctrine alike of the oldest and of the newest philosophy, that man is one, and that you cannot injure any member without a sympathetic injury to all the members.*
>
> —Ralph Waldo Emerson

When our lust to dominate others for our own benefit is left unchecked, when civility doesn't cause us to surrender our self-interest for the sake of others, and when we're controlled by our desires at the expense of others, we become less free, less our full, best selves. As we are tempted to harm others on the way to meeting our needs, we will find we are disgusted with ourselves. We will become self-alienated. It doesn't matter how vigorously we deny or ignore it: some foundational level of our soul is disquieted when we debase our humanity through viciousness toward our fellow persons.

For Augustine, we're born with the *libido dominandi* and the *incurvatus in se*. This means that we will inevitably harm others to meet our own needs at some point in life. It's in our DNA. The raw stuff of humanity is defined by self-love first and affection for others second. Humanity's default state, Augustine thought, was defined by "disordered loves." But through cultivation, education, training, and habit, Augustine thought that we could "rightly order our loves." He saw this ordering of loves as putting God and others before ourselves—which he called *ordo amoris*—and felt that it should be the goal of any education worth its salt.

Augustine was a student of Plato, and he built upon Plato's idea of a just individual soul building a just society. Plato thought that the just person was one whose reason, or head, had learned to rule their passions—including their lust to dominate—through their courage, or chest. A just person has cultivated this arrangement of the soul. They've become civilized by diminishing their base, primitive instincts. A society of just persons, for Plato, is what builds a just, and civilized, society.

We'll explore this concept of ordering human passions in our next chapter on the timeless principles of civility, and in our penultimate chapter exploring civility and education.

Augustine was hardly the last to make this observation about the human condition. As noted in the introduction to this book, in his "Letter from Birmingham Jail" Martin Luther King, Jr., used the framework of Martin Buber's "I–it" and "I–thou" distinction to describe how humankind's selfishness causes us to see and treat others as *things* instead of *people*. Johann Fichte and G. W. F. Hegel described this instrumentalization of persons through the language of the "other." Karl Marx used the term "commodification." Martha Nussbaum refers to it as

> *"Segregation," to use the terminology of the Jewish philosopher Martin Buber, substitutes an "I–it" relationship for an "I–thou" relationship and ends up relegating persons to the status of things.*
>
> —Martin Luther King, Jr.

"instrumentalization." The will to dominate others and instrumentalize them is ingrained within us. It arises when we allow our self-interest to remain unchecked and untempered by the duty we have to others. It begins when we see people as objects to be dominated and lose sight of people as they really are—beings with souls, dignity, and intrinsic moral worth.

The Architecture of Civilization: True vs. Faux Civilization

Historically, the words "civility," "civil society," and "civilization" have been used interchangeably to describe a state of being opposite that of barbarism. These words have often been weaponized to justify a society's perceived superiority on the grounds of its cultural or infrastructural achievements and complexity.

People have long looked to such superficial things to judge other cultures as lesser and distinguish themselves as better. But that is merely the "pursuit of luxury and a false civilization," as the French Revolution leader Mirabeau wrote. The civilization of a nation is not located in impressive architecture or institutions. It is instead located in the character of its people. Civilization is the cumulative effect of individuals' decisions to take the humanity of their fellow persons seriously.

Consider a modern ruler who tried to define his nation as a civilization through

> *People only want to accomplish [the civilizing process] for other nations, and also, for a period, for the lower classes of society. To the upper classes of their own society, civilization appears a firm possession.*
>
> —Norbert Elias, twentieth century German-Jewish sociologist

beautiful and extravagant national architecture. Saddam Hussein built over eighty ornate palaces across Iraq during his reign. He built one of his palaces in Babylon, where King Nebuchadnezzar II had built his vast palace of six hundred rooms as well as the famous Hanging Gardens of Babylon during the seventh century BC. Saddam razed two-thirds of the historic city to make the foundation for his new palace. He enlisted more than a thousand workers and had sixty million bricks made. Each brick was inscribed: IN THE ERA OF SADDAM HUSSEIN WHO REBUILT CIVILIZATION, AND WHO REBUILT BABYLON.

Iraq is the location of ancient Mesopotamia, the region of the world that housed the ancient civilizations of Sumer and Babylon and gave us *The Epic of Gilgamesh*. In building his palace on the site of ancient Babylon, Saddam's aim was to redefine his empire as the *new* cradle of civilization. He misunderstood civilization as being composed of extravagant shows of power through beautiful buildings and sophisticated urban designs. Saddam showed himself to be a latter-day Gilgamesh: a leader of a community of people in the cradle of civilization, but a barbaric leader nonetheless. He failed to recognize that, in employing violence, murder, torture, and otherwise capricious abuses of power—not to mention his systematic persecution of vulnerable ethnic minorities—his reign would never be civilized, nor would his city be the cradle of any true civilization.

Our desire to see ourselves, and people similar to us, as better than those around us—as Saddam sought to do with his architectural feats—is a perennial, harmful expression of human self-love. The word "barbarism"—a term often

A decent provision for the poor is the true test of civilization.

—Samuel Johnson, eighteenth-century English writer, lexicographer, and creator of the first English dictionary in 1755 weaponized toward the "other"—derives from the ancient Greek word *barbaroi,* meaning "all who are non-Greek." The Greeks had the unfortunate habit of assuming that their language, customs, and culture were the most sophisticated in the world, and of dismissing all other groups as not just culturally deficient, but morally inferior.

The Greeks were hardly the last people to "otherize" those who were different from them. We are all inclined to make such judgments. We are all susceptible to preferring people to whom we are related and people we like over people who are dissimilar to us and who do not benefit us. These sentiments point to an important truth about civility. We have obligations to friends and to family, but we also have more general obligations to the rest of mankind, and civility helps us uphold our duties to the generalized other. True civility, true civil society, and true civilization are about our humaneness to our fellow persons—friends, family, and strangers alike.

Civility obligates *kindness* in its literal sense: treating strangers and visitors with the benevolence with which we would treat our *kin*. The word "kind" is etymologically related to the word "kin," as in "kinship," derived from the Old English word for "family," "rank," and "race." Being kind is literally about treating a stranger with the benevolence one would offer a family member, a person of the same social class, or someone from the same tribe. Incivility and barbarism all consist of being hostile and cruel to

> *Our culture divides people into two classes: civilized men, a title bestowed on the persons who do the classifying; and others, who have only the human form, who may perish or go to the dogs for all the "civilized men" care.*
>
> —Albert Schweitzer, twentieth-century Alsatian-German polymath and humanitarian

the stranger, to those in need, and to those who are powerless and unable to repay acts of kindness.

Alsatian-German doctor, theologian, philosopher, and Nobel laureate Albert Schweitzer spent over two decades reflecting on the nature of true civilization. As a young man, Schweitzer's conscience was sensitized by the plight of colonial Africa. Horrified by the brutality of colonial powers toward the people of Africa and the European occupiers' cavalier disregard of human life, he emerged as one of the twentieth century's harshest critics of colonialism. He saw the transparent self-interest and imperialism that motivated European colonial powers, disguised beneath the name of spreading "civilization" to other nations. Schweitzer wrote,

> Oh, this "noble" culture of ours! It speaks so piously of human dignity and human rights and then disregards this dignity and these rights of countless millions and treads them underfoot, only because they live overseas or because their skins are of different color or because they cannot help themselves. This culture does not know how hollow and miserable and full of glib talk it is, how common it looks to those who follow it across the seas and see what it has done there, and this culture has no right to speak of personal dignity and human rights. . . .

He saw the Western world's hypocrisy: its claims to support human rights and dignity rang hollow in the face of its ruthless colonial legacy. Schweitzer wanted to change the way the world understood civilization, and how it viewed humanity. He decided to start with himself. "My life is my argument," he was fond of saying.

In 1913, Schweitzer opened a hospital in Lambaréné, a

Reverence for Life affords me my fundamental principle of morality, namely, that good consists in maintaining, assisting, and enhancing life, and to destroy, to harm, or to hinder life is evil.

—Albert Schweitzer

small town in what was then a part of French Equatorial Africa and what is today the West African country of Gabon. Immediately upon its opening, thousands of people traveled hundreds of miles to reach the hospital and seek much-needed medical care. When World War I broke out in 1914, Schweitzer and his wife, Helene, were German citizens in French-occupied territory, and were placed under supervision by French authorities. During that time, they were able to continue their work serving Africans in need of medical care. In 1917, they were sent to internment camps in France, from which they were released in 1918.

After his release, Schweitzer processed his years of instability and tumult by writing about his firsthand experience in Africa. He wrote about the barbarity of colonialism, exposing the sham of this atrocity committed in the name of "civilization." He offered an account of true civilization in his book *The Philosophy of Civilization*. In this work, Schweitzer said that there were two definitions of civilization: the material and the ethical. The material view defined civilization purely according to its creative, artistic, technological, cultural, and other material attainments—in other words, the sort of superficial attributes that Saddam Hussein thought defined civilization. For Schweitzer, the material view was false civilization. He favored the ethical definition as true civilization, which he defined as a "mental attitude" premised on "reverence for life"—a phrase he coined for the view that saw human life, and all life in general, as intrinsically valuable.

In an argument similar to Martin Luther King, Jr.'s, Schweitzer said that to perpetuate and foster life is an unalloyed good; to degrade it is an unalloyed evil. Individuals in a society must adopt a *weltanschauung*—a "theory of the universe," or worldview—that respects personhood and the intrinsic dignity of the human being in order to be a true civilization. Reclaiming a high view of personhood begins with appreciating the capability and potential within each of us. After that, Schweitzer says, we become inspired to realize our potential in ways that benefit our fellow human beings and the world around us and bring about social, cultural, and scientific advancements.

Who can describe the injustice and cruelties that in the course of centuries the peoples of color of the world have suffered at the hands of Europeans? . . . If a record could be compiled of all that has happened between the white and the colored races, it would make a book containing numbers of pages which the reader would have to turn over unread because their contents would be too horrible.

—Albert Schweitzer

In other words, the things that lead to achievements in culture, technology, and infrastructure are by-products of a society that values the intrinsic worth of human life. They do not make a true civilization—a true civilization, one that values the dignity of the person and nurtures his or her potential, makes it. Once a society has lost its reverence for life—once it has come to see its value as a civilization in purely material terms, and degraded the personhood of its own citizens or other groups—it begins to decay. Only a vigilant commitment to a reverence for life can prevent civilization from descending into barbarism and chaos, Schweitzer argued.

But how can one begin the process of transforming their society from a faux civilization into a true civilization? Schweitzer understood that big, heady concepts such as civilization are intimidating and abstract, but that everyone has a role to play in preserving these values and transforming a society's values for the better. "Everyone must find their own Lambaréné," Schweitzer asserted. Everyone has their own sphere where they can practice a reverence for life, esteeming and preserving its intrinsic beauty in all of its forms. Each one of us has a role to play in defending against inhumanity, cruelty, and barbarism, and in reviving true civilization, he felt.

Saddam Hussein was one of many leaders who misused the language of civility, civil society, and civilization. Such leaders misunderstand true civilization. Civilization depends on the disposition, or "mental attitude" as Schweitzer might say, of civility: a citizenry of individuals who respect the fundamental human dignity of their fellow human beings. It's not wealth, sophistication, or complexity that make a society civilized. Civilization is compassion for the weak, oppressed, and vulnerable. It is kindness in the face of animosity. It is decency and benevolence toward our fellow human beings, especially the vulnerable, other, stranger, and outsider. It's practicing reverence for life, in all its forms—but especially valuing the dignity of the human person—that makes a society truly civilized.

Civility, Self-Control, and Civilization

A German-Jewish sociologist, Norbert Elias, may seem an unlikely figure to offer lessons about both the art of timing a book launch and the way civility and manners can support the project of civilization, but he does in fact do just that. He published his magnum opus, called *The Civilizing Process*, in 1939, the year that Hitler invaded Poland and began the Second World War. Divided into two volumes—*The History of Manners* and *Power and Civility*—the rather dense book offers an explanation for how, between the Middle Ages and his era, Europe had become more *civilized*. For Elias, the Renaissance—and the work of Erasmus of Rotterdam in particular, whom we'll meet in our next chapter and throughout this book—marked a particularly poignant shift toward greater social control and personal restraint. By "civilized," Elias meant less violent, more peaceful, and more fastidious about rules of etiquette.

Elias scoured etiquette manuals from across European history and found that, over this period of time, these books increasingly suggested that readers cultivate habits of self-control—both physical and emotional. For Elias, self-control—or restraining our selfish will to dominate others and do whatever we want—is the secret to living peacefully together in civilization. This shift toward people possessing greater self-control and valuing it in others, Elias argued, started from the upper echelons of society—beginning with members of the court, whence we get our word "courtesy"—and moved downward, disseminating through the intellectual, middle, and lower classes.

For Elias, the civilizing process that he observed through examining changes in social norms meant that people consciously moved *away* from nature and *toward* culture. They wanted to distance themselves from the raw stuff of humanity and make themselves into something more suitable for social life. Elias wrote, "In

A man who knows the court is master of his gestures, of his eyes and his face; he is profound, impenetrable; he dissimulates bad offices, smiles at his enemies, controls his irritation, disguises his passions, belies his heart, speaks and acts against his feelings.

—Jean de La Bruyère, seventeenth-century French philosopher

the course of the civilizing process, [people] seek to suppress in themselves every characteristic that they feel to be 'animal.'"[2]

Interesting though Elias's theory was, Germans of the day were not interested in reading a book of Jewish authorship—and Hitler was certainly not interested in a book that suggested there was virtue in curbing the will to dominate. The rest of the world was preoccupied with looming global conflict, and not eager to talk about manners when civilization itself seemed to be on the precipice of collapse. The wounds caused from the senseless loss of human life during World War I were still fresh. Many remained skeptical of any notion of human progress, let alone a linear march toward "civilization." In the years leading up to Elias's book's release in 1939, people were confronted with the reality that cruel, barbaric, and inhumane behavior is lurking just beneath the surface of us all. Inhumanity and barbarism, past and present, were looming.

Elias's argument about the comparative looseness of medieval manners, when contrasted to those of later centuries, is overstated. He paints a mistaken picture of medieval Europeans as being slaves to unrestrained emotional and physical impulse and violence. He claims that their "shame threshold" was low, so they had no problem eating with their hands, belching, passing gas, or even relieving themselves in front of others without a second thought.

In his research on European manners, however, Elias overlooked key texts from the medieval era's courtesy and etiquette genre, such as the delightful twelfth-century etiquette handbook by Daniel of Beccles, *Book of the Civilized Man*, a text we'll look at in greater depth in our next chapter.[3] Elias makes sweeping judgments that this period lacked any care about refinement and polish, but his claim is exaggerated because his sources were limited. Finally, as we'll see in our next chapter, figures of the European Renaissance were not the first to see that self-control was necessary to the project of human community. In our survey of civility handbooks from cultures and eras the world over, we'll discover that thoughtful people have come to this conclusion independently across time and place.

Finally, Elias suggests that the history of Europe was one of linear progress toward civility, with his present being at the pinnacle of civilization. But that claim does not hold up to scrutiny today, nor did it when it was published. He published his book five years after he had been forced to flee his home in Frankfurt, Germany, after hearing a radio broadcast delivered by Joseph Goebbels, who vowed to his audience that the National Socialists would rid the country of the "Red Jewish menace."[4] Not quite the stuff of true civilization.

Could the world really be said to be more "civilized" if, as Elias's book was published, the most sophisticated country in the world was on the cusp of committing the most unthinkable barbarism? Descriptively, Elias is wrong. His era was not necessarily any more "civilized" than those prior. We should be skeptical of people and theories that claim that the present is morally or culturally more "evolved" than past eras.

Despite poor judgment about when to publish a book—his work was relatively unknown for decades—Elias's work would come to win deserved esteem for correctly recognizing that how we, and those around us, act has serious implications for the project of civilization. Our decision to exercise self-restraint—to suppress our innate self-love so that we may achieve our potential in community—is the hallmark of civilization. He astutely observed that, as people come together, they tend to want to distance themselves from their natural urges, both physical and emotional, and concertedly cultivate a persona appropriate for life in community. They tend to *cultivate* themselves—to continue our garden metaphor—by taking the raw stuff of humanity and refining it into something more fruitful and productive.

How they do so may differ between eras and places—which accounts for the changeability of manners and fashion, norms of cleanliness, eating, and more—but despite these superficial differences, there is remarkable continuity in the substantive norms that people across time and place have arrived at. This is because the ingredients of human relationship, community, and civilization itself—subduing our ego so we might thrive in society—have remained the same.

Civilization Is Civility Writ Large

Watch your thoughts, they become your words; watch your words, they become your actions; watch your actions, they become your habits; watch your habits, they become your character; watch your character, it becomes your destiny.

—Lao Tzu, sixth-century BC Chinese Daoist philosopher

Plato thought of a political regime as "man writ large." The soul of the *polis*—society—was determined by the soul of its people. The same can be said about civility and civilization: the character of a people determines the character of a society. As Lao Tzu wrote, our individual actions determine our habits and ultimately our character. And our character as individuals is what can make our society barbaric, or make it civilized. The extent to which a society embodies norms of civility—norms that subvert the ego in order for the social to flourish, norms that respect the dignity of *all* members of the human community, especially the different, the stranger, and the most vulnerable—determines whether it can rightly be called a *civilization*.

Civilization and barbarism, both Enkidu and Gilgamesh, exist in simple and sophisticated human arrangements alike because they exist in the human heart—*every* human heart. And every human heart has within it the *libido dominandi*—the will to dominate others in ways large and small.

Many assume that the social realities we enjoy—equality under the law, relative peace, prosperity—are *natural*, the default state of humanity. But this is not the case. Civilization and community are not foregone conclusions. They are the work—the cultivation—of thousands of years of intellectual history, political theory, and institutional development. These institutions are supported by a vast aggregation of individual, voluntary social interactions. And such interactions are in turn supported by individuals who consciously cultivate and nurture a respect and even love for their fellow human beings.

> *The line separating good and evil passes not through states, nor between classes, nor between political parties either—but right through every human heart . . . even within hearts overwhelmed by evil, one small bridgehead of good is retained. And even in the best of all hearts, there remains . . . an uprooted small corner of evil.*
>
> —Aleksandr Solzhenitsyn, twentieth-century Russian dissident and philosopher

The self-love that tempts us to instrumentalize others—to use them as means to our ends, or to be kind only when it benefits us—is like gravity. The pull toward dehumanizing others is ever-present and powerful. We must be vigilant to defend against it. When it comes to the battle between civilization and barbarism within each of us, we must ask ourselves: Which will we allow to win?

The Same, Yet Different: Incivility Today

A friend of mine was once asked a rather pointed question: "Are you a Protestant or a Catholic?"

Unwilling to be essentialized and boxed in by the query, he answered: "I'm actually Buddhist." He hoped his response would open up the questioner's mind, and show him that the world couldn't be reduced to the dichotomies through which he saw it.

Undeterred, the questioner replied, "Yes, but are you a Protestant Buddhist or a Catholic Buddhist?"

We live in a divided moment. We bring our divisions to every interaction, and impose them on the world and the people around us.

In human nature and human history, our self-love divides us. This is the ultimate challenge to civility. Often, once we've projected our divisions onto others, only then do we decide whether they deserve our respect. This is hardly the reverence for life necessary to build a truly civilized society.

The stuff of a civilization consists largely of its substantive norms.

—Robert Ellickson, Walter E. Meyer Professor of Property and Urban Law at Yale Law School, *Order Without Law*

Yet our current moment does feel particularly divided, and differs from the past in many important ways. New social, cultural, and economic changes—including novel modes of communication, and unprecedented wealth that can promote excessive materialism—have made our divisions worse and corroded relationships and traditional communities, as well as religious houses of worship, neighborhoods, and families. Our digitally mediated interactions—for some, the most common mode of communicating—make it easier to depersonalize and dehumanize others than has been the case in past eras. We're bombarded by messages from print, radio, and television outlets about why we are different, as well as why we should fear those who differ from us. Social media has diluted our sense of community, leaving us with many virtual friends or followers but fewer quality bonds of affection. Our consumerist and capitalistic society conditions us to apply a consumer mindset to all relationships in our lives, viewing others in terms of what we can get from them, and walking away when our needs are not met.

In reality, we have important duties toward family, friends, and even the strangers with whom we coexist. We also have an obligation to be good stewards of the natural world and the environment around us.

The physical makeup of our communities is also different than it was in past eras. Instead of front porches and communal living rooms, we have private backyard patios that allow us to curate our community and those we permit into our lives. (We'll explore this shift and cultural metaphor in our chapter on civility and civil society.) Instead of riding the subway together, we have cars. When we do ride trains together, we avert our eyes and pretend we are entirely alone, barely acknowledging those around us. More Americans live in densely populated areas of the country, and fewer Americans can access common spaces, such as parks, which support leisure, recreation, human interaction, social trust, and a sense of neighborhood and community.[5]

> *One of the most dangerous errors is that civilization is automatically bound to increase and spread. The lesson of history is the opposite; civilization is a rarity, attained with difficulty and easily lost.*
>
> —C. S. Lewis

We increasingly lack a basic understanding of American—let alone global—history. A recent study found that out of fifty states, only in Vermont could a majority of residents pass the citizenship test that the United States government requires all newly naturalized citizens to pass.[6] Without knowing our own history, and without being able to situate our story in the greater story of the human experience, we are unmoored from the wisdom of the past, an important source of guidance that can help us navigate the challenges of our present. Our history, instead of giving us a shared story and identity, as it has for human cultures across time, is among the most divisive topics in our public discourse and inhibits our ability to effectively remedy the perniciousness of racial injustice in America's present. All of these forces have contributed to our feeling of a uniquely divided moment. They have depleted our metaphorical reserves, leaving us all running on emotionally empty tanks and less gracious or eager to find common ground in our necessary exchanges about difficult questions of our day.

In many ways, these challenges—new technologies disrupting social life, the seduction of presentism (the uncritical assumption that the present is all that matters), materialism, and political division, among others have always been with us in some form or another. Yet they insidiously affect our lives, clouding our ability to appreciate the fragility of our civilization, our social fabric, the bonds of community, and the inherent dignity of the human person. They overwhelm us as we become desensitized to their malignant effects.

What's Past Is Prologue: History as Caution and Comfort

Despite these differences from past eras, we are as much in need today of opportunities to "unself," as twentieth-century

Irish novelist and philosopher Iris Murdoch said, as we have ever been. We must dim our "fat relentless ego," she wrote—we must conquer the self-love that threatens civility and the human social project in all times and places—if we are to see civility revived.

History is a powerful teacher, and can serve as both a caution and a comfort to us. History is a comfort because, contrary to what we might feel and what some claim, we are not, in fact, living in the most uncivil era ever. Incivility originates from a part of the human spirit that we all share. It emerges from a facet of our nature defined by self-love and a lust to dominate our environs. History is a caution because of the fact that abuse and violence are coeval with our species. Gilgamesh, the power-hungry protagonist of the ancient epic, was based on a historic king of Uruk and is an early example of the harm caused when humankind's will to dominate is allowed to reign.

He certainly, however, is not the last example. Tyrannical souls punctuate the human historical record and today's newspaper headlines—as well as our everyday experience. But the capacity for harming others resides also within the soul of each of us—something we must ever vigilantly defend against. Human society, and civilization itself, is fragile. History, including the rise and fall of dictators and empires, cautions us of this. When we forget civility, and the basic respect for personhood that it requires, we put our communities, and by extension our capacity to fully flourish, at risk.

Looking to the past can help guide us now. We have a bias toward the present. Old ideas are easily forgotten and seem innovative when rediscovered. But human progress, the revival of civility, and civilization itself depend on memory and remembering the people and occurrences that have come before us. For this reason, we must regularly refresh our minds at the wellspring that is the wisdom of human history.

Whoever has experienced the power and the unrestrained ability to humiliate another human being automatically loses his own sensations. Tyranny is a habit, it has its own organic life, it develops finally into a disease. The habit can kill and coarsen the very best man or woman to the level of a beast. Blood and power intoxicate . . . the return of the human dignity, repentance and regeneration becomes almost impossible.

—Fyodor Dostoyevsky, nineteenth-century Russian novelist

Comparing our era with eras of the past also helps to clarify the timeless challenge to civility—human self-love—and helps dispel the fog as we identify solutions suited to our current needs. To restore and reenergize civility will require innovation. We must take the best of the old and what has worked for people across time and place—which is why we'll explore the wisdom of some of history's greatest civility handbooks in our next chapter. We must repurpose this timeless wisdom so that it might meet the unique needs of the present.

Returning to our metaphor of civility and civilization as a garden, the plot of land we are each born to is beyond our control. For the early portion of our lives, we undergo this first cultivation unquestioningly. But as we grow, we're empowered to think critically about the seeds that were sowed within us in our formative years. We must learn to distinguish between the seeds in our soil. We can uproot the thistles and nourish the flowers. If the seeds of certain flowers don't exist, we can plant them, to the end of cultivating a beautiful and thriving garden—and civilization. As Robert Louis Stevenson wrote, "Don't judge each day by the harvest you reap but by the seeds that you plant." We can only control the seeds that we plant, and the seeds that we choose to nurture with our habits and resources. But as we'll learn throughout this book, those small, everyday choices make a big difference.

In beginning our exploration of civility with the story of Gilgamesh and Enkidu—a story that represents how the ugliest aspects of human nature can be transformed by the promise of human kindness and life in relationship—we have already begun our search for the timeless principles across history and culture, and started our exploration of the power of each of us to create a more civil present and future. We'll continue this effort in our next chapter, which will offer us a road map for how we might rediscover the soul of civility.

2

A Timeless Solution

Twenty-four hundred years before Christ, there lived a wealthy and powerful statesman named Ptahhotep. Ptahhotep was an adviser to Pharaoh, the leader of ancient Egypt—the most sophisticated civilization in the world. Ptahhotep had made it to the pinnacle of earthly success. He had spent his career in the room where it happens—where big, world-altering decisions are made. He had helped shape the course of the world's most advanced society. He had tasted the best and finest things that money and power could buy. Ptahhotep was even set to succeed Pharaoh as ruler of Egypt.

The Greek word for "person" is *prosopon*, meaning "he who stands in front of someone else's eyes."

But in a move similar to that which would, millennia later, make President George Washington the stuff of democratic legend, Ptahhotep turned down the offer of absolute temporal power. The original gentleman farmer, he instead chose to withdraw from public life and live out his days, quietly and honorably, in retirement.

And there, Ptahhotep began to reflect on the ingredients of the life well lived. After enjoying the best that earthly life offered, Ptahhotep realized that what truly mattered were the sacrifices one made in order to live in community with others. He wrote a letter to Pharaoh's son distilling his insights into joyful living, in hopes that the son might take the lessons to heart and lead Egypt with wisdom and grace. He could never have anticipated that, in writing down his pithy thirty-seven maxims on civility as the building block of human community, he was writing what is today the oldest book in the world.[1]

Ptahhotep's book was read not only by Pharaoh's son, but by people across Egyptian society and throughout world history. What is now known as *The Teachings of Ptahhotep* distills and immortalizes timeless principles of civility, offering wisdom for how to restrain and overcome our selfishness and desire to dominate so that we can live well with others.

Ptahhotep's advice on how to live well with others is as relevant and practical today as when the book was written nearly forty-five hundred years ago.[2] In our last chapter, we explored how *The Epic of Gilgamesh*, the oldest story in the world, explains the root causes of incivility. Now we discover that the oldest book in the world is a meditation on civility, too. This is no coincidence. The challenge to community—humanity's inherent self-love—has always been with us. Across history and culture, thoughtful people like Ptahhotep, through experience, observation, and reflection, have come to appreciate the role of civility in promoting human community. Every society

> *[Human nature is] deviant, dangerous, and not correct, unruly, chaotic, and not well ordered . . . prone to cruelty and villainy . . . lasciviousness and chaos . . . struggle and contention.*
>
> —Xunzi, third-century Chinese philosopher and student of Confucius

has needed and relied on the Ptahhoteps of their day to re-mind them of the timeless principles of civility, those endur-ing guidelines to living well with others.

Each of Ptahhotep's teachings is remarkably consistent with other how-to civility manuals throughout human history, in-cluding those published currently. The explanation for this con-tinuity, as we learned in our last chapter, is that as long as human beings have existed, they have chosen to live communally. And as long as humans have lived communally, our selfishness has threatened community and caused strife and division. As *The Epic of Gilgamesh* teaches us, as Ptahhotep teaches us, and as our current divided moment reveals, this tension is not exclusive to any historical moment. It is as present in our own era as it was four millennia ago. *The Teachings of Ptahhotep* wrestles with this universal problem: How can we overcome our selfish natures so that we can live with others?

The Epic of Gilgamesh answered that we must harness the transformative power of friendship to help us curb our baser, self-interested instincts so that our social natures can thrive, and that we might achieve our full potential as human beings. The Gilgamesh story implies that the highest and best life is the one in relationship others. Ptahhotep agreed, and went a step further by giving specific pieces of advice for how to achieve this good life in community—pieces of advice that comprise the timeless principles of *civility*.

What Civility Is and Why We Need It

As we have learned, civility is the disposition of respecting the fundamental dignity and worth of our fellow human beings. It involves knowing who we are and what our place is in the world. *Teachings* demonstrates how to put these ideas into action.

"Do not be proud and arrogant with your knowledge," *Teachings* begins, condemning human vanity, a recurring and perpetual expression of our human selfishness. The second teaching advises restraint for the sake of community: "If you meet a disputant in the heat of action . . . pay no attention to his evil speech. . . . Your self-control will be the match for his evil utterances." Teaching four relates to our duty to do kindness to those who can do nothing for us in return,

The edifice of your pride has to be dismantled. And that is terribly hard work . . . Lying to oneself about oneself, deceiving yourself about the pretense in your own state of will, must have a harmful influence on your style; for the result will be that you cannot tell what is genuine in the style and what is false.

—Ludwig Wittgenstein, twentieth-century Austrian-British philosopher

the hallmark of true civility: "Wretched is he who injures a poor man." Kindness toward others—including the stranger and those who cannot do anything for us in return—allows us to flourish.

As teaching thirty-three states, "Be generous as long as you live. . . . Your kindness to your neighbor will be a memorial to you for years, after you satisfy their needs." Ptahhotep's *Teachings* articulates that the timeless principles of civility embody ideals of self-sacrifice, which are necessary for community and friendship to flourish. Honoring the gods was central to keeping our pride in check, Ptahhotep thought, and it is a recurring theme in the maxims.

The maxims condemn slander. For instance, teaching eight instructs, "Do not malign anyone, great or small," and teaching twenty-two advises, "Don't repeat slander nor should you even listen to it." Gossip was as harmful to the human social project four millennia ago as it is today.

Numerous maxims outline reminders about how to combat many common expressions of our selfishness, such as greed, envy, and the all-too-human tendency to be cruel to those who are weak and vulnerable. Number nineteen: "Above all guard against the vice of greed. . . . Greed is the compound of all evils." Number twenty: "Do not covet more than your share. . . . Poor is the person who forgets his relatives. . . ." Number twenty-one: "Love your wife with ardor. Do not be brutal. Good manners will influence her better than force."

Besides caring for our family, Ptahhotep reminds us that we have obligations to our neighbors and the broader community. Twenty-two: "Help your friends with things that you have, for you have these things by the grace of God. If you fail to help your friends, one will say you have a selfish Ka [the invisible alter ego in ancient Egyptian religion]. . . . If you do praiseworthy deeds, your friends will say 'welcome' in your time of need."

> *Don't be mean toward your friends. They are like a watered field, and greater than any material riches you may have, for what belongs to one belongs to another.*
>
> —Ptahhotep

Ptahhotep would not have had to write down his precepts if everyone in his era had been following them already. Ptahhotep, and the other civility writers we'll meet in this chapter, wrote their teachings because their cultures needed to be reminded of these principles for life. Ptahhotep did not create his maxims out of thin air. He derived them by observing human behavior and documenting what conduct brought misery, and what led to personal and societal harmony. Notwithstanding the diversity of human cultures and practices, there are certain unchanging truths about the human experience, many of which *Teachings* encapsulates.

Throughout this chapter, we'll explore the timeless principles of civility that have been shaped and refined by many minds over time. These people came from different walks of life. Some were powerful, wealthy, educated, admired, and famous. Others we know little about, other than that they wrote thoughtful reflections on the stuff of successful human social life. Some of the things they wrote were the products of a millennia-long dialogue; some of these sources borrowed liberally from one another. Some came to the same insights as others had before them, only landed on them independently. The fact that many came to the same conclusions about good living separately from one another implies the timelessness of the problem—selfishness—and the timelessness of the solution—civility. Collectively, they reveal truths about the human experience that offer us important advice about living well together, and we can continue to learn from them today.

The *Mahabharata* and the *Ramayana*—two ancient Sanskrit epic poems and sacred texts of the Hindu faith, composed around the fourth century BC—offer important insights into universal principles of living well with others.[3] The *Mahabharata* is considered the longest poem ever written, at 100,000 lines of verse and 1.8 million words—three times longer than the Bible, and over seven times the combined length of the ancient Greek epics *The Iliad* and *The Odyssey*, texts to which the *Mahabharata* is often compared. Avoid greed. Be a true friend. Do not do harm to those in need. Fight the temptation to be

> *They are forever free who renounce all selfish desires and break away from the ego-cage of "I," "me," "mine" to be united with the Lord. This is the supreme state. Attain to this, and pass from death to immortality.*
>
> —*Bhagavad Gita*

prideful. The *Mahabharata's* numerous stories and vignettes affirm that happiness depends on countering our selfish nature. This message is especially central to the *Bhagavad Gita*—a text within the *Mahabharata* and the most famous Hindu sacred work—which calls readers to renounce the self for a more noble, fulfilled life.

Isocrates was an orator in fourth-century BC Athens who had a knack for hitching his wagon to the wrong horse. He was a sophist—meaning he offered his rhetorical guns to the highest bidder, not unlike today's lawyers—which made him something of a villain in his contemporary Plato's book. He solicited the aid of Philip II of Macedon to lead an attack against the Persian Empire. But Philip instead decided to take over Greece, ending Greek self-rule for the remainder of antiquity. Isocrates—disgraced and not exactly becoming the hero of Greek history that he had yearned to be—starved himself to death in despair.

Despite his rather pitiful end and his poor political judgment, Isocrates was a staunch defender of the Athenian aristocratic tradition of *arête,* meaning virtue or excellence, best cultivated through the love of wisdom, or *philosophia,* including the practical application of ethics.[4] He was the "Miss Manners" of the ancient Greco-Roman world, and his work illustrates ageless principles of civility. Instead of books and syndicated newspaper columns, Isocrates wrote many letters to his friends and their children reflecting on the time-tested principles of living well with others.

Isocrates wrote in a cultural milieu that borrowed liberally from the traditions of other civilizations. These include ancient Mesopotamia, which gave us *The Epic of Gilgamesh,* and also ancient Indian and Egyptian cultures. It's not entirely surprising, then, that Isocrates' advice echoes Ptahhotep's *Teachings.* Isocrates, along with many other ancient Greek thinkers, including Aristotle, revered the Egyptians' sophisticated philosophy and culture.[5]

In one letter, sent to the young son of one of his friends, Isocrates shares his ideas about how the young Demonicus might best succeed in life. According to Isocrates, our ability to rise above our selfish nature in order to live well with others is what makes us human, and our choice to do so is the secret ingredient of a harmonious life.[6] Like Ptahhotep, Isocrates understood the power of maxims. He thought that they were the most effective tool for countering our default inclination toward selfishness, and that saturating our minds through repeating and memorizing important truths for living well with others could help us overcome the selfish gravitational pull in our nature. Like Ptahhotep, Isocrates insisted on cultivating and maintaining an other-oriented disposition: "Be courteous in your manner, and cordial in your address. It is part of courtesy to greet those whom you meet; and of cordiality to enter into friendly talk with them."

Isocrates encouraged proactive kindness and recommended that we discipline our baser impulses for the sake of community: "Consider that no adornment so becomes you as modesty, justice, and self-control; for these are the virtues by which, as all men are agreed, the character of the young is held in restraint."

Isocrates also emphasized trustworthiness and condemned gossip. Why? Because speaking ill of people behind their backs—saying things about others you would never say to them personally—corrodes trust and social harmony. "Guard more faithfully the secret which is confided to you than the money which is entrusted to your care," Isocrates wrote. "For good men ought to show that they hold their honor more trustworthy than an oath."

The undercurrent of all the advice that Ptahhotep and Isocrates offer is that we must combat our innate self-love, care for those in need, and show humanity to our friends and enemies alike. This is the soul of civility, and such advice rather remarkably appears and reappears in similar manuals and philosophical reflections on good living across human history.

We can see these themes, for example, in *The Huainanzi*, an ancient Chinese text dated from before 130 BC that expresses the ideals of ancient Daoism. *The Huainanzi* offers advice for a harmonious and just society in which all people flourish. One section, called "The Ruler's Techniques," is a handbook for future leaders who,—as in Ptahhotep's *Teachings*—fall into what is called the "mirrors for princes" category. The essay observes that the ideal ruler has a "humane and sincere heart"—in contrast to a heart inclined to dehumanize, abuse, or deceive others. And once again, the author instructs the reader that self-control is necessary in order to suppress our selfish urges so that the social can flourish: "[The ruler] practiced personal economy in his actions and made clear the humaneness of mutual love so as to harmonize and pacify [the people]." Care for the vulnerable and needy is prized as well: "Humane princes and enlightened rulers are restrained in what they take from those below. . . ."

The Huainanzi is also expressly humanistic, noting that humankind is different from other forms of life and uniquely deserving of respect: "To be thoroughly loving toward all sorts of [living] things yet not love humankind—this cannot be called humaneness." We also see in *The Huainanzi* the value of mutual benefit—an expression of the Golden Rule, as we are familiar with it in the West—surface once more: the ruler's "inner sense of reciprocity is reflected in his [outward] feelings. What he does not wish for himself he does not do to others."

The word "humaneness" in these excerpts is a translation of the Chinese character *ren,* which connotes the virtue of other-oriented behavior—quite contrary to our uncultivated nature, but quite necessary for our collective flourishing. *Ren* is a difficult concept to translate, but it has also been rendered as "benevolence" and "common humanity." The Chinese character for *ren*

(仁) is a composite of two characters—the character that means "person" (人) and the character that means "two" (二). Reminiscent of the African concept of *ubuntu* and other concepts that reveal the value that cultures across time and region have placed on community, *ren* points to a powerful reality: our "humanness" can only be fully realized in relationship with others.

Ren was a central concept to the philosophy of Confucius, who lived in fifth-century BC China in the Yellow River Valley, a region of the world considered to be another cradle of civilization.

British mathematician and philosopher Alfred North Whitehead noted that the "European philosophical tradition consists of a series of footnotes to Plato." Many have said the same is true of Confucius, only for the Chinese philosophical tradition: the entire history of Chinese literature—plays, novels, and more—is a series of footnotes to Confucius and the *Analects*. His philosophical and ethical ideas have formed the basis of East Asian culture and society.

We know little about the historical Confucius beyond the fact that he led a professionally frustrated life. He yearned to have political influence during his lifetime. He hungered to see his teachings adopted from the top of society down so that they could help people. He had a "trickle down" theory of social change that began with cultivating the character of leaders: elites with integrity would naturally work toward the benefit of all people. He spent over a decade traveling across China trying to convert rulers to his ideas, and persuade them to adopt him as an adviser.

When he failed to do so, Confucius was at first discouraged that he was not able to put his ideas into practice. But he returned to his home of Lu, south of Beijing, and resolved to do what he could with the rest of his life to bring about positive social reforms. He spent the remainder of his life talking with his disciples, and teaching his local community his vision of an ethical and humane world.

Confucius would not live to see the effect his ideas would have on government leaders. For many years, the entrance exam to become a government official in China was to memorize the entirety of the *Analects*! For Confucius, known simply as "the sage" throughout Chinese history, the best life was the social life, and the social life required developing a demeanor of kindness and benevolence toward others. We find in Confucius's *Analects*—a collection of dialogues, maxims, stories, and aphorisms thought to have been compiled by his students—that the virtue and kindness of one person can elevate and improve the lives of those around him or her—and society, too.

Confucius knew that we live in an incredibly complex and social world where roles and duties change all the time. Instead of giving people principles to memorize, he wanted to give them guidelines to live by and to help them navigate the often ambiguous and fluid project of life in community. He understood that changing our disposition toward others was more effective than memorizing a list of rules, and would more reliably cultivate a shared effort to elevate social life together and improve civility in society.[7]

In addition to *ren,* another central Confucian idea is *li,* or public ritual, decorum, propriety, and good form. The concept of *li* suggested that there was an appropriate style for completing every task, and that even the mundane and menial parts of our day could be made sacred and infused with beauty if we brought the appropriate mindset to them. According to *li,* manners are essentially communicative, akin to the rules of grammar, a theme

> *One is inspired by poetry, strengthened by rituals, and perfected by music.*
>
> —Confucius

we'll explore in Chapter 9 on civility and citizenship in a digital age. They are not necessarily right or wrong. They just *are*.

Major thinkers in world history—from Confucius, to Buddha, to Aristotle, to Jesus Christ, Mohammed, and beyond—all cited human selfishness as the root of suffering and social discord. They did this because they were astute observers of the human experience. They knew that reminding their followers of the need to overcome their selfishness for the social project would help lead them—and help them stay—on the path to the good life.

Central to the Christian tradition in which I was raised is the notion that human beings are sinful and selfish. Our word "sin" is related to an ancient Greek archery term for "missing the mark, or target." We sin when we fall short of an ideal. Jesus Christ's teachings encourage followers to subjugate these baser parts of our nature that cause us to fall short—to "die to" our fallen nature, and to become "a new creation" in faith in Jesus Christ. When Christ was asked which is the greatest commandment, he replied, "Thou shalt love the Lord thy God with all thy heart, and with all thy soul, and with all thy mind. This is the first and greatest commandment. And the second is like unto it. Thou shalt love thy neighbor as thyself. On these two commandments hang all the law and the prophets."

Known as the "dual commandment," this mandate is essentially one single, unified call for people to love things in their

> *[The idea that] "a person is a person through other people" strikes an affirmation of one's humanity through recognition of an "other" in his or her uniqueness and difference.*
>
> —Michael Onyebuchi Eze, philosopher of race and reconciliation, on the essence of *ubuntu*

In the Islamic faith tradition, the concept of al-adab encompasses a set of protocols and proper manners, and is also defined as humanity, humaneness, decency, and respect—an ethos toward others which informs proper decorum and manners.

proper order: God first, others second, ourselves last. The opposite of selfishness—elevating ourselves above others—is sacrifice: giving of ourselves for the betterment of others. Christ not only taught sacrifice as an antidote to selfishness—he *lived* it, ultimately offering his own life as an example. Relatedly, in the Jewish tradition from which Christianity sprang, the concept of *chesed* describes adherents' duty to engage in acts of kindness toward others, derived from the understanding that human beings are created in God's image. It is a mandate to do as God would do.

Moving ahead a few hundred years, we see the same ethical advice in popular European manners manuals of the early Middle Ages. Petrus Alfonsi was a Jewish convert to Christianity who lived in eleventh-century Islamic Spain. Born and raised in Al-Andalus, the Muslim-ruled area of the Iberian Peninsula, he was intimately familiar with the Jewish, Christian, and Islamic traditions. He wrote the *Disciplina Clericalis*, which distilled popular Eastern wisdom for a Western audience in a collection of fables and adages. He wrote the book first in Arabic, and then in Latin and other languages as the demand grew.[8]

Alfonsi's ability to bridge these cultures earned him enormous esteem and popularity. He lived in a time of growing factionalism and division between the major cultural, religious, and ethical traditions of his day—Judaism, Christianity, Islam, and Greek and Roman philosophy. Not unlike the goal of this book, Alfonsi's aim was to show what these traditions had in common, and emphasize their humane and humanizing attributes.[9] Though he was a Christian—and his conversion from Judaism earned him many enemies—his work was neither for, nor enjoyed by, an exclusively Christian audience. Alfonsi believed that insights into living well could be derived from many different sources—Eastern and Western, pagan and Christian alike—and that anyone who practiced certain universal ethical precepts could lead a life of flourishing and happiness.

In addition to relying on maxims, Alfonsi also favored the long-standing tradition of storytelling for moral instruction, where narrative brought to life the themes of time-tested wisdom and proverbs. Alfonsi saw himself as merely a messenger, distilling from observation and study different ethical traditions that helped people lead full, rich, and meaningful lives. He didn't create these guidelines—God did. After all, he wrote, "For in anything invented by man, there is no perfection."[10] Citing the Hebrew Bible and Arab poetry, the *Disciplina Clericalis* begins and ends with advice on the fear of God, reminiscent of a core aspect of Ptahhotep's advice. This mandate to fear or respect God implicitly advises humility, anticipating the all-too-human tendency of thinking ourselves to be the center of the universe.

I have been mindful of the fact that in order to facilitate remembrance of what has been learnt, the pill must be sweetened by various means, because man is by nature forgetful and has need of many tricks which will remind him again of those things he has forgotten. For that reason, then, have I put together this book, partly from Arab proverbs, counsels, fables, and poems. . . .

—Petrus Alfonsi, *Disciplina Clericalis*

Alfonsi writes, again cautioning against human hubris: "For the philosopher says, 'He who seeks glory in a field of which he is ignorant will be proved quite clearly a liar.' Another philosopher says: 'Agree with what is true and do not enquire whether you discovered it or some other person.'"[11] Alfonsi determined the secrets of harmonious social living by drawing from the best traditions of his day, illustrating the rewards and punishments of virtue and vice, which he communicated through narrative and precept. His winning formula of intermingling proverbs and story entertains, educates, and ennobles all at once.

Daniel of Beccles was the Emily Post of twelfth-century England. While Ptahhotep wrote about broad, high-level principles, Beccles's *Urbanus magnus*—sometimes referred to as *Liber Urbani*, or *Book of the Civilized Man*—left no aspect of human life untouched. At nearly three thousand lines, ten times longer than any other contemporary book on the subject, it is the most substantial "courtesy poem" in any language and was enormously popular. Written to "old King Henry" (probably Henry II), its tone is that of a father's advice to a son, but it was intended for women, aristocrats, and laymen alike. The poem opens, "Reader, read, and reread me if you wish to be adorned with good manners, if you wish to be respected and to lead a civilized life as a noble householder." It outlines best practices for "elegance of manners" (*gracia morum*) at the table, including over three hundred lines on what to drink and eat. Beccles also offers some recipes for good measure, and suggests the ideal frequencies for bathing, exercise, and copulation—seasonally adjusted, naturally.[12]

Beccles was a fan of basic decencies, such as refraining from attacking one's enemy while they relieved themselves.[13] He advised children's obedience and deference to their parents: "It is an immense crime to hate your own parents. It is an ignoble

and perverse child steeped in wickedness who defiles them."
And Beccles recommended that we lead our lives with an eye to
general harmony with others: "You should avoid violating civil
peace with crime. Hold dear to your neighbors, it is worth being
kind to them; there is no greater praise than being pleasing to
your neighbors."

The overarching theme is self-control—surrendering oneself for the sake of others. To this end, it suggests specifics
about when, where, and how readers should defecate, urinate,
spit, belch, and pass gas in society. Self-control, Beccles emphasized, was the secret ingredient to *pax in urbe,* or the social ideal of living at peace with one's neighbors and fellow
citizens.

Apparently 1216 was a bad year for civility in the German
Middle Ages. One Thomasin von Zirclaere, an Italian trans-
plant to Germany, was so fed
up with what he saw as the
degraded state of common
decency and manners of the
Germans he was surrounded
by that he spent a frenzied
ten months composing an
epic poem on manners called
Der Wälsche Gast, or *The Italian Guest.* This outsider had

> *When you belch, remember to
> look up at the ceiling!* [. . .]
> *Only the head of household is
> entitled to urinate in the hall!*
>
> —Daniel of Beccles, twelfth-
> century manners writer

decided that adaptation to his new environs was not an option:
Germans would have to improve their manners if they were to
keep their new Italian companion.

At this point, we can see a trend: manners writers, including yours truly, brandish their pens when the barbarity of their
surroundings becomes too much to bear. It's not always the case
that finger-wagging books become bestsellers—especially not

ones written by cultural outsiders with an eye to reforming insiders. But Thomasin's polemic hit a cultural nerve: his fifteen-thousand-line poem was enormously popular with the young people he wrote it to instruct.[14]

The Italian Guest was the most important didactic work of the German High Middle Ages. The poem was so popular that it is preserved to this day in twenty-four illuminated medieval manuscripts—works of art, some of which took years for transcribers to adorn and complete. Thomasin drew from Christian and pagan sources, from Pope Gregory I to Aristotle and Cicero and more.

Thomasin urges young noblemen and-women in his readership to model their lives and conduct after the great mythic and historic heroes of the recent and distant past—including Charlemagne, King Arthur, Gawain, Percival, and the Knights of the Round Table, as well as Biblical heroes such as Job, David, Moses, and more. He encourages them to live their lives drawing inspiration from past heroes, and with an eye to setting an example for the rest of society. For Thomasin, ethics and etiquette, manners and morals, right conduct and right character were inextricably bound.

Thomasin was uncommonly democratic for his day. He claimed that true chivalry isn't merely a label for a knight who "breaks a lance" in the joust. Instead, it is a title anyone who pursues virtue and justice can claim as their own. His formula for the good life is to oppose our selfish nature at every turn: be humble, chase justice, and avoid pride, envy, anger, and overindulgence. Above all, aim for moderation and constancy in all things. He viewed the human condition as we have so far in this book: each person by nature seeks primarily their own well-being, an instinct that we must rise above in order to achieve the promise and possibility of social life together.

Cato's *Distichs*, a Latin textbook for children that consisted of a series of rhymes meant to inculcate manners and morals in young pupils, may be the most influential handbook of the Middle Ages.

This textbook was for many years incorrectly attributed to the famous Roman historian Cato the Elder, but it is now attributed to the relatively unknown Dionysius Cato. The work was revived during the Middle Ages and became an influence, though now underappreciated, on centuries of thinkers to come. Luminaries from Geoffrey Chaucer and Cervantes to Benjamin Franklin learned civility by the *Distichs*'s instruction.[15] Chaucer's *The Canterbury Tales*, for example, makes frequent reference to the *Distichs*, often to affirm that the failure to have read the famous manual marked someone's education as incomplete.

Much of the *Distichs* reiterates the practical ethics with which we are now familiar, exploring the theme of restraining self-interest for the sake of community. Forgive quickly and freely; don't hold grudges; don't gossip. Keep your temper: "Temper in fighting rival claims eschew: temper bars minds from seeing what is true."

Franklin, nourished by Cato's teachings as a child, said the book was "very proper to be put in the hands of young persons,"[16] and even

> *What one sees on the outside is not without significance, for it always signifies what is on the inside, too.*
>
> —Thomasin von Zirclaere, thirteenth-century Italian writer of the German courtesy poem *Der Wälsche Gast*

> *If you can, even remember to help people you don't know.*
>
> *More precious than a kingdom it is to gain friends by kindness.*
>
> —Cato's *Distichs*

In most places that I am acquainted with, so great is the present corruption of manners, that a printer shall find much more profit in such things as flatter and encourage vice, than in such as tend to promote its contrary. . . . I confess, I have so great confidence in the common virtue and good sense of the people of this and the neighboring provinces, that I expect to sell a very good impression.

—Benjamin Franklin, in his preface to the 1735 printed edition of Cato's *Distichs*

printed his own translation in 1735.[17] In the preface to his edition, Franklin noted that he wasn't sure printing an old manners manual was a wise business move, but said it was worth reproducing good and virtuous content for its own sake. And, besides, as the preface states, he had faith in the American people to know a good thing when they saw it—and, ideally, buy his book! Franklin's flattery did the trick: his edition sold well, and was a well-known textbook in the American founding era.

Facetus was the title of another beloved twelfth-century courtesy poem inspired by Cato's *Distichs*, which remained widely used until the fifteenth century. *Facetus* offers advice on everything from table manners to dress to how to be a good conversationalist. "He who speaks badly of women is a boor (*rusticus*), for truly we are all born of women," *Facetus* wisely advises.[18] The Latin word *rusticus*, whence we get our word "rustic," was important to *Facetus* in particular and to medieval courtesy books in general. A "rustic" person was someone who hadn't yet made the sacrifices necessary to live happily with others.

In addition to *Facetus*, Cato's *Distichs* also influenced the intellectual superstar of the European Renaissance, Erasmus of Rotterdam. Known as the "Prince of the Humanists," Erasmus was the original cosmopolitan. He left his hometown of Rotterdam in the Netherlands at a young age, and for the remainder of his life rarely spent more than two years in any one location. He referred to himself as a "citizen of the world," a term he popularized. He loved people, good conversation, and learning, and had a general joy for life. This gentleman-scholar was the most coveted dinner guest in all of Europe.

There can be no high civility without a deep morality.

—Ralph Waldo Emerson

Erasmus was intellectually courageous, but had a peace-loving disposition. He translated a copy of the Christian New Testament from the original Greek—an extraordinary intellectual feat. This process highlighted many errors in a copy of the Bible, called the Latin Vulgate, that was used throughout the Western church for hundreds of years. The Catholic Church was nonplussed by Erasmus's discovery. Though he was a lifelong Catholic, he wasn't afraid to show the church areas in which, to put it mildly, it needed to improve. (He hoped to reform it over time through improved access to education.) His ideas for reform inspired a young Martin Luther—it's said that "Erasmus 'laid the egg' of the Protestant Reformation that Luther 'hatched.'"

These were radical days, which was unfortunate, because Erasmus was not a radical in any way, shape, or form. There was no room for a moderate middle course at this moment in history. Erasmus earned enmity from Catholics and Protestants alike but today is relatively forgotten, having established and inflamed no polarized religious tribe that kept his memory alive. In this way, Erasmus is a model of civility to us today.

Erasmus was acquainted with the mores of the most refined royal courts in Europe. He was also well-traveled—he made a point of relocating every few years for the duration of his life—when travel wasn't an easy undertaking, which meant that he had regular interactions with non-nobility, too. He had relied on Cato's *Distichs* to prepare him for his regular encounters with kings and commoners alike, and so treasured the book that in 1514 he, as Benjamin Franklin would centuries later in the New World, published his own edition. Sixteen years after that, Erasmus wrote his own manual, inspired by *Distichs*, entitled *A Handbook on Good Manners for Children*. Written in Latin, his book was an immediate international bestseller and was quickly translated into every major language in Europe. Erasmus's book became the continent's most influential guide on civility for several centuries.

That Erasmus—the greatest intellectual luminary of his day—chose to dedicate time to manners shows how important it was to people of the Renaissance era. Like Ptahhotep, Isocrates, Daniel of Beccles, Thomasin, and Cato, Erasmus framed his civility manual as instructions to a young man in his life—a Dutch prince—though he also wrote it "for all young people." Those who lament the decline of common courtesy and manners in today's youth will find a champion in Erasmus, who was convinced—like Thomasin von Zirclaere and many others before him—that *he* was living in the most uncivil era. "There was no one except one old man who greeted me properly, when I passed in the company of some distinguished persons," Erasmus lamented, decrying the state of modern manners.

As the father of Christian humanism, Erasmus believed that piety was the first step in a child's education. Like the great thinkers of antiquity by whom he was influenced, Erasmus cared primarily about cultivating good character and nobility of the soul. Like St. Augustine, whom we met in our last chapter, Erasmus thought that a classical education in the humanistic tradition and in the liberal arts was the best remedy for disordered loves—which, as we learned from St. Augustine in Chapter 1, is the default state of humanity in which we put ourselves before others or God. The humanistic tradition that Augustine and Erasmus were formed by and which they fostered involved reading famous works of literature and philosophy. It helped children develop habits of overcoming their selfish nature and their *libido dominandi,* and "rightly ordered" their loves.

Like Augustine, Erasmus understood that all people are born with disordered affections, that we naturally elevate ourselves and our needs above others, and that it is only through instruction, example, and practice that our loves can be put in their proper place. An education in Christian humanism helped students reorder their loves correctly. For Erasmus, this meant putting God first, others second, and ourselves last.

In our penultimate chapter, on cultivating civility through education, we'll return to this idea of how ordering our loves can apply to our modern secular educational culture and usher in greater civility. Manners and common courtesy are important means of practicing rightly ordered loves, because they help us cultivate the habit of considering others alongside and before ourselves in our everyday interactions. Erasmus knew that basic consideration of others when it came to ordinary interactions was an important way of expressing inner character.

Like the ancient Greek and Roman thinkers whom he admired, and like the other thinkers and writers we've explored in this chapter, Erasmus knew that virtue and true freedom of the soul consist of self-governance, controlling one's baser impulses and passions in the name of a higher principle—namely, friendship and community with others. He referred to manners as "one of the most basic elements of philosophy." Erasmus's *Handbook* is the only etiquette book of which I am aware that is organized by anatomy, with each section addressing a different part of the body and noting the correspondingly appropriate and ill-advised conduct.

"It's polite to say 'Christ help you' to another person when they sneeze," Erasmus wrote in the section on the nose. He condemns laughing to oneself when with others so as to not make others think they are being ridiculed. Try not to burp in public. Don't pick your teeth with your knife. Sit up straight at the dinner table. Try not to scratch yourself in public, lest people think you have fleas or lice—more relevant, perhaps, in the sixteenth century than today, but still an apt reminder!

Don't relieve oneself in front of others; do so privately. Don't lick your fingers at the table, or lick your plate. Avoid talking with your mouth full. Erasmus was even an early opponent of manspreading: "Sit with your knees together—not wide open."

Keep your hands on the table at dinner, not hidden in your lap, Erasmus recommends. Erasmus was the protagonist in Norbert Elias's story about the history of manners in Europe, which we explored in our last chapter. Erasmus noted that there is violence and vulnerability inherent in eating a meal with someone. Sharp utensils and knives are potential instruments of harm. Doing what one can to communicate trust and transparency while dining with someone—such as making sure your hands are always visible—is a common piece of advice found across cultures. Elias pointed to Erasmus as the first manners writer to define a standard that required people "to mold themselves more deliberately than in the Middle Ages."[19] Erasmus gave instructions to readers about aspects of life together that were far more specific than past etiquette writers offered, Elias argued, and suggested that this greater focus on control of how we eat—and how we wield potential weapons at the dinner table—reduced the anxiety, fear, and disgust that had previously defined communal dining, and helped to promote the project of social harmony and civilization.

Neither Erasmus nor Elias was the first to note how manners mitigated both disgust and violence when dining and promoted friendship and community. Virtually every culture has norms around how to consume a meal, because they help regulate an otherwise perilous—or simply gross—encounter with others.

As you wash your hands, so, too, clear troubles from your mind. For it's not good manners to be gloomy at dinner or to make anyone else miserable.

—Erasmus of Rotterdam, sixteenth-century intellectual superstar of the European Renaissance

Erasmus is presciently sanitary. He suggests turning away from others when one must sneeze or wipe one's nose—and recommends doing so into a handkerchief. His advice in avoiding contagion, physical and emotional, lest one weaken the community, is lovely and timeless. Once again, we see a prohibition against gossip: "Harming the reputation of someone not present is a great offense." He advises conducting oneself in a way that promotes trust: "It's disgraceful to bring out into the open, as Horace says, something that someone has revealed unwittingly. . . . I hate a drinking companion with a good memory." He took a puzzlingly strong stance against winking. In the chapter on the right conduct of the eyes, he contends, "It's inappropriate to wink at another person. For what is it other than doing yourself out of an eye? We should leave that gesture to tuna fish and one-eyed mythical metal workers."

"Greedy gobbling is the way of ruffians," Erasmus wrote, cautioning against stuffing one's mouth so full that one spews its contents on others.

The guiding principle behind every piece of Erasmus's advice is that the key to good manners is to counter our default tendency to ward off selfishness and pride, and to instead cultivate a disposition of charity: "Readily ignore the faults of others, but avoid falling short yourself."

As we learned in our last chapter, human community and civilization itself are exquisitely fragile. Our relationships with others, though, give us the motivation to overcome the selfishness endemic to our natures so that community can survive. Society is supported or degraded by how we live every day. Civility writers the world over have noted this, and reminded us that the less we disgust, antagonize, and generally vex one another, the better it is for civilization—and all the better for us.

Decades after Erasmus lived, one Giovanni della Casa took up the theme of the precariousness of social life. His book *Il Galateo: The Rules of Polite Behavior*, published in 1558, like Erasmus's book before him, had broad, cross-cultural resonance. Within two years of publication, it had been published in Milan, Rome, Florence, and Bologna, and in the years that followed, it was eagerly received by readers in France, Germany, and Spain.

On the one hand, some of della Casa's advice reflected his personal taste and view of beauty and appropriateness. He adopted the aesthetic ideal of his Renaissance peers, valuing balance, the high potential of human beings, and classical visions of beauty. Most of his principles of public conduct reflect this specific vision of attractiveness. But he was also steeped in classical culture—he spent a year of his life doing nothing but translating Cicero and other Latin writers from antiquity!—which at its best sought to cultivate both humanity and humaneness in students. Della Casa was influenced by Plato's theory of forms and Aristotle's "golden mean." He drank deeply from the ancient writers, such as Marcus Aurelius, who had many thoughts on how the weaknesses of the human condition can present barriers to friendship and human community.

As in the texts previously discussed, we observe in della Casa an acute sensitivity to the way in which our self-love is a constant barrier to community. Revealing another set of norms that are remarkably constant across time and place, della Casa pays special attention to the unhygienic and the just plain obnoxious.

"Don't lean over and sniff someone else's food," he suggests. "It's gross, and nose debris could fall in." This, della Casa rather sensibly worries, could distract from the conversation and conviviality of friendship—perhaps something of an understatement.

As previously noted, many of these authors borrowed liberally from one another. In another example of this, della Casa's *Il Galateo* provided the source material of a Jesuit etiquette manual, a version of which eventually found its way into the hands of a young George Washington. When Washington was thirteen years old, he hand-copied 110 rules of civility, which we'll consider in our next chapter. Today, these rules are often cited and published as Washington's own work, but they were in fact part of a long lineage of ethical writings and conduct literature, a lineage we have explored in this chapter. Washington was transcribing rules from the Jesuits. The Jesuits drew from della Casa's *Il Galateo*. Della Casa's work drew heavily from Greek philosophy, such as Aristotle's *Nicomachean Ethics*, which in turn was influenced by the Egyptians—and the vizier Ptahhotep, who wrote on civility in 2350 BC.

The civility authorities we have explored so far in this chapter—from Ptahhotep to Isocrates to Confucius to Daniel of Beccles to Thomasin von Zirclaere to Petrus Alfonsi and Cato, Erasmus, della Casa, George Washington, Aristotle, and back to Ptahhotep—all make one important observation: relationships, like civilization, are fragile. Minimizing the threats to them by restraining our selfishness, and considering how our presentation and conduct affect others, buttresses both friendship and community.

All of these authors tightly link our personal conduct to the project of human society. They link our outer conduct with our inward character, a theme we will unpack in greater depth in our next chapter. The enduring popularity of the civility-book genre speaks to the timelessness of the problem these writers seek to address: none of these authors would have had to write a book on civility if civility were not a problem in their era! Incivility has been and always will be with us, because human selfishness will always be part of us. The question is whether we will, in reviving this rich lineage, choose to build on their vibrant tradition and apply their wisdom to our own lives now.

We're a doggedly social species. Our sociability is even embedded in our language.

The Greek word for "person" is *prosopon,* meaning "he who stands in front of someone else's eyes." The Latin expression of *prosopon* is *persona,* the root of our word "person." Pro-social behavior has been praised across time and place; meanwhile, selfish, antisocial behavior has been consistently condemned. *Polis* means "city" in Greek. The opposite of *polis* is *idiótes*—which means "individual," "private person," or someone who refuses to take part in public affairs—and is the root of our word "idiot."

This survey of civility handbooks also illustrates the timelessness of humanity's efforts to overcome the challenges of life together. For millennia our species has reflected on how we can manage to build true civilization together—a society founded on comity, collaboration, peace, and harmony. Human history shows that, with the proper motivation—and with the right reminders from authors such as those we've explored in this chapter—we are resilient, committed, and capable of overcoming our basic selfishness and reaping the fruits of life in community.

In addition to manners manuals, virtually every culture has wisdom literature that offers advice for both leading a good life *and* getting along well with others. This is because people across time and places have known

Do not do unto others whatever is injurious to yourself.

—*The Gathas*, the writings of Zarathustra, founder of the Persian religion of Zoroastrianism, composed between 3000 and 2000 BC

that life with others *is* the good life—and that harmony with others is neither natural nor a foregone conclusion. That is why this body of literature consistently encourages us to rise above our natural instinct toward unmitigated self-love. Life in community requires continuous effort, but it promises something better. We see this in the Golden Rule, for example—a teaching that is central to the Christian and Zoroastrian traditions, as well as many others—which appeals to our self-interest to help others. We observe this teaching in the Books of Proverbs and Ecclesiastes in the Hebrew Bible, the Dharma of the Buddha, the *Bhagavad Gita*, the *Masnavi* of the Persian Islamic poet Rumi, and more.

Time and time again, these works offer the same recommendations. Honor God. Have compassion for those less fortunate than you. Respect the wisdom that comes with age. Pursue virtue. Hold on to things of this world loosely. Avoid greed. Be honest in your dealings with others. Forgive quickly. Show grace frequently to your fellow man. Be aware of the shortcomings in our nature—and strive to overcome them.

These reminders are repeated over and over, often within the same text. Why? Because our selfishness makes them easy to forget. Self-sacrifice is not our natural way of thinking or taking action. The Book of Proverbs from the Hebrew Bible goes so far as to charge us to "bind [these teachings] around our neck," as we are prone to forget them. We must be trained, and frequently reminded, to think of others alongside ourselves.

Within any place, person, continent, or culture there is the capacity to build or detract from civilization. We can let our selfishness and *libido dominandi* run unchecked, or we can rein it in. The choice is up to us, and our individual choices can have important consequences, for bad or for good.

> *A generous friend*
> *gives life for a friend.*
> *Let's rise above*
> *animalistic behavior*
> *and be kind to one another.*
>
> —Rumi, thirteenth-century
> Persian-Islamic poet

As we discussed in Chapter 1, the challenges to civility and civilization in our current era are both the same—because of the unchanging selfishness in our nature—and also very different than in past eras. Yet one constant is the agency we each have to choose to reclaim our sphere of influence, to be part of the solution in how we can control each day. If we didn't have agency, the efforts of Ptahhotep and those like him—individuals across history who sought to persuade people to act in more noble, selfless ways—would be futile.

We can't change the world or how other people behave. But we can change ourselves. Changing ourselves can make a big difference toward elevating and rehumanizing our use of technology, healing our public discourse, nourishing the beauty in our environment, recovering community, neighborliness, and friendship, restoring the bonds of affection between citizens, and restoring civilization itself—all of which we have seen diminished, undervalued, and strained in recent years.

The potential to create a civilized society—to usher in a new era of civility, empathy, and compassion that cherishes the value of *every* human life—lies within each of us. Thoughtful writers from Ptahhotep to George Washington believed this, and we should, too.

We'll continue to explore what recovering the soul of civility looks like and why it matters to our lives in our modern, democratic context in the next several chapters. I hope you'll join me there.

Part II

WHY CIVILITY?

3

Integrity

While I was working in Washington politics, one particular experience taught me about the shortcomings of politeness, the importance of civility, and that appearances are not always reality. I had the privilege of working alongside members of America's disability community. On a visit to an educational program for adults with disabilities in the Washington area, I was invited to join a meeting between a student, her parents, and her teachers. The student in question sat at one end of the room—a young, petite girl, aged twenty, named AC, who had been born with Down syndrome. AC looked frightened and alone. At the other end of the table sat administrators and members of her support staff. Her parents were present telephonically via a loudspeaker in the middle of the table.

There'd been an "incident," an administrator began to explain. Even just hearing that word spoken in that tone made my heart drop and my pulse begin to race, reminding me of the times growing up when I had found myself in trouble. The prior evening, the administrator shared, AC had put a towel on her head to emulate the hijab that a member of her support staff wore. This was interpreted by the institution as an act of intolerance and led to the present disciplinary meeting. "Coming to college is a brave thing to do," the administrator empathized, speaking to AC. "It's also very challenging, because of the way one inevitably encounters diverse people, beliefs, and opinions."

AC trembled, and then erupted into tears.

"I can't do this!" she cried. "I have Down's. I need to go home. I can't be at school because I have Down's."

After a moment, AC's mother, Laura, consoled her daughter. She reminded AC that her two sisters had faced the same frustrations and challenges when they'd first left for college. "But they didn't have Down's!" AC exclaimed.

Laura continued, explaining to the room that this outburst was likely a manifestation of AC's broader, lifelong struggle to accept her Down syndrome.

"Our family believes in God, and we have always reminded AC that she was created by God and he created her just the way she is—perfect and loved by him," Laura reflected pensively. "She has always had difficulty accepting that."

Laura explained to the room that, growing up in the Midwest, AC had enjoyed little exposure to people wearing religious and cultural head coverings. Putting the towel on her own head was not an act of malice, but of curiosity, of joyful exuberance in learning about her novel environment, and becoming like a new friend.

"This isn't about a struggle for AC to accept beliefs that differ from her own," Laura said. "It's related to her lifelong struggle to accept herself and her disability—and accepting a loving God, who made her this way."

This experience, and my time serving and learning from people with disabilities more broadly, taught me that what we see is not always what we get. How people, or situations, first appear are not perfectly correlated with truth. AC's teachers thought her conduct was intolerant. In truth, it was an act of curiosity, and was also related to a lifelong inward struggle of self-acceptance. Outward acts are an imperfect proxy for a person's inner character. People can seem good but be bad, as I had learned in government. I knew many people who understood how to comply with and manipulate social norms in order to achieve their own ends. Conversely, one could misinterpret a person's actions as intolerant even if they were not.

Compliance with external social norms—or politeness—is not a reliable way to assess someone's inner goodness or character. Sometimes, people do not comply with social expectations through no fault of their own. They may have physical challenges, developmental delays, difficulty remembering social rituals, or trouble interpreting social cues. These are not reasons to punish people. Unfortunately, we are often intolerant of socially atypical people and behavior, and excruciatingly hard on people who do not fit the mold. We must cultivate a greater sense of understanding, grace, and forbearance for difference, and for people who do not comply with conceptions of politeness. Choosing civility is a solution to this. We can start by putting politeness—or the form of an act—in its proper place, and elevating civility—the substance and motivation behind it—instead.

The Challenge of Information Asymmetry

There is an inherent information asymmetry in life. When it comes to living with others, all we have to go on are people's outward actions, including how they dress, speak, and act. We cannot ever fully know another's heart, mind, or character. We can, often do, and often must make assumptions based on first impressions. But first im-

For the Lord sees not as man sees: man looks on the outward appearance, but the Lord looks on the heart.

—I Samuel 16:7

pressions aren't always reliable, and are often deceptive. A suave and charming couple could turn out to be nothing more than low-stakes con artists. Conversely, someone who is brusque, unkempt, or simply uninitiated in certain proprieties may have a good and earnest heart. Appearances are imperfect stand-ins for reality.

> *If you will only take the trouble always to do the perfectly correct thing, and to say the perfectly correct thing, you can do just what you like.*
>
> —George Bernard Shaw, twentieth-century Irish playwright

Having a polite and polished exterior is not enough to indicate the goodness of a person. Compliance with norms of goodness and decency *can* help make us good. But an inordinate focus on polished exteriors—on dressing well or adhering to the rules of politeness—can foster hypocrisy, too. Hypocrisy, a manifestation of our selfish nature, is when one preaches one set of values—the values that one expects others to live by—and then lives by a different standard.

Knowing the rules of politeness—including how to dress, what to say, how to act—is not enough. We must practice civility and cultivate *integrity*—which will help us flourish both personally and communally.

Integrity vs. Hypocrisy

Integrity is self-coherence. The word derives from the Latin root *integer,* which means "intact." Integrity, as its etymology suggests, describes inner sturdiness, or wholeness of self. It's the ideal state that my mother described to us growing up of outward actions reflecting inner character. Civility fosters integrity—it promotes all parts of one's self fitting together—because it emphasizes having correct motivation and internal disposition toward others and the world, and cultivating habits and actions aligned with that inner state.

Hypocrisy, on the other hand, is self-contradiction, as when we fail to practice what we preach. Hypocrisy derives from the Greek *hupókrisis*, meaning "stage acting" or "pretense." Hypocrisy elevates the act, pretense, or appearance of truth without the reality. Politeness fosters hypocrisy because it emphasizes external appearance and compliance with the rules instead of internal character. Politeness does not care for the disposition or motivation behind looks, words, and conduct. It elevates the *appearance* of virtue without the *substance*. While hypocrisy is the enemy of healthy human relationships, integrity is essential for human flourishing.

Socrates said to his followers: "Watch that you be not obedient and disobedient toward God at the same time." And they said: "Explain to us what you mean," and he said, "Put aside hypocrisy. For it is hypocrisy to pretend in men's presence to obey God, but in secret really not to believe. . . . To prevent this from happening, do everything with a pure heart, lest you seek to gain glory."

—Petrus Alfonsi, twelfth-century writer and Jewish convert to Christianity from Islamic Spain

Moral habits that promote human flourishing are virtues. They empower us, and fortify us from the inside out, and strengthen society. Moral habits that divide us—within ourselves and between ourselves and others—are vices. Moral habits founded on virtue promote integrity, or a character and outer conduct that are in alignment. Civility promotes the virtue and integrity that enable us to get on well with others, because it helps us develop a correct outlook of others and the world: one that takes personhood and basic respect for others seriously. It helps us practice actions that cohere with, and reflect, that inner disposition. Politeness, however, promotes hypocrisy by eschewing motivation, and making people feel as if complying with the rules of etiquette alone is enough. Even some of most pro-polish figures in history knew that the outward form of an act was insufficient, and could be used for deceit.

If all men knew what others say of them, there would not be four friends in the world.

—Blaise Pascal, seventeenth-century French polymath

The nineteenth-century British social reformer Lord Shaftesbury called faux, insincere politeness "froth"—a visual I adore and word I think is due for a revival.[1] Froth for Shaftesbury was what some today might call "smarm," or "bullshit," and he had an entire home regime in place for people to prevent it from taking root in their lives.

Social life at times requires artifice. If everyone did and said exactly whatever they wanted to, the result would be chaos, anarchy, and suffering. If there were total transparency between people—if everyone knew everyone else's worst thoughts and deeds—we wouldn't ever want to be around anyone at all.

Does society require hypocrisy, then? No. It requires integrity.

Integrity is distinct from *authenticity*. Integrity doesn't require us to act out every private thought and feeling. Sometimes, counterintuitively, integrity requires a disconnect between our inner feelings and our outer conduct. But this disconnect exists to serve others. Integrity expresses itself in action based on deeply held core values—for example, the value of friendship and respecting those around us—rather than temporary feelings or selfish desire.

When we find ourselves in a disagreement with a friend, spouse, or sibling, we will often bite our tongues instead of saying *exactly* how we feel. This is inauthentic. But it's not hypocritical.

In fact, it's acting with integrity, because the disconnect between our outer conduct and our inner feeling serves a higher, selfless purpose: maintaining a deeper connection. We restrain ourselves from an outburst of anger in the heat of the moment—an authentic display of our inner feelings—because we would like to preserve the relationship. Our feelings, moods, and opinions are fluid. Often, they are self-interested. How we feel about someone or a situation when we are angry may change once we allow ourselves time to relax and cool off and consider other perspectives alongside our own. Integrity sometimes means *not* acting on the basis of our inner feelings. As we learned in Chapters 1 and 2, our relationships with others motivate us to restrain our selfish needs so that we might fulfill our higher social needs. How we feel in one moment does not define who we are. Integrity calls us to act in accordance with our deeply held inner values, even when we do not feel like doing so.

By contrast, the problem with hypocrisy is not that it promotes a disconnect between inner feeling and outer conduct. Hypocrisy is problematic because we betray our moral commitments in order to serve ourselves. A person may flatter their boss—telling them they are attractive, well-dressed, and a great golfer—while secretly

> *Wouldn't the social fabric come undone if we were wholly frank with everyone?*
>
> —Molière, seventeenth-century French playwright, *Le Misanthrope*

> *Hypocrisy is a tribute vice pays to virtue.*
>
> —La Rochefoucauld, seventeenth-century French writer

despising and seeking to undermine them, an example of the self-serving nature of hypocrisy at its finest.

Hypocrisy is harmful because it dispenses with one's purported values for personal gain and convenience. It instrumentalizes others instead of respecting them, using them as a means to one's selfish ends. In focusing on the expression of an act alone—instead of the substance and motivation *behind* the act—politeness fosters hypocrisy. Integrity and civility place the interest of others above one's immediate desires for the longer-term benefits of being in relationship and community. They surrender the ego so that our social nature can flourish.

Civility's other-oriented disposition promotes integrity, because it refuses to allow human selfishness to dictate how we act. It instead guides our actions based on a higher, more principled and noble part of our self—the part of our self that values community and sees other human beings as intrinsically worthy of respect. Both civility and integrity defy transient and base inner feelings in the name of acting in accordance with a higher value. But developing character and maintaining integrity are hard. It's often easier to get the credit and reap the benefits of appearing good than it is to be good—a challenge to the civility and social trust that binds society, and a problem we've been dealing with as a species for a long time.

The Society of the Spectacle

We'll explore later in this chapter examples that show we are just as susceptible to elevating image and appearance over reality as we were in past eras. At least one thinker, however, has argued that contemporary society is even *more* prone than past ones to embracing simulacra over reality. In his 1967 work *The Society of the Spectacle*, French philosopher Guy Debord contended that we've exchanged authentic relationships for false, intermediated ones. Our word "spectacle" derives from the Latin *spectaculum*, which means "public show," and *spectare*, which means "to watch, view, or behold." Debord thought appearances—and merely viewing others—were all we cared about. "All that once was directly lived has become mere representation," he wrote.

The spectacle is not a collection of images; rather, it is a social relationship between people that is mediated by images. . . . In a world which really is topsy-turvy, the true is a moment of the false.

—Guy Debord, twentieth-century French philosopher

Debord observed a phenomenon that would become only more pronounced in the age of the internet and social media. As a card-carrying Marxist philosopher, he was concerned with capitalism's effects on consumerism and acquisition. Debord argued that in past eras, people prioritized authenticity and *being* in their social lives. The influence of a progressively consumerist culture, however, caused people to care less about *being* and more about merely *possessing*. And in the future, Debord contended, people would begin to care even less about *possessing* and more about merely *appearing*.

The society that cared more about *having* and *appearing* than about authentically *being* was, for Debord, the *spectacular* society. People in the spectacular society care less about substance and more about style. All human relationships are expressed and mediated through objects and images. This "relationship by proxy," he warned, takes a profound toll on the quality of human life, at both the individual and societal level. In a spectacular world of image-mediated relationships, everyone has a persona—or, as in our day, a brand, a social media profile—that represents the self-image that one wants others to perceive. People are no longer people, but commodities. As Martin Luther King, Jr., and Martin Buber would say, what should be "I–thou" relationships have devolved into "I–it" relationships.

And it's not just Fortune 500 companies or social media influencers who care about their public personas or online presence. We all do. We're told at every turn of the importance of cultivating and maintaining our personal "brand." We've become so focused on how we seem to the world that we've impoverished our character, and forgotten why leading authentic lives is important both for our own well-being and for that of others. In a spectacular society, our relationships are drained of their life-giving power because they are based on a falsity, mediated by hollow images and appearances instead of grounded in integrity and truth. For Debord, the antidote to the society deceived by spectacle is "to wake up the spectator who has been drugged by spectacular images." Perhaps we can awaken from our spectacular stupor by learning from spectacles in our own era that have been thoroughly unmasked.

What Simon Leviev, Anna Delvey, Billy McFarland, and Elizabeth Holmes Have in Common

Ample modern-day examples support Debord's thesis that we are a spectacular society. Our world is awash with confidence men and women, archetypes we'll explore shortly. Simon Leviev, Anna Delvey, Billy McFarland, and Elizabeth Holmes are a few of many recent examples.

Simon Leviev paid for his extravagant lifestyle with an online-dating Ponzi scheme. Posing as an Israeli diamond heir, he wooed his marks with expensive gifts and lavish vacations in private jets. His Instagram profile, which documented every detail of his luxurious life, only enhanced his allure to his marks. At some point in the relationship, he would ask for a loan because of an imminent threat to his life. He would use that money to wine and dine his next mark. Known as the "Tinder Swindler," which is also the name of the Netflix documentary about him, he was estimated by authorities to have scammed dozens of women out of tens of millions of dollars.

Anna Delvey arrived on New York City's social scene in early 2010.[2] She flashed hundred-dollar bills, sported designer clothes, and spoke in an unidentifiable, affected pan-European accent. As long as she was footing the bill at the city's best restaurants, no one was too concerned about the provenance of her wealth. Posing as an heiress to a multimillion-dollar fortune, Delvey led an extravagant and cosmopolitan life among the global elite, one defined by luxurious travel, fine dining, art, and fashion. Her Instagrammable life was the envy of New York's social elite: everyone wanted to be friends with Anna. That is, until she stopped paying her bills.

Over several years, Anna Delvey—whose real name is Anna Sorokin—scammed hotels, banks, and friends in New York City out of hundreds of thousands of dollars. She was ultimately arrested and as of this writing is currently serving prison time for her crimes. Her story, dramatized in the Netflix series *Inventing Anna*, seems too sensational to be true, but it convicts our society's obsession with spectacle.

Billy McFarland had a dream of producing the best music festival in history. Fyre Festival, however, became "The Greatest Party That Never Happened," as the eponymous Netflix documentary is subtitled. Billy sold Fyre as a luxury music festival on the glittering white sands of a remote private island in Exumas, Bahamas—which, the festival's promoters bragged, was once owned by Colombian drug lord Pablo Escobar.[3]

Reminiscent of what Debord called the "shimmering diversions of the spectacle," videos advertising the festival—featuring supermodels laughing, dancing, and drinking on the beach and on yachts in bikinis—were plastered across Instagram. They promised prospective attendees "the best in food, art, music, and adventure."[4] Rappers such as Ja Rule, a festival co-organizer, lent Fyre celebrity cachet. Instagram was alit with videos and endorsements from supermodels such as Emily Ratajkowski and Instagram "influencers" such as Kendall Jenner, Bella Hadid, and Hailey Bieber.

But the Fyre Festival was smoke and mirrors. After paying up to thirteen thousand dollars per person to be there, attendees arrived on the Bahamian island eager for an opulent getaway. They were instead greeted by chaos, carelessly assembled FEMA disaster relief tents, and warm, limp cheese sandwiches.[5] It was a far cry from the glamorous experience that social media had promised them. Attendees were seduced by the glistening promotional images. As Debord would have put it, images had supplanted the real—that is, until the real became too dire to deny.

No discussion of spectacle would be complete without discussing Elizabeth Holmes, former CEO of Theranos—and also the subject of the award-winning 2018 book *Bad Blood: Secrets and Lies in a Silicon Valley Startup*, the 2019 HBO documentary *The Inventor: Out for Blood in Silicon Valley*, and the Hulu miniseries *The Dropout*. Holmes was an attractive young CEO who claimed to be starting a revolution in blood testing and medical treatment. She dressed in black turtlenecks, like Steve Jobs, assuming the appearance of the famous disruptor, inventor, and in-

> *Celebrity [is the] the spectacular representation of a living human being. . . . Being a star means specializing in the seemingly lived. . . . Celebrities exist to act out various styles of living and viewing society, unfettered, free to express themselves globally.*
>
> —Guy Debord

novator she admired. She named the Theranos blood-testing machine "the Edison," after Thomas Edison.

At its peak, Theranos was a nine-billion-dollar company with the backing of some of America's most powerful and influential men on its board, from George Shultz—economist, diplomat, and one of the two people in US history to have held four different Cabinet-level posts—to former defense secretary Jim Mattis, former Wells Fargo CEO Richard Kovacevich, and former secretary of state Henry Kissinger. When Jim Mattis was asked what drew him to Holmes—what caused him to throw his weight behind her project—he answered: "integrity."[6] In the end, however, Holmes's claims about what her blood-testing technology could do were proven to be untrue. A federal jury eventually found her guilty of defrauding her investors out of hundreds of millions of dollars, and she was subsequently sentenced to eleven-plus years in prison.[7]

What ties these stories together? Each of these figures was remarkably charismatic. They had a knack for earning people's trust, including winning wealthy, influential, and powerful people to their cause. They were malevolently innovative and creative. They were willing to cut corners in order to win. They each relied on *spectacle*—including leveraging the power of appearance and social media—to succeed. And spectacle allowed them to succeed in our world, at least for a while. Our spectacular society—where people elevate appearance over substance—enabled Simon Leviev, Anna Delvey, Billy McFarland, and Elizabeth

> *[The spectacle] says nothing more than "that which appears is good, that which is good appears." The attitude which it demands in principle is passive acceptance which in fact it already obtained by its manner of appearing without reply, by its monopoly of appearance.*
>
> —Guy Debord

Holmes to defraud and deceive thousands of people out of millions of dollars. To achieve their selfish ends, they used *polish* and *politeness* to present a façade of someone others wanted to be around. They lacked *civility*, which forms the character of a person whose heart is genuine and oriented toward others. Each of these people relied on hypocrisy, not integrity.

The world is rife with pretenders—those who cultivate the image of something they are not. While this tendency is not new, we have tools and technologies today, such as social media, that enable us to create cultivated images and reach wider audiences with personas that do not represent reality. We should pause before placing our faith in those who rely primarily on charisma and charm to achieve their ends, as it is far too easy for such people to deceive others, and possibly themselves, along the way.

Personality Ethic vs. Character Ethic

There are two types of people in life: those who rely on *personality ethic* and those who rely on *character ethic*.[8] The character ethic relies on integrity, on charm, methods, techniques, and spectacle. This sounds like politeness, doesn't it? Character ethic, by contrast, depends on deep changes within each of us, and a proper orientation of the heart. It relies on integrity, or on all parts of the self making sense together. It relies on civility.

Personalities are what people can see on the surface. They are what, and how, we present ourselves to the world. They include how we speak, such as the affected European accent Anna Delvey adopted; how we curate our image on social media, such as Simon Leviev and Billy McFarland did; and how we dress—Elizabeth Holmes and her black turtlenecks. Personalities are only skin-deep. If they are different from our true, core selves, the result is hypocrisy.

Character is deeper, and is composed of our values, our motivations, and our disposition toward others. Character is one of those things that people cannot see, at least not directly. Yet character cannot remain completely invisible forever. Living life without character is like trying to navigate through Paris with a map of London. It doesn't matter how skilled you are at the *techniques* of map reading. It doesn't matter how polished your personality ethic

> *False face must hide what a false heart doth know.*
>
> —Shakespeare

is. Without a good map, or a solid foundation of good character, you will be limited in where you can go and what you can achieve.

Integrity and Hypocrisy in Philosophy and Art

Great artists and thinkers across history and culture have appreciated that polite manners and a polished appearance are not enough to make a person good. The ancient Greeks believed in the unity of beauty, goodness, and truth. What was beautiful was good and true, and what was good and true was beautiful. They tended to be *totus teres atque rotundus,* which means "polished and rounded off," in their ethical views, and did not strictly separate manners from morality.[9]

Human beings, they thought, were wholly transparent to one another: what one *saw* of another person was what they *were.* A person's true character was on clear display. If one wanted to deceive others about who he was, it was possible— but only in the short term; in time, one's true character would be revealed. The concept of *kalos kagathos* was important to the ancient Greeks, and was also an educational ideal in the Middle Ages. It embodied the idea of appearance and personal conduct that extended from a sound inner character. The term is a composite of the Greek words for "beauty," *kalos* and *agathos*, meaning "virtuous" or "good." In his famous book *Paideia*—which we'll return to in our chapter on education—Werner Jaeger describes *kalos kagathos* as "the chivalrous ideal of the complete human personality, harmonious in mind and body, foursquare in battle and speech, song and action."[10]

We find an echo of this idea of the inseparable relationship between a person's conduct and character in the work of Confucius and the Chinese philosophical tradition. For Confucius, there was no distinction between manners and morals, between inner character and outer conduct. Right action was always an extension of right belief. One's conduct with others—in politics and in communal life generally—was an extension of inner character and morality.[11] Confucius suggests that we should live a life of virtue—which we do by following the *dao*, an East Asian concept of "the way" or the natural order of the universe—for its own sake. It might not lead to immediate gain or gratification, but a life in harmony with the *dao* and virtue is its own reward. Personal moral cultivation is the foundation of a functioning society, Confucius thought. The concept of *chun tzu* that he develops throughout the *Analects* describes the person whose character is one of virtue and kindness to others, and who, as an extension of his good character, acts well in accordance with justice and his duties to others.

> *Look at the means a man employs, observe the path he takes, and examine where he feels at home. In what way is a man's true character hidden from view?*
>
> —Confucius

Around the same time that Giovanni della Casa's popular *Il Galateo* was making the case for common decency and civility for the masses, Baldassare Castiglione's *The Book of the Courtier* (1528) was being read in the aristocratic halls of Europe, instructing the elite in the ways of polish and politeness. Castiglione wrote the handbook to help ambitious courtiers foster an appearance of sophistication so as to curry favor with superiors.

Sprezzatura, the art of effortless effort, wrote Castiglione, is "a certain nonchalance," and was central to his argument about ideal courtier conduct. The opposite of *sprezzatura*'s studied carelessness was *affectazione*, or the affectation of pretense. For Castiglione, the true courtier didn't just *pretend*—or *affect*—to be talented in all things. They truthfully *were* exceptional in all realms.

Castiglione, in keeping with the Renaissance ideal of a humanist education, encouraged his readers to cultivate themselves to the fullest. He wanted them to be well-rounded, well-read, and well-versed in many different activities, as the humanistic vision of education prescribes. The potential for abuse of *The Courtier*'s principles was apparently widely accepted: Castiglione's book ended up on the list of banned books on the Catholic Index. When Irish author James Joyce read—and apparently adopted the teachings of—*The Book of the Courtier*, his brother told him he had become more polished, but less sincere. But Castiglione hedged against the accusation of hypocrisy—which focuses on the external *form* of conduct alone—by encouraging internal and external coherence. The outer show of talent ideally reflected an inner reality and character.

> *Avoid* affectazione *in every way possible . . . and practice in all things a certain* sprezzatura *so as to conceal all art and make whatever is done or said appear to be without effort and almost without any thought about it.*
>
> —Baldassare Castiglione, author of *The Book of the Courtier*

The Victorians were convinced that one's conduct revealed one's character. Victorians were fastidious about proper table manners, personal hygiene, dress, appearance, and elegant conversation, because they connected them inextricably with morals. "Civilities of private life were corollaries of civilized social life," wrote historian Gertrude Himmelfarb in her book *The De-moralization of Society*. Appearance mattered because, even if it did not perfectly correlate with a virtuous inner reality, it affirmed the legitimacy of Victorians' values.

Jane Austen appreciated that appearance is not a reliable representation of character, nor are manners a reliable representation of morals. A favorite target in her novels was the hypocrisy of her own Georgian period. In *Sense and Sensibility*, John Willoughby is handsome, well-mannered, and well-bred. But his polished exterior is purely pretext. He lacks integrity, which we discover when he seduces, impregnates, and then abandons the young and vulnerable Eliza. After deserting Eliza, Willoughby proceeds to misrepresent his intentions with Marianne Dashwood, only to abandon her, too, in search of a wealthier wife.

Austen's Willoughby couldn't be more different from her most famous male protagonist: Mr. Darcy. In *Pride and Prejudice*, Darcy is haughty, curt, and downright rude toward Elizabeth Bennet, the novel's female lead. For this reason, Bennet despises him. She assumes that his lack of politeness means that he is a cruel person of poor character. She accuses him of lacking the "gentlemanlike manner" appropriate for a man of his station in life, and even turns down his proposal of marriage because of his lack of polish. Yet Mr. Darcy surprises Elizabeth by showing her and her family great kindness, even saving Elizabeth's sister from disgrace. Mr. Darcy wasn't po-

> *One may smile, and smile, and be a villain.*
>
> —William Shakespeare

lite. He didn't always follow the rules or assume the appearance of propriety. But in the end, he was kind and civil in the truest sense, and when it mattered most.

A recurring theme in Austen's novels is that problems can arise when we fixate on the form instead of the substance, the rules of politeness instead of civility. She reveals through her characters the imperfect correlation between manners and morality. A person can follow the rules of dress, taste, decorum, and politeness to the letter—as Willoughby did—and still be cowardly and cruel. Conversely, one can flout the rules—as did Mr. Darcy—and still be decent and kind.

Lord Chesterfield's *Letters*, written in the eighteenth century to his illegitimate son with advice about how to use polish and charm to win social success, is illustrative of someone using manners and the appearance of goodness for calculated ends. "It is by manners only that you can please and consequently rise," Lord Chesterfield wrote. When Samuel Johnson read the letters, he dismissed them as "the morals of a whore, and the manners of a dancing master."

The "affable villain" or the "wicked cultured character" prevalent in cinema and pop culture shows the broad resonance of this theme. Hannibal Lecter, for instance, is among the most exquisitely polite and cultured figures in popular fiction and Hollywood film, yet a cannibalistic serial killer. He is refined and sophisticated. He quotes Marcus Aurelius and William Shakespeare. He hangs his charcoal sketches of Florence, produced from memory, in his prison cell. He enjoys Johann Sebastian Bach's *Goldberg Variations* while flaying one of his victims.

Many a Bond villain is polished, sophisticated, and refined. Dr. No enjoys fine art and even steals Francisco Goya's portrait of the Duke of Wellington, and Auric Goldfinger enjoys classing things up with a splash of gold, including women and servants. They're elegant, but they plan world domination. Interestingly enough, Ian Fleming, the author of the James Bond book series, while portraying his villains as having sophisticated tastes, also frequently depicts them with a physical deformity. This reflects their inner, moral deformity of character, which no amount of taste or polish could cover up: a third nipple, no earlobes, a face marked or scarred. Fleming's depictions of his villains instantiate the view of the ancient Greeks, Confucius, and the Victorians, wherein one's appearance reveals a person's true—though invisible—inner character.

In his essay "What Is Art?" Leo Tolstoy argued that all art is moral. All true beauty serves the project of education and moral instruction. Anything or anyone that appears beautiful, but is cruel or unjust, is an impostor.

It's not always easy to tell the impostor from the true, the spectacular from the real. It's difficult to know when there exists a mismatch between people's external appearances and their internal character. We should not mistake culture and refinement for either character, virtue, or morality. There is infinite variety in matters of taste and beauty, but cruelty toward others is almost always understood as ugly and contemptible.[12] While we should limit our judgments of others on matters of discretion, cruel and callous conduct toward our fellow human beings—or toward any form of life, for that matter—is always contemptible. Tastes, and what people deem fashionable and elegant, change with time. The tenets of integrity, good character, and civility—which involve respect for and kindness toward others—are timeless.

The Charlatan

In the Greco-Roman world, hypocrisy was exemplified by the charlatan. Charlatans were philosophical pretenders who wanted the social esteem and cachet of a philosopher without doing the hard work of really being one. In the ancient world, philosophers exhibited recognizable attire and mannerisms. Socrates, for example, didn't bathe, dressed in rags, and refused to wear shoes because he thought that focusing on material things distracted him from the more important world of ideas and matters of the soul. Cynic philosophers in the Roman Imperial period dressed in rustic wool cloaks and wore sandals, carried wooden staffs and wrapped leather wallets around their waists, maintained long, unkempt beards, and avoided bathing. They also delighted in flouting social conventions.

When I saw that many of [the charlatans] were not in love with philosophy, but simply coveted the reputation of the thing, I got angry.... I found their preaching directly opposed to their practice.

—Lucian of Samosata, second-century Syrian satirist and comic writer

Charlatans adopted the mannerisms and appearance typical to philosophers—spurning social norms and doing outrageous things—but they did so purely to get attention, not because they held any principles that informed their disregard for convention. They pretended to love wisdom, but they really loved only pleasure, money, and fame. They did not care about improving the lives of their students through learning, as true philosophers did. They used the disguise of a philosopher to enrich themselves at their students' expense. This is what made them hypocrites: their inauthenticity was self-serving.

Hypocrisy in America

Alexis de Tocqueville noted the honesty and candor of American manners when he embarked on a nine-month trip to America in 1831. Officially traveling to study America's prison system, the twenty-six-year-old French aristocrat also had an *unofficial* goal: he wanted to discover firsthand the promise and pitfalls of American democracy. There was generational trauma in the Tocqueville family from the French Revolution, during which Alexis lost many family members—including, very nearly, his own parents. Though he was skeptical of democracy, Alexis understood that democracy was the future.

As a French aristocrat, Tocqueville was familiar with the complex social rituals typical in Europe. He knew that the outward, ornate show of manners of a nobleman could obscure an ugly heart. When he visited America, he found our rustic manners refreshing, because at least they were honest. When it came to interacting with Americans, Tocqueville learned, what you see is what you get.

There was a tight connection between form and substance. We trusted others because we were trustworthy. We've long taken pride in this aspect of our national character.

Our trustworthiness was of particular importance during the nineteenth century, an era of great social and cultural changes, such as urbanization.[13] People moved en masse from *gemeinschaft* to *gesellschaft*—from smaller-scale "community" to larger "society." Suddenly people moved from towns where "everyone knew everyone" to cities where they suddenly found themselves dependent on countless anonymous strangers in

But no, you say, what makes a cynic is a contemptible wallet, a staff, and big jaws; to devour everything you give him, or to stow it away, or to revile tactlessly the people he meets, or to show off his fine shoulder.

—Epictetus, second-century Greek philosopher, poking fun at people who thought they could gain the social credibility of being a philosopher just by dressing like one their daily life. No longer able to rely on the close-knit social networks where everyone knew everyone else personally, by family name, or by reputation, people were forced to develop and depend on a shorthand for trustworthiness. That shorthand was first impressions, outward appearance, and manners. A person who dressed well and followed the rules could be trusted. One could confidently form a relationship or do business with them.

Handbooks on manners exploded during this era of American history.[14] Familiarity with prevailing etiquette became inextricably bound to the American dream: with a little work and dedication, anyone could cultivate the character, and the manners, that led to making friends and building success. They could then rise through the ranks and prosper.

The large-scale shift from the small town to the big city made the problem of information asymmetry in social life—where one cannot fully know a person's inner character—even more severe. Then, a group of opportunists emerged to make matters worse. The nineteenth-century "confidence man"—the origin of our modern term "con man"—threw Americans for a loop.[15] The confidence man preyed on Americans' trusting nature.

A common con went like this: the confidence man would

> *Democratic manners . . . form, as it were, a thin, transparent veil through which the real feelings and personal thoughts of each man can be easily seen. . . . I know it has happened that the same men have had very distinguished manners and very vulgar feelings; the inner life of courts has shown well enough what grand appearances may conceal the meanest hearts.*
>
> —Alexis de Tocqueville, nineteenth-century French writer and statesman

> *Manners are of more importance than laws. Upon them, in a great measure, the laws depend. The law touches us here and there, and now and then . . . [manners] give their whole form and color to our lives. According to their quality, they aid morals, they supply them, or they totally destroy them.*
>
> —Edmund Burke, eighteenth-century Anglo-Irish statesman, orator, philosopher

eagerly greet a perfect stranger as if they were old friends, inquiring earnestly into their family and general well-being, only to bid farewell and make off with their interlocutor's pocket watch or wallet. The fact that a polished and refined gentleman could be a swindler cast doubt on Americans' faith in our "what you see is what you get" ideal. Our external polish and politeness, which had become a proxy for virtue and goodness, was no longer a reliable indicator of trustworthiness. The confidence man undermined the commonly held view that manners could accurately convey character.

Appearances and manners are not perfectly correlated with inner goodness and morality. People who have bad intentions can seem to be good. An inordinate focus on the rules of politeness can foster hypocrisy, because politeness focuses on the *form* of actions. Civility, on the other hand, focuses on the *substance* of an action; civility is about having the right motivation behind our conduct. Politeness thus focuses on *seeming* good, while civility focuses on *being* good—on true virtue as opposed to the appearance of it.

The idea of habits having the effect of internalizing virtue finds expression in the Confucian concept of *li*, an idea we examined in the last chapter. *Li* notes that people and character are formed by custom, propriety, and decorum.[16] Habit and ritual can help restrain our worst impulses—and help us live happily with others—if we let them.

In his book *Civility: Manners, Morals, and the Etiquette of Democracy*, Yale Law professor Stephen Carter argues that civility promotes the integrity necessary for democracy. This is because civility, he says, is "a set of sacrifices we make for the sake of our common journey with others, and out of respect for the very idea that there are others . . . who are every bit our equals before God." Civility requires conducting oneself with integrity—a mode where our outer actions are aligned with our inner values. Carter says that this coherence happens in large ways and small—respecting others in recognizing their fundamental human rights, and respecting others with our manners.

Carter points to the "purification" process that Martin Luther King, Jr., and his followers used in their nonviolent civil protests. Adherents to the philosophy of peaceful, nonviolent resistance knew that rebelling against an oppressive status quo would subject them to violence. But they chose the high ground. They chose to conduct themselves more justly than their oppressors. Their aim in doing so was to prick the conscience of their nation, exposing America's hypocrisy. Their goal was to confront and sensitize their fellow citizens to the deep injustices of institutional racism. Purification violated the rules of politeness. It also invariably meant suffering for those who followed its method. Yet it was an act of great civility—and integrity. It went against the protesters' true desires—after all, who would want to endure such abuse?—but they did it anyway because of their affection and respect for those whose opinions on racial segregation they sought to change.

Lessons from Jesus Christ on Why the Rules of Politeness Promote Hypocrisy

The life of Jesus Christ helps explain why *being* good is more important than *seeming* good. Christ was constantly exposing the hypocrites of his day. He taught that a correct *disposition*—one of compassion and love for others—matters more than complying with the rules of right conduct alone. Jesus understood the potential perils of an inordinate focus on appearance and politeness. He scathingly critiqued the religious hypocrites of his day, who were smug in their self-righteous compliance with prevailing rituals. But he knew that their fastidiousness was merely a cover for their selfishness.

When the Pharisees accused Jesus of breaking the religious law by not washing before eating, he responded, quoting the Book of Isaiah in the Hebrew Bible: "These people honor me with their lips, but their hearts are far from me. They worship me in vain; their teachings are merely human rules." He accused them of letting human traditions become more important than the commands of God.

> *What comes out of a person is what defiles them. For it is from within, out of a person's heart, that evil thoughts come—sexual immorality, theft, murder, adultery, greed, malice, deceit, lewdness, envy, slander, arrogance, and folly. All these evils come from inside and defile a person.*
>
> —Mark 7:20–23

Christ's disciple, Judas Iscariot, betrayed him while complying with the polite custom of the day: giving him a kiss on the cheek.

Jesus understood that doing good and helping others is more important than unthinkingly following the rules. When rules got in the way of helping others, he disregarded them. The Pharisees weaponized the rules against Jesus when he healed a man's withered hand on the Sabbath—a day where the rules required rest. He responded: "I ask you, which is lawful on the Sabbath: to do good or to do evil, to save life or to destroy it?"[17]

Christ's life and teachings remind us that a person's disposition, the state of their heart, matters far more than their compliance with social norms. Jesus understood that it was a reality of the human condition for people to look for ways to make themselves feel superior to others. He knew that people like rules to follow, and that rule following was an easy way for people to feel smug in comparison to those around them.

Yet he also understood that rule following alone is insufficient to make a person good. Appearing to act well while allowing one's heart to remain angry and bitter, as the Pharisees did, is the epitome of hypocrisy. Christ was unequivocal about the importance of maintaining the *spirit* of the law over the *letter* of the law. Christ had no problem calling them out for their duplicity: "Woe to you, teachers of the law and Pharisees, you hypocrites!

You [Pharisees] are the ones who justify yourselves in the eyes of men, but God knows your hearts. What man values God hates.

—Luke 16:15

You give a tenth of your spices—mint, dill, and cumin. But you have neglected the more important matters of the law—justice, mercy, and faithfulness. You should have practiced the latter, without neglecting the former."[18]

For Christ, it was a person's attitude—the condition and orientation of their inner life—that was most important. He approached things contextually, because he realized that rules could easily be abused and a blind application of them could be counterproductive. Politeness and its rules are easy to follow. They let us avoid the hard work of changing our hearts. As the Pharisees in Christ's day exemplify, if we are creative, we can figure out how to follow the rules while still being as selfish as ever.

He said to them, "If any of you has a sheep and it falls into a pit on the Sabbath, will you not take hold of it and lift it out? How much more valuable is a person than a sheep! Therefore, it is lawful to do good on the Sabbath."

—Matthew 12:11–12

Why Hypocrisy Hurts Both the Other and the Self

In our first chapter, we discovered how our unchecked self-love and the *libido dominandi* hurt others and corrode the human social project—but how they also hurt us. The same is true for hypocrisy, an expression of our self-love, a manifestation of our tendency to use others for our own benefit. Hypocrisy is a lose-lose game. Hypocrisy hurts others because it deceives them, and by deceiving others, it disrespects them. It hurts hypocrites themselves because, while they may be able to fool others with their pretense and appearance, they cannot fool themselves. Sixteenth-century English statesman Sir Walter Raleigh defined a compliment as "a courteous and court-like kind of lying." Eighteenth-century Anglo-Dutch philosopher Bernard Mandeville thought that good manners

Flattery corrupts both the receiver and the giver.

—Edmund Burke

were nothing more than fanning the selfishness of others and concealing one's own.

Two and a half millenia before Christ, Ptahhotep cautioned his readers: "Do not listen to the words of flatterers or to words that puff you up with pride." He warned people to be wary of those who offered fawning praise, because such praise kindles the selfishness that poses a threat to everything from personal relationships to civilization itself. Three and a half millennia later, seventeenth-century English Puritan writer John Bunyan bemoaned "the poor and beggarly art of complimenting." Why? Because the "more the compliment, the less the sincerity." Unlike acting with civility and integrity, being hypocritical and falsely polite with others hurts them because it constitutes lying to them. And lying to others disrespects them and their dignity as persons.

Second, hypocrisy hurts the hypocrite. Wise people across history have argued that virtue—and living with integrity and civility—were their own reward. Vice and hypocrisy, by contrast, were their own punishment. This is because they viewed hypocrisy and vice as diseases of the soul, symptomatic of disordered passions that placed the self above others. Hypocrisy is bad for our psyche.

Vanity working on a weak mind produces every kind of mischief.

—Jane Austen, eighteenth-century Anglo-Irish statesman and philosopher

Adam Smith, in *The Theory of Moral Sentiments,*

There are two ways man may wrong another, by force and by fraud. A man may be violent as a lion or crafty as a fox. Both are inhuman kinds of behavior, but fraud is the more odious. Particularly to be deplored is the hypocrisy of those who under the guise of respectability practice the worst acts of deception.

—Cicero, first-century BC Roman orator, philosopher, and statesman

wrote, "Man naturally desires, not only to be loved, but to be lovely." We yearn to be loved. We desperately crave the esteem of others. We're willing to flatter, fawn, and even deceive in order to get it. We also yearn to be lovely—that is, we want to be *deserving* of the respect of others. If we go about gaining the esteem of others by lying or by other deceitful means, we will always know that the adoration we receive isn't deserved.

When a person is divided within—when one thinks of themselves as a good person but acts unjustly to others—the *psyche*, the Greek word for "soul," suffers. That cognitive dissonance—the gap between who we think we are and who we are—will take its toll. As we've learned and will learn throughout this book, when we hurt others—in ways great or small, through violence or by lying to them through hypocrisy—we hurt ourselves, too.

How to Create More Integrity and Civility in Ourselves and Society

Information asymmetry in social life has always existed, and it always will. We can never know with complete certainty the state of someone's soul or character.

We should reject politeness and hypocrisy, and embrace civility and integrity. We can do so at both the individual and the societal level. Max Beerbohm's 1897 *The Happy Hypocrite: A Fairy Tale for Tired Men*, is basically the inverse story of Oscar Wilde's 1890 novel *The Picture of Dorian Gray*, and reveals to us a path of less hypocrisy, more integrity, and greater harmony of society and the soul.

Lord George Hell enjoyed every vice, and was someone who had gained status and wealth in society by being willing to do anything, and use anyone, to get ahead. But he fell in love with a virtuous woman, Jenny Mere, who had pledged to marry only a man with the face of a saint. Undeterred and determined to win her hand, Lord George tried to take a shortcut to integrity—similar to the one that Simon Leviev, Anna Delvey, Billy McFarland, and Elizabeth Holmes chose. He purchased the mask of a saint, which he affixed to his face. When, donning his newly masked face, he proposed to his beloved Jenny Mere, she accepted.

Their marriage marked a point of moral conversion for Lord George. He renounced his ill-gotten wealth and began to lead a morally upright and simple life. He decided to become worthy of his new, very righteous, wife. Soon after their marriage, another suitor of Jenny Mere appeared and exposed Lord George, demanding that he remove his mask so that she might see his true, vicious countenance. After a struggle, Lord George took off his mask. He was petrified, knowing that without his mask, his life of sin would be evident and he would lose his beloved.

Something shocking happened instead. When his face was revealed, his complexion *had become like the mask of the saint he was at first only wearing*. Wearing the mask had begun as a lie. His virtuous conduct was at first pretense and hypocrisy to win the hand of the woman he loved. But his virtuous and selfless outer actions eventually transformed his vicious inner character into a virtuous one.

We can build our integrity and inner character by practicing and forming habits of sacrifice and civility—as Lord George Hell did—in our lives. We must strive to close the gap between appearance and reality. Character is habit long continued. As individuals, we can each choose what inner character we want to cultivate with our outer actions. Every choice we make forms our character, and character is important because it determines our destiny. We can also create broader social cultures of integrity and civility. One way to cultivate a culture of integrity and civility is to change what we value as a culture. Instead of focusing on the polish, spectacle, charm, appearance, and form, we can decide as a culture to see beyond that, and to value substance and virtue instead. We can do this by praising and rewarding people who demonstrate character, integrity, and civility wherever we see it—and by creating a culture that honors those who embody the soul of civility.

How to Build Trust, Civility, and Integrity

1. Remember that civility promotes the virtue and integrity that enable us to get on well with others because it helps us develop a correct outlook on others and the world: one that takes personhood and basic respect for others seriously.

2. Remember that being good is more important than seeming good. Live your life that way, and model it for others—especially children—around you. Your integrity and civility will ennoble all you meet.

3. Character is habit long continued. Moral habits founded on virtue promote integrity, character, and outer conduct that, grounded in virtue, are in alignment. Remember

that moral habits that promote human flourishing are virtues. Moral habits that divide us—within ourselves and between us and others—are vices.

4. Resist the urge to make assumptions about people based on appearances alone. Remember that we can never perfectly know a person's inner state and motivations, and never will. As we've learned, those who are polished and refined are not always good, while those who flout convention don't always do so out of malice. Try to see past appearance and get to know a person's heart.

5. Avoid rewarding spectacle with our attention, and instead choose to elevate substance over style.

6. Remember that being hypocritical hurts others but also ourselves. Have candid, civil, and respectful conversations with friends and colleagues about things that bother you. Don't let things go that breed resentment and cause you to be hypocritical. Resist engaging in Shakespeare's "mouth-honour," or being outwardly kind but inwardly resentful, or engaging in Lord Shaftesbury's "froth," or faux civility.

7. In a spirit of charity, call out your loved ones when you hear them saying things they don't mean, or see them acting in ways that contradict their values. "Cut out that mouth-honor," you might say to them. Or my personal favorite, "That's downright frothy." (Can we get these on T-shirts?)

8. We can build trust with others and within ourselves by becoming trustworthy, and cultivating integrity. We can start by following through with promises to ourselves and to others. For instance, only say "Let's get lunch" or "Must do coffee soon" if you mean it. Words lose their meaning when we abuse them, and we hurt ourselves and others when we aren't honest.

4

Freedom, Democracy, and Human Flourishing

Men are qualified for civil liberty in the exact proportion to their disposition to put moral chains upon their own appetites. . . . Society cannot exist unless a controlling power upon will and appetite can be placed somewhere, and the less of it within, the more there must be without.

—Edmund Burke, eighteenth-century Anglo-Irish statesman and philosopher

When incivility becomes a problem, public leaders are sometimes tempted to impose civility by force. These efforts are rarely either welcomed by citizens, or effective in their ends. In the early 2000s, Mayor Michael Bloomberg launched a campaign against rudeness in New York City.[1] Subway riders and showgoers could be fined fifty dollars for inconsiderately resting their feet on a bench or for using their phones during movies or Broadway shows. The city's noise code was overhauled to crack down on loud nightclubs and barking dogs and to promote neighborhood peace. Cell phones were banned in movie theaters, and smoking was banned in public places.

Other New York City officials, emboldened and inspired by Bloomberg, took aim at impoliteness at sporting events, arresting, fining, and imprisoning people for spitting or throwing objects onto the field. One man was sentenced to nine weekends in jail, fined two thousand dollars, and banned for three years from Shea Stadium.[2] Still other local officials went further. Children under ten were prohibited from attending movies after 10 P.M., in an attempt to prevent disruption to people's moviegoing experience. Parents who shouted during their children's sporting events could be banned from them.

Manners experts, apparently tired of being ignored by the public, praised these measures and elevated New York City as a shining example to other metropolises. "I cannot applaud it enough," said Letitia Baldrige, the White House social secretary during John F. Kennedy's administration. "My hands are tired from clapping."[3]

New Yorkers and local parents did not quite like being "civilized" by their local government. While proponents argued that just having these laws on the books in the first place was enough to improve behavior, the laws went largely unenforced and were soon recognized as entirely ineffective.

Bloomberg and New York's technocrats aren't the only ones who have attempted to socially engineer civility. Nor are they the only ones who failed. Across the pond, British prime minister Tony Blair's 2006 "respect action plan" also exemplified an unsuccessful effort to enforce civility from the top down. The campaign's goal was to prevent and combat all forms of "antisocial behavior"—from crime to bad manners. It included imposing a nighttime curfew, with a salty fine of eighty pounds sterling (over one hundred US dollars) for violators, and a "national parenting academy" that aimed to help parents "recognize their responsibilities" in civilizing their children.[4]

The plan's more controversial proposal sought to address "nuisance behavior" by giving authorities the remarkable unilateral

We are justified in enforcing good morals, for they belong to all mankind . . . [but] we are not justified in enforcing good manners, for good manners always mean our *manners.*

—G. K. Chesterton, twentieth-century English writer

power to temporarily evict people from their homes for three months. If a bureaucrat deemed a person discourteous, perhaps noisy or disruptive, or their home a "property from hell," that person could be given the boot from their own hearth, even if they *owned* the home.[5] While the government assured the public that such a measure would be a "last resort," the potential for abuse alarmed many. Detractors argued that Blair's "respect" agenda wasn't terribly respectful of English people's basic civil rights, and verged on totalitarianism that unnecessarily made criminals out of everyday citizens.

Civility and Freedom

We take for granted the many freedoms we enjoy. The ability to move, leave our jobs to pursue better opportunity, worship where and how we want, and more, however, have not always been part of the human experience. We often overlook the moral underpinnings, as well as the norms of restraint and self-sacrifice, that support the freedoms we enjoy in contemporary, democratic societies.

By regulating the manifestations of our self-love, civility supports our personal and political freedom. When too many of us fail to exercise civility, people will begin calling for the government to restrain us through laws and regulations. Civility promotes the virtue and self-government that allow us to thrive in community, uninhibited by either tyranny or fear of our fellow citizens.

Our selfishness poses a problem for our freedom. If we cannot individually control ourselves, others, including our political leaders, will impose controls upon us. Sociologist Edward Shils called this dynamic "the antinomy of liberalism": within a free society, we have the freedom to undermine our freedom. Our freedom and flourishing are sustained through our routine exchanges and nourished through the decisions we make every day to respect our fellow citizens.

> *For as good manners cannot subsist without good laws, so those laws cannot be put into execution without good manners.*
>
> –Niccolò Machiavelli, sixteenth-century political theorist

Civility: The Social Contract That Supports the Social Contract

As we explored in the last chapter, civility helps us become more trusting of others by helping *us* become trustworthy. In addition to removing the low-grade discomforts of everyday life, a subject we'll shortly explore, civility supports our freedom on personal, institutional, and societal levels.

For the ancient Romans, the *civitas,* or city, was composed of a group of *cives*—citizens united by common laws. The laws of the *civitas* offered citizens the rights of citizenship, but also bound them to certain obligations. These rights and obligations among citizens were the premise of the *civitas.* Each citizen was born into the laws, rights, and duties of the *civitas,* and each citizen had to abide by them to remain part of it.

Several prominent seventeenth- and eighteenth-century political theorists—such as Benedict Spinoza, Thomas Hobbes, John Locke, and Jean-Jacques Rousseau—developed the concept of a "social contract," an agreement about the unwritten mutual duties between citizens and government. Formal political arrangements—such as the *external constraints* on government, including laws passed by Congress—are important. Equally important, however, are the *internal constraints* that individual citizens place on *themselves* to govern how they interact with their fellow citizens. While the social contract pertains to the *vertical* relationship between citizens and their government, civility is the unwritten, unspoken contract that governs *horizontal* relationships between us.

In short, civility is the social contract that supports the social contract. Without it, our free way of life will cease to exist.

Because of this, democracy depends on civility. In his book *The English*, Jeremy Paxman wryly claims the English invented manners "to protect themselves from themselves." We learned in Chapter 2 that the English didn't invent manners—in fact, they're coeval with the human species, and the subject matter of the oldest book in the world, *The Teachings of Ptahhotep*, given to us from ancient Egypt. But Paxman rightly notes why our social norms support the social contract: civility requires us to commit to living in community, to protect ourselves from the worst elements in our nature, and to make certain sacrifices to maintain life together.

> *Civility and incivility are the words you reach for when you want to suggest that the behavior you're concerned about isn't just a breach of manners, but a threat to the health of the civic sphere.*
>
> —Geoffrey Nunberg, twentieth-century American linguist

As we've learned, our self-love and love of others—our selfish and social natures—have been in tension as long as human communities have existed. To restrain mankind's selfish impulses and allow its social nature to flourish, communities have created formal and informal institutions so we can live together. Formal institutions include laws and systems of government. Informal institutions involve the unwritten cultural norms that help us navigate social life.

The formal institutions of the United States—federal, state, and local governments, the courts, and more—were established by our founders to limit the negative consequences of people's innate drive toward self-preservation. Our formal institutions deter and protect us from thieves who might want to rob us and companies that might want to defraud us.

> *Only a virtuous people are capable of freedom. As nations become corrupt and vicious, they have more need of masters.*
>
> —Benjamin Franklin, eighteenth-century American inventor, writer, and statesman

But these formal institutions by themselves are insufficient for a free and flourishing society. They only address the most egregious examples of our innate selfishness. To prevent petty acts of selfishness in our everyday interactions would require a much more invasive role for government than most people, including New Yorkers and Londoners, are willing to tolerate. To avoid government overreach, we need *informal* cultural norms of self-governance and self-sacrifice—norms that encourage honesty, demonstrate trustworthiness, and promote consideration of the needs and well-being of our fellow citizens. Formal institutions, such as laws and courts, can promote the selflessness needed for social living. But it's up to us to sustain it.

Few states are ruined by any defect in their institution, but generally by the corruption of manners; against which, the best institution is no long security, and without which, a very ill one may subsist and flourish.

—Jonathan Swift, eighteenth-century Irish writer

John Fletcher Moulton, a nineteenth-century English barrister, mathematician, and judge, observed that there exists a middle ground between the realm of the things we do with unrestricted freedom and those things we do because they are prescribed by law. He called this domain the "obedience to the unenforceable." This is where our actions are influenced by a sense of what we view as good, moral, and proper—our unofficial code of duty to our families, friends, and fellow citizens and persons.

For Moulton, this code is where "the real greatness of a nation, its true civilization," lies. The more society relies on self-regulation—and the less it relies on law, coercion, conflict, and litigation—the freer it is. The more often people *choose* to respect and care for their fellow citizens and persons—especially the weak and the vulnerable—the more civilized they are. A free society depends on its citizens deciding to do the honorable and virtuous actions even when they have the opportunity *not* to do so. Moulton was neither the first nor the last thinker to make this observation.

Lord Kames reminded the young King George III in 1762 that "depravity of manners will render ineffectual the most salutary laws." Montesquieu, among the most important intellectual influences on America's framers and founding, wrote that manners are those habits that are not established by legislators because they are unable to do so. He argued that wise and humble lawmakers must recognize that not everything can be corrected by law and policy, and that they should stick to their own lane: echoing John Locke, he wrote that while laws govern the body, custom governs the heart— the motivation, the disposition—of a citizen, and that a ruler has no business legislating matters of the heart. He argued that it is bad practice to try and change by law what should be changed by custom.

Where the manners of a people are gone, laws are of no avail. They will refute them, or they will neglect them.

—James Burgh, eighteenth-century English statesman

Ancient Roman society did not have a written constitution, and instead relied on standards of custom, morality, and manners that they called the *mos maiorum*—or the "old ways." Most are etymologically related to our concept of "morality," and also give us our word "mores," or social norms. The old ways were an unwritten code of conduct, the lifeblood of the civic and moral norms that animated their republican system of government and allowed it to survive.

We hear echoes of Norbert Elias's ideas once again. In his second volume of *The Civilizing Process*, called *Power and Civility*, Elias argues that the increase of personal, individual constraints, from the Middle Ages to the Renaissance and beyond, supported the liberal democratic project. A tightening of social norms and expectations—through peer-to-peer accountability at first, and later by government—contributed to the development of the modern nation-state. A country could grow only once there was domestic peace and the horizontal relationships between citizens were regulated. External controls of the state were supported by the individual citizen's internal self-restraint—both of which are necessary for the liberal project.

Our own formal institutions also rely on unwritten rules and customs. Civility encompasses many of these unarticulated norms, and is essential to keeping governmental coercion from intervening in every social interaction.

The Manners Police Chronicles

Traveling from New York and London, inland from the edge of the Continent, we find a more moderate—and effective—governmental effort to elevate the conduct of citizens. Paris's politeness crusade, which took place between 2012 and 2013, deployed social shame in an attempt to elevate the public behavior of its citizens. In using softer, informal social norms to promote civility—instead of resorting to the coercive power of the state through law and fines— Paris saw far greater success than either New York or London.

This may surprise some readers, but according to some visitors, Paris has a rudeness problem. Paris's technocrats became worried that it would begin affecting the city's bottom line. France welcomed 89 million visitors in 2018, more than any other country in the world, and the vast majority of visitors come in through Paris.[6] Yet Parisians have long enjoyed a notorious reputation among foreign travelers for their discourtesy. A Tripadvisor survey of travelers voted the City of Lights Europe's rudest city, with the least welcoming locals, the most discourteous taxi drivers, and the most demeaning waiters.[7] For city officials, the time had come to act.

Authorities learned that it wasn't only visitors who took issue with incivility in Paris. Survey data revealed Parisians themselves were fed up with ill-mannered behavior in one another. In a 2012 survey conducted by RATP, the city's transport authority, 97 percent of respondents said that they had witnessed discourteousness from their fellow passengers at least once in the last month.[8] In response, RATP launched a poster campaign to shame Parisians back to some level of propriety. The intent of the politeness crusade was to "reeducate" locals in courteous social behavior.[9]

Posters, such as the one below, were displayed on Paris's metro trains and in stations. A common trope was likening social transgressors to animals of various types. For example, one poster showed horrified onlookers looking at a lazy sloth, and aimed to encourage Parisians to adopt more considerate behavior. The poster says, GET LAZY AT PEAK HOURS, AND YOU RISK 2 OR 3 COMPLAINTS. Each poster had a consistent call to action: "Let's stay civilized down the line."

A poster from Paris's transport authority's politeness campaign.

Other posters depicted a woman with the head of a hen speaking loudly into a phone that was on speaker while on the train; a man with the head of a llama spitting on the train platform; a man with a frog's head jumping a turnstile without paying his fare. In yet another, a buffalo shoves his way into a crowded train. In addition to the posters, the transit authority created a survey online where riders could complain about the uncouth behavior of their peers. This formal outlet to vent apparently offered catharsis, and was very popular with Parisians.

Then, in 2013, Paris's mayor and the Chamber of Commerce entered the battle for greater civility. On the heels of the transit authority's politeness poster campaign, the mayor decided it was time to encourage Parisians to make a greater effort to ensure visitors felt welcome.

City officials tried to manufacture Parisian politesse by publishing a six-page manual called "Do you speak Touriste?"[10] Thirty thousand copies of the booklet were printed and distributed to people in Paris's service industry, including taxi drivers, hotel managers, people in sales, and waiters. The booklet contains basic greetings in eight languages including Chinese, German, and Portuguese, as well as advice on norms, customs, and habits of people from different national backgrounds.

The booklet "Do you speak Touriste?" published by the Paris city government, offers advice on the best way to interact with Les Américains: they visit Paris to learn to appreciate its refinement, to see many beautiful spectacles, and experience full-service.

The booklet is full of culturally specific recommendations. It reminds readers that Americans are "technophiles" who will always be in search of the nearest Wi-Fi hot spot.[11] They have high expectations of customer service, and will appreciate personalized suggestions. Chinese visitors like to shop for luxury items, the booklet offers, and a brief wave and acknowledgment while they are shopping will please them. Japanese visitors are demurer and will not complain until they are back in Japan. Italians love it if you show interest in their children, and tourists from other parts of France don't like being treated like tourists, so don't go out of your way for them, the booklet suggests.[12]

Harnessing the power of social shame, Paris's 2012–2013 politeness campaigns worked: 63 percent of respondents to a survey commissioned by RATP who had admitted to being rude said the ads caused them to reflect about their poor conduct on public transit. Many tourists also reported improved experiences interacting with Parisians in the hospitality industry.

We can learn several lessons from the stories about the efforts of New York, London, and Paris to foster greater civility in their cities. First, if people don't voluntarily comply with basic norms that help support society, the government *will* take action. Second, as we saw, there are better and worse—more and less effective—types of state action. State action that coerces

> *On every occasion of misbehavior, we hear people cry, there ought to be such or such a law made; whereas, upon inquiry, it is perhaps found that there are already several unexceptional laws upon the head standing; but, through want of manners, a mere dead letter.*
>
> —James Burgh, eighteenth-century British writer and politician

people will often be resented and resisted. But, if France's example is any indication, state action that appeals to our sense of propriety and social duties can be effective—a bit of useful intel for local officials with civility problems on their hands.

Examples of state overreach in the face of incivility abound. In recent decades, a draft law was introduced in the Israeli Knesset that would have made *cutting in line* a criminal offense.[14] Going further back in history, English common law recognized a concept called *scandalum magnatum,* which essentially provided a legal remedy to protect English peers in the House of Lords (roughly equivalent to United States senators) from having mean things said to them—and seventeenth-century courts were not shy about imposing heavy fines for this offense. Imagine if American courts issued a fine for every unkind thing said about a politician! The US debt—which was recently tallied at thirty-one trillion dollars—might very well disappear overnight.

Montesquieu said that *honor,* or ambition, is the "principle"—or defining characteristic common to citizens—of a monarchy. *Fear* was the principle of despotism. And *virtue* was the principle of republics. Modern democracies—the lineage of what Montesquieu called republics—depend on virtue, or moral habits that promote personal and social flourishing. The aforementioned attempts by modern, democratic city government officials to force people to be kind and considerate to one another illustrate that the less we restrain our immediate desires for the sake of others, the more people and politicians

> *Liberty cannot be preserved, if the manners of the people are corrupted; nor absolute monarchy introduced, where they are sincere.*
>
> —Algernon Sidney, seventeenth-century English politician

will call for laws to regulate our social interactions, which will inevitably weaken our democratic, limited government.

As we've explored, countries around the world understand the importance of civility, and the virtue it promotes, to flourishing and freedom—and have taken better and worse approaches toward promoting civility and common decency. A free society requires *civility*—the voluntary, inner, moral constraints on our actions—from its ordinary citizens.

Civility and Human Flourishing: On Virtuous—and Vicious—Cycles

A lack of civility in modern life is pervasive in our world today, and our cable news outlets and newspapers never let us forget it. But we experience the lack of civility most acutely in our daily lives. Giovanni della Casa, whom we met in Chapter 2, was a perceptive observer of human nature. In his book *Il Galateo*, he reminds us that the timeless principles of civility are grounded in unchanging traits of good character, such as empathy for others. His theory of how civility supports our freedom and flourishing was inherently aesthetic. We are interdependent, and della Casa understood that what we absorb through our senses influences our mental and emotional states. Whether we care to acknowledge it or not, what we do and say invariably affects those around us. He anticipated the discovery of "mirror-neurons,"

> *[Spitting] is a nauseating habit not likely to make anyone love you, but rather, if someone loved you, he or she would fall out of love right there.*
>
> —Giovanni della Casa, sixteenth-century Italian etiquette writer, making an important point about both civility and love

When the elements of truth and right are developed in the social doctrine of a welfare, the folks are raised to another plane. They become capable of extending their constructive influence on a man in society. These we call the mores. The mores are the folkways, including the philosophical and ethical generalizations as to societal welfare which are suggested by them, and inherent in them, as they grow.

—William Graham Sumner, nineteenth-century American sociologist

which explain why we intuitively feel emotions that we observe in others. This gives each of us an incredible power to either promote or weaken our community with our daily conduct.

Our everyday behaviors are regulated by unspoken, subtle guidelines that have developed over time to make coexistence not just tolerable, but enjoyable. If we choose to do life with others, instead of in complete isolation, we do not have unlimited freedom. We don't have the right to categorically disregard the comfort of others by doing whatever we would like. Counterintuitively, true freedom comes with self-imposed restraints on our words and conduct for the sake of others—the only path by which we might become fully human, and truly free.

Della Casa explicitly links manners with this project of human community. Like the Victorians discussed in the last chapter, he adopted a theory of manners that resembles the modern French idiom *la petite morale*, or "little morals." He saw morals and manners as two sides of the same coin, united in their purpose of making life together possible. He saw them as means by which we might become free from our baser nature and impulses, forging, as English philosopher Roger Scruton put it, "a society of cooperative and mutually respectful individuals out of the raw material of self-seeking animals."[15]

We are not isolated, self-sufficient monads. Our everyday interactions can either elevate or degrade our experience of living in society together. Our considerateness toward others promotes mutual trust, and in turn, our freedom and flourishing.

Small, gracious acts toward one another spark a virtuous cycle.[16] We see a need arise, such as someone trying to open the door with coffee in their hand. We act on our duty to meet that need, and hold the door open for them. If duty is deployed, and duly recognized with a simple *Thanks*, both parties move on with their day. The person doing the kindness feels *virtuous* and is encouraged to be kind again in the future. The person who received the kindness feels *safe*, and is inspired to pay the kindness forward in a future interaction. All is well with the world. This simple, virtually costless exchange is a small but important thread weaving and sustaining the entire social project.

Social life is a dance of a thousand social rituals that coordinate our interactions with each other, each day. Best-case scenario, they go according to plan, and we think little of them.

But what if, as sometimes happens, instead of being thanked, the person who held the door open is *scorned*—or worse, *ignored*? We're at first surprised that things did not go as expected. Then, we often feel rejected, offended, and angry. We resent feeling overextended—we were kind when we didn't have to be—and made to feel invisible. It feels like the good deed has been thrown back in our face.

> *To affect the quality of the day, that is the highest of arts. Every man is tasked to make his life, even in its details, worthy of the contemplation of his most elevated and critical hour.*
>
> —Henry David Thoreau, nineteenth-century American philosopher

You can never confuse him with anyone else, since the neighbor . . . is all people.

—Søren Kierkegaard, nineteenth-century Danish philosopher

We often over-extrapolate from single instances like this and make generalizations about society and others. "People just don't care for one another anymore"; "What has happened to the world?"; "That person must be a horrible human being."

Now a vicious cycle has begun. Many may question the rituals of courtesy they have been conditioned in, and not only second-guess themselves the next time they feel the urge to hold the door open for someone, but second guess the wisdom in *all* the trust-building norms our culture values. You may stew about the offense, and carry the mistrust and hurt throughout your day. Having that exchange might put one in a bad mood, and one might feel tempted to displace their negative emotions onto someone else, passing on the unkindness by being short with their colleague, barista, or taxi driver. They might think twice before doing *anything* nice for others for a while. "What's the point? Society is in decline anyway," one might reason.

What could have been an impersonal, albeit kind, exchange that filled our emotional reserves and gave us a nugget of motivation to support the social project that day has now drained us of our emotional energy, become deeply personal, and caused us to want to give up on society altogether. "They did not thank me *on purpose*," we might reason. "They *meant* to hurt me."

People are thoughtless all the time. This means that situations such as this will happen. We must cultivate the practice of "unbundling" situations: instead of seeking to fit them into a story about how horrible people and the world are, we should choose to see them as one-offs.

Overlooking ways to be thoughtful toward others is a missed opportunity to sow seeds of trust and goodwill that can pay dividends across time and place. Forgetting to thank others for small kindnesses is, too. Conversely, being thoughtless can corrode the social project beyond the isolated incident, causing people to lose faith in society and others.

Whether or not we want to accept it, we rely on one another. Life in society means moderating our selfishness, and requires negotiating our needs and those of others. More than memorizing a list of rules, cultivating a disposition of civility—of fundamentally respecting others—will help us navigate the potential minefield, and reap the high benefits of life together. There are certain basic principles of getting along with others every day. Our very civilization is held together by small, common courtesies, which is why such small, simple daily acts matter. As della Casa wrote, "Don't be looking like you consider the things discussed above as trivial and of small moment, for even light blows, if they are many, can kill."

Civility Vigilantism: The Larry David Effect

Our interactions with others brighten or degrade our lives. They promote trust or sow discord. They motivate us to continue our efforts to sustain this project of civilization and democracy, or they compel us to give up on it altogether.

We're interconnected. Our decisions impact one another. We are all familiar

Manners are what vex or soothe, corrupt or purify, exalt or debase, barbarize or refine us, by a constant, steady, uniform, insensible operation, like that of the air we breathe in.

—Edmund Burke, eighteenth-century Anglo-Irish statesman

Good manners are made up of petty sacrifices. If they are superficial, so are the dewdrops which give such a depth to the morning meadow.

—Ralph Waldo Emerson

with the irksome person who chooses to ignore the obligations they have to others—to pretend they are alone on an island, and not in society—and the grief caused as a result. Imagine this scenario. At LaGuardia Airport on a bright winter morning, a man removes his left shoe and sock. He extracts a set of clippers from his briefcase, and proceeds to trim his rather protruding toenails. He appears oblivious to the revulsion on the faces of his fellow travelers.

What would Larry David do?

Larry David, creator of *Seinfeld* and television's favorite curmudgeon, is the most astute modern observer of civility. His show *Curb Your Enthusiasm* is a comedy of manners. *Curb* reveals the social norms we take for granted by having its characters constantly *break* those norms. Larry highlights our hypocrisy when he calls people out for not upholding their end of the social contract of civility—double-parking or cutting in line—only to frequently violate the contract himself. He confronts people for large and small social infractions—as many of us often *want* to do, but don't—taking his complaints to often unhealthy extremes.

He reminds us that we can tell how powerful a norm is by how strongly we react when it's broken. He reveals how interdependent we are when he calls someone out for a social faux pas, and we cringe and writhe in discomfort—even though we're only watching him through a TV screen. Larry David is our foremost educator in manners, all while making us laugh and cringe in equal measure. In producing a show about commonly broken social norms, Larry David is our foremost modern defender of freedom, civility, and civilization itself.

Were Larry David at LaGuardia Airport when this gentleman began trimming his toenails, he would not hesitate to confront the offending man for his breach of this basic rule of doing life in society. "Are you kidding me?" he'd shriek in shock and horror. "Don't be disgusting!"

The cringeworthy confrontations that have made Larry David famous also remind us of the role of peer-to-peer accountability in a free society. The Larry Davids of the world keep the worst expressions of our selfishness in check so that the government and policy makers don't have to. As we learned earlier in this chapter, if enough people are inconsiderate for long enough, the state will take action.

Larry David constantly grapples with the same question that Ptahhotep did forty-five hundred years ago in ancient Egypt: Given mankind's innate self-love, how do we do life together without disgusting or harming one another?

Norms of civility are informal and sublegal. When they're broken, usually there are not manners police around to enforce the norms. They are voluntary, and complied with out of charity—a unique privilege of a free society. In democratic regimes, without a monarch or nanny state to monitor and compel our every move, we must be stricter in how we impose restraints on ourselves, and more aware of how our actions impact others. In order for a society to flourish, individuals must check their selfish inclinations and make a conscious effort to be thoughtful.

A world composed of too many civility vigilantes like Larry David would be intolerable. But a world without

> *There is still some memory of the strict code of politeness, but no one knows quite what it said or where to find it.*
>
> —Alexis de Tocqueville, nineteenth-century French writer and statesman

any—a world of civility anarchy or one where a centralized state monitors our every interaction, as Bloomberg and Blair attempted to do—is a worse one indeed.

Peer-to-Peer Accountability and Social Grace

Self-proclaimed norms authorities across history—the Larry Davids of other times and places—have long believed in holding one another accountable. One eighteenth-century Victorian manners book, for example, instructs children to "reprove thy companions as oft as there shall be occasion, for any evil, wicked, unlawful, or indecent action or expression."[17] Erasmus of Rotterdam, whom we met in Chapter 2, similarly advises, in his *A Handbook on Good Manners for Children*, "If a friend does something wrong without realizing it, and it seems important, then it's polite to inform him of it gently and in private."

Peer-to-peer accountability is important in a free society. But equally important, if not more so, is that we approach our daily exchanges armed with a healthy measure of social grace. A world full of people with the social litigiousness of Larry David—where everyone constantly demands that everyone else conform to their own sense of social justice or mercurial sensibilities—is the stuff of nightmares. If everyone confronted everyone else for every perceived social infraction, real or imagined, society would disintegrate. Our innate self-love means that we're all bound to break norms from time to time, which is why we must maintain an ample reserve of grace for others, and be ready to give it freely.

John Locke was adamant that children be taught to tolerate injustice and moderate their own pride.[18] He did *not* want a society of Larry Davids: touchy on points of honor, quick to take offense, too swift to avenge insults, and eager to right every wrong. But just as we forgive the shortcomings of others, we also must be vigilant in monitoring our own manifestations of self-love, and reining in our will to dominate. Erasmus's concluding maxim is once again apt: "The key to good manners is that you should readily ignore the faults of others, but avoid falling short yourself."[19]

In the West, we tend to think of freedom as freedom *from* constraints. Yet, as we've learned in the previous two chapters, freedom—both social and personal—is supported *within* constraints, too. This is true politically, but self-imposed restraints on our conduct—self-discipline, in other words—foster freedom socially as well.

Norms free our minds so that we do not have to negotiate every social situation anew. With social constraints in some areas—for example, when it comes to what utensils we use, who sits or eats first, how the table is arranged—there is freedom in other areas, freedom to relax and let personality shine and friendship flourish.

We can be free and flexible—we can flourish in community—only when some areas of life are fixed, and only when we voluntarily submit ourselves to these fixed norms. As Roger Scruton wrote in his primer on beauty, "Fleeting

Manners and customs are those habits which are not established by legislators, either because they were not able or were not willing to establish them.

There is this difference between laws and manners, that the laws are most adapted to regulate the actions of the subject, and manners to regulate the actions of the man. There is this difference between manners and customs, that the former principally relate to the interior conduct, the latter to the exterior.

—Montesquieu, eighteenth-century French philosopher

joys and brief encounters become eternal values when we set them in ritual and stone."[20]

The timeless principles of civility are like the frame of a painting, or the guidelines of music and grammar: within the frame and constraints, we can be creative, flourishing, and free. Edmund Burke wrote that civility is "drapery" that "covers the defects of naked shivering nature." Human beings are, by nature, raw and none too attractive. But cultivating the fertile ground of our souls—with an eye toward sowing and nurturing seeds of civility, integrity, grace, and forbearance—supports personal and relational flourishing within the garden of civilization.

As Dr. Johnson wrote, one can break the rules only once one knows them. But we should also be willing to suspend them for a higher principle. Rather than the *letter* of the law of politeness, we should instead be informed by the *spirit* of civility and social grace.

Thankfully, the norm that prohibits the gentleman at the airport from grooming himself in the terminal seems to pass the test of universality, and comprises the timeless principles of human flourishing. Daniel of Beccles, whom we met in Chapter 2, advised in his bestselling medieval-era

There are three distinct kinds of judges upon all new authors or productions; the first are those who know no rules, but pronounce entirely from their natural taste and feelings; the second are those who know and judge by rules; and the third are those who know, but are above the rules. These last are those you should wish to satisfy. Next to them rate the natural judges; but ever despise those opinions that are formed by the rules.

—Samuel Johnson, eighteenth-century English writer, lexicographer, and creator of the first English dictionary conduct work *Book of the Civilized Man*, "Avoid cracking fingers and thumb; avoid removing your shoes or washing your feet, or trimming your nails, or shaving your beard in the presence of lords and ladies." Going back a bit further in history, seven hundred years before Christ, the Greek poet Hesiod instructed, "At the abundant dinner of the gods, do not sever with bright steel the withered from the quick upon that which has five branches."[21] By this, he revealed that certain principles of maintaining life in community together truly are timeless: when it comes to cutting finger- or toenails in public—don't.

How to Promote Civility, Freedom, Democracy, and Human Flourishing

When you wake up in the morning, remember—and continue to remember throughout the day:

1. As we voluntarily choose to think of our fellow persons and citizens alongside ourselves, remember that we nourish our democracy, and cultivate the garden of civilization. Civility is the social contract that supports the social contract. Remember the examples of Mayor Bloomberg's politeness campaign in New York City, Tony Blair's respect campaign in London, and Paris' politeness efforts: kindness by choice diminishes the possibility that our public leaders will impose civility by force.

2. No interaction is neutral. We never know where people are or what they're going through, and each interaction is an opportunity to debase or elevate someone's day and life. Consideration of others helps us survive in community; kindness toward others helps us flourish. Maximize life's everyday junctures. Become artisans of the common

good. When you encounter someone, you're interacting with another human being—a miracle of life, a person with irreducible dignity and worth. Don't take that for granted. Celebrate it by elevating and making the most of small encounters.

3. When you're tempted to be offended by someone's thoughtlessness, try to interpret the incident in isolation: there is no cosmic, orchestrated plot against you. Thoughtlessness is not malice. Most people are tired enough merely surviving, trying to meet their own basic needs and those of their loved ones. Our baser, selfish natures prompt us to tell stories to ourselves that place us at the center as the victim. Remember that this is our selfish nature in action, and it's usually not accurate.

4. Reclaim the superpower of unoffendability. When someone says something that you do not like, or find offensive, reclaim your power over the situation—and save your emotional energy—by choosing not to be offended.

5. You do not have a moral duty to right every wrong that you encounter in the world. Sometimes, you may be tempted to channel your inner Larry David and call someone out for not upholding the unwritten social contract of peaceful coexistence. Sometimes there is a place for that. But most people don't have the stamina that Larry David does for everyday litigiousness. Remember Erasmus's mandate, that the root of all civility is to "readily ignore the faults of others, but avoid falling short yourself."

6. No matter where you are or what you're doing, the small things matter. Living in society means that everything we do affects others. Even not doing things—as we learned in our thought experiment about holding the door open for

others—can significantly impact another. We are a highly codependent species. Channel your inner della Casa, and don't roll your eyes at reminders to be thoughtful in the small ways, "for even light blows, if they are many, can kill."

5

Civil Society

While working in Washington politics, I yearned for more peaceful and less divided pastures. We moved to Indianapolis, Indiana, not far from my husband's family roots.

I didn't expect our move to the Midwest to illuminate for me how inextricably bound civility is with human flourishing, a healthy civil society, and our free and democratic way of life, but it did. When we moved to Indianapolis, I was at first relieved by what I *didn't* find. There wasn't the overt hostility, toxicity, and divisiveness that had defined my time in government service, nor was there the saccharine, superficial, and manipulative politeness.

The human condition is the same in all times and places—including Washington, DC, and Indianapolis. But Indianapolis is less of a company town than Washington, a city where virtually all aspects of life revolve around politics and proximity to power, which can inordinately exacerbate darker aspects of the human personality that we all share.

The absence of hostility, toxic politeness, and constant talk about the divided nature of our republic that I discovered in Indianapolis was refreshing. But it wasn't quite enough to make the city feel like home. Then, one day, I received an unexpected invitation.

"I'm Joanna Taft," said the tall, socially fearless woman with a blond bobbed haircut and ready smile after church one August afternoon. She immediately reminded me of my mother, in more ways than one. "Would you like to *porch* with us sometime?" she asked.

This marked the first time I had heard the word "porch" used as a verb.

For Joanna, "porching" is about reviving the community living room. The porch is a quasi-public "third place," a neutral ground where people from different backgrounds can encounter and befriend one another.[1] In a seminal essay for the *Palimpsest*, Richard H. Thomas documents how during the half century beginning in 1890, Americans began to change the architectural arrangement of their homes: porches moved from the front of the home to the back, becoming the modern patio. Thomas argued that the home is a personal and cultural statement about the way a society and culture is organized and oriented, and that this architectural shift—from front porch to patio—tracked a social one: a move from the communal to the individual, from a focus on public life to a preference for the private.

Though originally from the Washington, DC, area, Joanna chose to build a life in Indianapolis with her husband and family. She has used her porch to continue our garden metaphor, to cultivate community, and a haven from the hurriedness of modern life. It is a place to forge new friendships, an incubator of ideas to make the community brighter, a place to encounter and create beauty, a catalyst for further cultural and communal growth, and a venue where those who differ politically, racially, and culturally can form bonds and feel seen, known, and loved.

My husband and I joined Joanna on her porch that afternoon, a decision that would deepen my understanding of the practical benefits of civility. Much as I'd seen my mother

It's not about having a porch. It is a lifestyle. It's about embracing and facing the street and your neighbors.

—Joanna Taft, social innovator, founder of Indianapolis's Harrison Center, and "porcher"

do with countless others whom we had welcomed into our home growing up, Joanna asked us about our backgrounds, interests, and passions so that she could effectively introduce us to others and plug us into the community. Joanna's emotional and practical hospitality helped us discover and define our niche in our new community. Her civility—and the community it built—helped make Indianapolis feel like home.

We live in fractured days, lacking in harmony, civility, and comity. "Comity," an old word for courtesy and kindness, is related etymologically to the Sanskrit word for "smile." As it often does, etymology here beautifully illuminates a reality about both kindness and smiling: they unceasingly bring warmth, joy, and a smile to both giver and receiver. I realized that the civility of Joanna's front porch, as a place of joy and laughter, was a breeding ground of comity, a much-needed refuge from the broken state of our world.

In this way, Joanna's porch and other spaces like it are essential building blocks of civil society—and in turn, our democracy. But what is civil society?

The Uncivil Roots of Civil Society

Civil society refers to the voluntary relationships between people, the sphere in between, and distinct from, the individual and the state. English philosopher Thomas Hobbes

(1588–1679) understood civil society to be the transition from a state of constant war with one another to a state of relative peace and prosperity. Civil society encompasses person-to-person interactions, and therefore relies on civility. Yet who would have thought that our modern concept of "civil society" would have such uncivil roots?

When Scotsman Adam Ferguson coined the term "civil society" in his 1767 *An Essay on the History of Civil Society*, he did not anticipate the rather choice words it would earn from another famous Scotsman named Adam—one Adam Smith—or that it would spell the end of their friendship.

Smith cried plagiarism. He accused Ferguson of "having borrowed some of his ideas without owning them," an allegation that Ferguson adamantly denied.[2] Ferguson countered that he and Smith had merely drawn from the same intellectual well—probably the influential French political theorist Montesquieu—and that, yes, "Smith had been [there] before him."[3] Smith wasn't satisfied with that explanation and abruptly ended their longtime friendship.

Civil Society, Then and Now

Despite its rocky interlude between the two Scottish Adams, the idea of civil society has had remarkable staying power. It has sparked debate for thousands of years, and continues to do so today. Aristotle wrote about the *koinonia politike*—later translated into Latin as *societas civilis*, or "civil society." Civil society occurred when families and villages came together to help one another lead virtuous lives in community. It was synonymous with the *polis:* the best place for human beings to realize their potential and flourish.

Fourteenth-century Tunisian Muslim philosopher Ibn

*Human social organization
is something necessary.
The philosophers expressed
this fact by saying: "Man is
'political' by nature." That is,
he cannot do without the social
organization for which the
philosophers use the technical
term "town" (polis).*

—Ibn Khaldun, fourteenth-
century Tunisian Muslim
philosopher and early
theorist of civil society

Khaldun (1332–1406), influenced by Aristotle, formed
his own ideas of civil society.
He also thought human be-
ings were social, or political,
by nature. He coined the
concept of *asabiyah* (pronounced AH-sa-BEE-yah),
central to his work, and
which he argued was the
defining idea and tension in
human life and community.
Asabiyah is often translated
as "social cohesion," but it is
more nuanced than that. It
refers to the two-sided aspect of human nature: our
variable "group spirit," or social impulse, that has bonded people together in all times and places, juxtaposed against our will
to dominate others. "Aggressiveness is natural in living beings,"
he wrote.[4]

As we learned in our first chapter, this *libido dominandi* is
an expression of our foundational selfish nature. *Asabiyah* is, in
Khaldun's theory, the driving force in human history. Central
to *asabiyah*, and to how Khaldun conducted himself in his personal life, was *adab*—an Arabic word and Islamic concept that
we discovered in Chapter 2—which connotes respect toward
others expressed through words and deeds.[5] In his *Muqaddimah*, or introduction, Khaldun offers a history of mankind, the
most comprehensive account of the human experience by an Islamic author.[6]

An aspiring poet, Khaldun deployed his mastery of language
to make his argument. As human communities developed from

rural and simple arrangements to sedentary, urban, and more complex ones, he worried that the increased wealth and the pursuit of luxury that defined more "civilized" states of life would feed our basic human selfishness, that it would nourish our propensity toward tribalism, partisanship, and division, and undermine *asabiyah,* the fundamental fellow-feeling that kept society together.

> *Prejudice and partisanship obscure the critical faculty and preclude critical investigation. The result is that falsehoods are accepted and transmitted.*
>
> —Ibn Khaldun

Four hundred years later, Ferguson followed in the footsteps of Ibn Khaldun and offered a sweeping history and philosophy of the human experience. Like Aristotle and Khaldun, Ferguson used "civil society" to mean *political society*—a community consciously formed around shared values. In his essay, he offers a theory of human relationships and human flourishing drawing from examples and insights across history and culture.

Ferguson saw that we were divided between selfish and social appetites.[7] He thought the best life was the social life, and that we must give up certain desires for the sake of society. Like a single thread in a tapestry, an individual part of an engine, or a single branch on a tree, Ferguson thought, when the individual person surrendered to community, he was enabled to fulfill his potential. The result was a beautiful, well-functioning whole.

Ferguson was concerned that the growth of markets, commerce, and trade during this time—which had unleashed unprecedented wealth and access to novel luxuries—could promote our selfishness and hurt the social project. He saw the good that commercial, manufacturing society offered—how it improved living standards and quality of life for many—but, like his onetime

Man is, by nature, the member of a community; [he is] no longer made for himself. He must forgo his happiness and his freedom, where these interfere with the good of society. He is only part of a whole.

—Adam Ferguson, eighteenth-century Scottish philosopher

friend Adam Smith, thought that markets could dislocate people from community, and alienate them from one another. Ferguson saw signs of civic degeneracy and weakened civic bonds caused by a culture that put capital accumulation before all else—and by a society which mistook wealth for wisdom, and pursued luxury instead of personal and public virtue.

Civil society—and human community generally, he thought—was in great peril.

A Nation of Joiners

Khaldun and Ferguson weren't the last thinkers to express concern about the state and future of communiy in modern society. Karl Marx lived and wrote contemporaneously with Alexis de Tocqueville, a figure we've met and will explore further shortly. Marx was also fretful that commercial society—saturated with egoism, the unbridled pursuit of self-interest, and a transactional commodification and utilitarian approach to people and relationships—gravely threatened *bürgerlichen Gesellschaft,* or civil society. Marx may be among the most famous thinkers to express this concern, but again, he was not the first.

The most significant influence on modern thinking around civil society is Alexis de Tocqueville, whom we met in Chapter 3. Tocqueville helped place the "spirit of association" at the center of American identity. During his visit to America from

France, he noticed that Americans held a general affection for mankind—they were filled with philanthropy, or "love of man-kind," in its truest sense—an attribute that he thought classical cultures lacked. He wrote, "In democratic ages men rarely sacrifice themselves for one another; but they display general compassion for the members of the human race."

The American philanthropic spirit expressed itself in many ways. For example, Tocqueville saw Americans solving problems together themselves. They didn't wait for or depend on the government to resolve them, as he claimed was typical in England and France. Instead, Americans formed "civic associations." He noted that civic associations were essential in a democracy, because they counterbalanced the power of political institutions.

> *Manners [in America] have neither the regularity and dignity frequent in aristocracies nor the qualities of simplicity and freedom which one sometimes finds in democracies; they are both constrained and casual.*
>
> —Alexis de Tocqueville, nineteenth-century French writer and statesman

We learned in our last chapter that we are governed by two social contracts. The first governs the vertical relationship between citizens and their government. The second governs horizontal relationships between citizens. This second social contract is why Tocqueville was so interested in civic associations, civil society, and civility. Civility nourished the second social contract, because it nourished relationships between citizens. It promoted a culture of trust, as well as norms of reciprocity and basic affection for one another. Norms of civility nurtured a complex, interactive, mutually reinforcing network of civic community and associational life that supported

American democracy. Adopting the disposition of civility led them to treat their fellow citizens with equal moral worth, and promoted collaboration across differences—political, cultural, geographic, and more—to support a common cause.

Tocqueville noted a tension at the heart of American social life—a tension that is also at the heart of human communities in all times and places. This tension was between individualism and communalism or, put another way, between our self-love and sociability in our nature. Left unchecked, individualism—in America and beyond—was a recipe for personal alienation and societal deterioration. It was also a threat to American democracy. Tocqueville noted that voluntary acts of kindness, including spontaneous efforts to "join" together and help one another in need, kept this individualistic impulse in check. Efforts to work together to solve a common problem became "schools of citizenship" where Americans developed the habits of democracy. Civility and civil society were the social glue that made the fragile project of American democracy work.

Nothing New Under the Sun

Aristotle worried that communities that became too large would undermine the trust needed for civil society. Ibn Khaldun and Adam Ferguson worried that commerce and luxury would corrode civic virtue and modern human community. Tocqueville worried that government overreach would do the same. He compared American civic life and local governance to a muscle that strengthened with exercise. When the government took over, that muscle of civility, self-governance, and spirit of association—so essential to the democratic project—atrophied.

Several decades later, another Frenchman, Émile Durkheim, despaired at the state of modern human communities, particularly those in his native France. Thanks to markets and the division of labor, he noted, France was wealthier than ever before. But why were people so unhappy? In his 1897 book, *Suicide*, Durkheim argued that the rise of *anomie* was to blame. Anomie is often rendered as "normlessness." It derives from the Greek word *anomos*, or "lawlessness." In Christian history, early translations of the New Testament translated "sin" as "*anomia*."[8] It is a state where each person decides what is right for him or herself, with social alienation resulting from the breakdown in the horizontal contract governing human community.

For Durkheim, anomie was *dérèglement*, or "derangement," as it prompted a constant mental panic and suffering that came with not knowing what was expected of you in society, or what you could expect from others. Anomie had caused a sharp rise in suicide in France. Anomie was the enemy of "collective effervescence"—a time when people spontaneously gather around a common cause. It had caused a breakdown in people's moral self-discipline—and the institutions, such as church and family, that taught self-control and the habits of self-governance. Reminiscent of Tocqueville's insight into America's "spirit of association," and our modern understanding of civil society, Durkheim knew that the quality of our basic interactions predicted whether we engaged in activities together, and whether we felt connected to those around us and our broader community.

Since Khaldun, Ferguson, Tocqueville, and Durkheim there have been many people decrying the decline of community. For Robert Nisbet, the greatest threats to community were a "centralized territorial State," ideology, and war. He wrote *The Quest for Community* in 1953 as the world was recovering from the trauma of the Second World War. Nisbet worried that the newly consolidated nation-state and globalization had displaced our loyalties from those around us to the anonymous outside world, leaving us personally and culturally impoverished. He

The quest for community will not be denied for it springs from some of the powerful needs of human nature—needs for a clear sense of cultural purpose, membership, status, and continuity.

—Robert Nisbet, twentieth-century American sociologist

posited that the nation-state married with ideology and expansionism—as the totalitarianism of communism and Nazism had just shown—was the death knell for family, church, and neighborhoods, as well as the bonds that supported them.

In his 1995 essay "Bowling Alone"—published as a book in 2000—Robert Putnam also argued that communal life was in peril. Americans weren't doing things together anymore, and the spirit of association that Tocqueville had praised—that democracy depended on—was dying. Examining the 1950s and 1960s through the early 1990s, Putnam looked at a number of metrics—from membership in Rotary Clubs to voting rates to philanthropic gifts to volunteering and more—and showed that Americans were decreasingly engaged with their neighbors and their communities. Putnam argued that in its citizens becoming less engaged with those around them—in turning inward by doing things alone, not volunteering, not voting, and giving less—American democracy was at stake. For Putnam, the rise of the television was to blame for this inward turn toward the self.

People have long feared how new social changes—such as commerce, the division of labor, a growing government, war, and new technologies such as television—would affect people's communal lives. In our own moment, many argue that technologies such as social media put communal life—and modern democracy—in peril.

Civic life and civility—both in America and beyond—have

endured ebbs and flows, dissipation and reinvention. Every era and human society will have grounds for concern about the survival of community, and different people looking at the same era can emphasize different cultural trends: for example, during the timeframe that Putnam dubbed a "golden age" for civic health—the 1950s—Robert Nisbet decried that community was in crisis because of the growth of government due to the war effort. Even during Tocqueville's day, often pointed to as a paragon of American civic life, there was civic churn at play: old civic institutions were dying, and new ones, such as the National Benevolent Associations and temperance societies, were forming.[9] As we learned in our first chapter, civilization and community are fragile. That we are social by nature drives us as a species to create relationships in all eras and places. That we are selfish means that the social project will always be precarious. As long as the tension between our social and selfish natures exists, civil society will never be safe.

How Civility Can Help Rebuild Trust and Civic Life

We've learned throughout this book how civility helps us subvert our selfishness so that our social nature can flourish. Civility is the building block of civil society, because civility is what makes people want to do things to be with and to aid one another. Civility is related to social capital, generalized reciprocity, social trust, and civic virtue—all concepts that support civic, democratic life. A decline in civility— the simple norms of self-sacrifice that help us do the tough stuff of life together—results in a decline in "joining" and an associated decline in "social capital." Decline in social capital results in decreased trust and generalized reciprocity in a society. When trust in a society deteriorates, citizens are less likely to do things for others. Why would we do things for others if we cannot trust that we might be helped when in need? This mindset promotes isolation and individualism, which in turn makes people less likely to go out of their way to help one another, or do things together, in ways big and small—from holding the door open for the person behind you to joining a bowling league or Rotary Club with them.

In low-trust societies, people expect immediate repayment when they do things for others. They carry a "What's in it for me?" mindset of cost versus benefit into every interaction. They try to get as much as they possibly can out of every exchange. They are constantly keeping score and trying to get and stay ahead. This is both exhausting and inefficient.[10] There are transaction costs to not trusting your community, such as the time and effort it takes to constantly count your change every time you make a purchase. Honesty and trust lubricate the inevitable friction of social life.

There's a difference between *thick* and *thin* trust. Thick trust is the trust we have in people we know well, including family and close friends. Time and familiarity with them have allowed us to make judgments about their trustworthiness. Thin trust is generalizable trust, or the trust we place in the countless strangers we interact with every day. Thin trust lowers the transaction costs in our anonymous society, and is built by our small acts of kindness and generosity toward strangers.

Restoring Community, Civility, and Trust in an Anonymous, Globalized World

We each have different concentric circles of relationships that connote distinct levels of intimacy. Each circle of association imposes different obligations upon us. Aristotle offers us a helpful framework for thinking about how our duties to others differ according to our relationships with them. He distinguished between three circles. First, the *oikos*—or family household, and the origin of our modern word "economics," which literally means "household management." The *oikos* is the level at which we have the most interaction, know best, and also, generally speaking, trust the most. Second, the village is the level of society that we don't interact with daily, but still depend on for our needs. We might compare this level to a modern neighborhood. Third, as we've already learned, is the *koinonia politike*—the *societas civilis* in Latin, "civil society," and *polis*—the larger, more anonymous, association of families and villages living in community.

For Aristotle, a thriving *polis* must not be too large. For effective self-rule among equals, a *polis* required a basic trust and familiarity among co-citizens. We daily interact with countless anonymous others, both digitally and in person. This is a necessary part of being in a modern, interconnected, and cosmopolitan world. We don't need to know every person we buy or sell from personally and intimately.

As we move through life and interact with friends and strangers alike, we intuitively adjust our interactions, and keep in mind that our different relationships require different interactions and obligations. Economist and social philosopher Friedrich Hayek noted that we must live in "two sorts of worlds at once": a world with people we know and have natural affection for, and a world with people we do not know. It is untenable for us to have the same duties to complete strangers as to our loved ones. But, because of our shared status as members of the human community, we still have some duties to strangers. The Stoics of antiquity describe this dynamic with their doctrine of *oikeiôsis*—meaning "appropriation" or "endearment." *Oikeiôsis* held that,

Part of our present difficulty is that we must constantly adjust our lives, our thoughts, and our emotions, in order to live simultaneously within the different kinds of orders according to different rules. If we were to apply the unmodified, uncurbed, rules of the micro-cosmos (i.e., of the small band or troop, or of, say, our families) to the macro-cosmos (our wider civilization), as our instincts and sentimental yearnings often make us wish to do, we would destroy it. Yet if we were always to apply the rules of the extended order to our more intimate groupings, we would crush them. So, we must learn to live in two sorts of worlds at once.

—Friedrich Hayek, twentieth-century Austrian-British economist and social philosopher

while we have duties to those closest to us, we also have a duty of benevolence to all human beings.

Civility supports civil society and modern democracy because it is—like civilization itself—*unnatural.* Francis Fukuyama explains in his book *The Origins of Political Order* that the strongest of human impulses is the desire to promote and preserve kinship ties. This impulse is arguably an extension of our inherent self-love and drive for self-preservation, discussed throughout this book. Love for one's family can be a great good, of course, but exclusively prioritizing one's own tribe, family, and kin over the rest of one's community is a recipe for corruption, nepotism, and dysfunction.

In his 1993 book *Making Democracy Work: Civic Traditions in Modern Italy*, Robert Putnam empirically concluded that northern Italy was more civically engaged, better governed, and more prosperous than Southern Italy. Why? The North had, over time, developed social and economic organizations, such as guilds and credit associations, that fostered "horizontal bonds," and created a culture where people trusted complete strangers, not just members of their own family. The South, by contrast, was defined by "vertical bonds." It was rigidly hierarchical, with those at the bottom dependent on the patronage of landowners and officials, not on one another. This ingrained a culture in the South that trusted family first and foremost instead of strangers beyond one's kin.

A world where everyone looks after themselves and their own first promotes a "two-tiered" system of morality: one set of norms governs our interactions with our family and friends, and another governs our interactions with the rest of humanity.[11] A world without the generalized trust to do business and form relationships with strangers and non-family members is a world where modern liberal democracy and free markets fail to function.

As we explored in our last chapter, modern democracies rely on formal economic and political institutions—such as our judicial, executive, and legislative branches of government—which are arranged to overcome this basic impulse to care for ourselves and our own first. Equally important are our *informal* institutions—our civil norms that see all persons as equal and worthy of treating well—that allow us to trust strangers.

[It is the] common sense of the poet, by a Greek derivation, to signify sense of public weal and of the common interest, love of the community or society, natural affection, humanity, obligingness, or that sort of civility which arises from just sense of the common rights of mankind and the natural equality there is among those of the same species.

—Anthony Ashley Cooper, 3rd Earl of Shaftesbury, eighteenth-century English writer

Let us suppose that the great empire of China, with all its myriads of inhabitants, was suddenly swallowed up by an earthquake, and let us consider how a man of humanity in Europe, who had no sort of connection with that part of the world, would be affected upon receiving intelligence of this dreadful calamity. He would, I imagine, first of all, express very strongly his sorrow for the misfortune of that unhappy people. . . . And when all this fine philosophy was over, when all these humane sentiments had been once fairly expressed, he would pursue his business or his pleasure, take his repose or his diversion, with the same ease and tranquility, as if no such accident had happened.

—Adam Smith, eighteenth-
century Scottish moral
philosopher

In his book *The Expanding Circle*, philosopher Peter Singer maintained that while we once cared primarily for our kin and a few close friends, we now have a more global concern that extends beyond our immediate tribe to people across the world from us. Thanks to the growth in human prosperity due to markets and technological advancements, we can travel and stay linked digitally, which allows us to more easily connect with others—and which in turn makes it easier for us to care for those whom in prior eras we may have disregarded.

Adam Smith might disagree with Singer's argument that we have a more global concern for others today than we had in past eras. Smith famously wrote about this phenomenon in his 1759 book *The Theory of Moral Sentiments*. He observed that when we hear about a catastrophe—such as an earthquake in China—we feel sorry for the suffering of those involved. But in no time at all, we are back to focusing on our daily lives and our own comparatively trivial problems. We don't lose sleep over every example of human misery we encounter. We couldn't cope if we did—especially in our modern media environment that tends to focus on the negative, inflammatory, and incendiary.

Smith's insight about how we respond to the suffering of those far away from us stemmed from his theory of *sympathy*, which is analogous to our modern conception of *empathy*. Smith, like Italian author-on-manners Giovanni della Casa from past chapters, anticipated the discovery of mirror neurons and observed that we have a fundamental connectedness to the emotions of others that makes us care about how others think and feel. This connectedness promotes a "fellow-feeling" we share with others that makes us prone to adopt the emotions of others. To some extent, we naturally view the world through the eyes of others—both strangers and those familiar to us.

This isn't all good. Life in our modern world is defined by countless exchanges with strangers, which makes empathizing with everyone we meet a challenge, if not impossible. We intuitively disengage our empathetic muscles so as not to emotionally exhaust and overextend ourselves. We must find an appropriate balance—one that safeguards healthy emotional boundaries while also cultivating the empathy that helps us stay aware of the humanity and dignity of everyone with whom we interact, strangers and friends alike. We must remember that because we are united in our humanity, we are more alike than unlike. For that reason, we owe to others a basic duty of civility.

We can each deploy the power of civility and help rebuild civil society right now. We can do so by cultivating integrity and being more trustworthy—an idea we explored in Chapter 3—and also by sowing seeds of goodwill in ways big and small.

Porching: The Link Between Civility and Civil Society

When Joanna Taft brought me into her fold after our move to the Midwest, she offered me a window into a small-scale rebellion against our cynical and atomized era that she was staging from her front porch. Her porch is an incubator of social trust, and a place where she converts strangers into friends, and friends into family. She has welcomed countless others onto her porch in the same way that she first welcomed me. She has used her wide network of relationships—fortified on her front porch—to make her community better.

Joanna shows us how to harness the power of civility to renew civil society, and how we might, too. Her fingerprints can be found on many wonderful civic and social institutions in Indianapolis. Her civility built the trust and relationships that aided her work with others in developing new community institutions. The Tafts were a founding family of The Oaks Academy, a classical Christian school in an underserved area of Indianapolis, along with other community leaders, including former governor of Indiana Mitch Daniels and many others. Twenty years on, The Oaks is now a network of schools and has become an institution that promotes much-needed social and economic equity and mobility in Indianapolis.

Joanna also helped open an art center, the Harrison Center, which supports local artists, connects them with patrons, creates beauty in the city, and helps weave its diverse neighbors into

[Manners] are a kind of lesser morality, calculated for the ease of company and conversation.

—David Hume, eighteenth-century Scottish philosopher

the fabric of the larger Indianapolis community. The Harrison Center received $2.2 million in grants to make building improvements that foster accessibility and bridge social and cultural divides. Joanna also helped to found a classical charter school, called Herron High School, with the aim of creating a new generation of art patrons in Indianapolis. Herron High School began in the basement of the Harrison Center, showing the generative nature of civility and civic life. As one initiative begets another, one person's civility begets civility in others.

The civility of Joanna, and that of countless others who nurtured these institutions of civil society, has made Indianapolis a beautiful city. Joanna would be the first to acknowledge that she did not do these things alone. But that's the power of civility: it harnesses individual potential and amplifies it by allowing us to achieve in community what no single person could accomplish alone.

Joanna's civility has enabled her to make friends with people outside of her immediate social circle, which has amplified her community-building power.[12] The term "gatekeeper" often invokes an air of exclusivity. It connotes people who are "in" keeping other people "out." This is what the rules of politeness often do. The very point of the rules is to separate the people who know them from those who do not. But there is a growing group of gatekeepers across the country who actively seek to throw the gates wide open—to let people in, and to help integrate them into the broader community.

There is a difference between "bridging social capital" and "bonding social capital."[13] Bridging social capital builds bonds of social capital *between*

So many of us want to live in big cities. We desire the amenities of and cachet of a large metropolis. But in our hearts, we all want to live in small towns. We each long to feel known and loved. That is why we porch.

—Joanna Taft

groups of people; bonding social capital builds social capital *within* a group. "Gatekeepers" in the *inclusive* sense—in the way my mother modeled, and in how Joanna approaches new people in Indianapolis—specialize in *bridging* social capital. They put civility into practice. It is their custom and practice to invest in others and build relationships wherever they go, which allows them to build the community and institutions that make for a truly *civil* society.

> *Bonding social capital constitutes a kind of sociological superglue, whereas bridging social capital provides a sociological WD-40.*
>
> —Robert Putnam, American political theorist

"Benjamin Harrison House"
By Indianapolis-based artist Alicia Zanoni

There is a rich tradition of both porching and porches in Indianapolis, and porching's civic roots run deep. Benjamin Harrison, who lived in Indiana, served as the 23rd President of the United States from 1889 through 1893. Harrison conducted one of the first "Front Porch" presidential campaigns. Hundreds of thousands of Americans came from across the country to listen to him speak from his front porch on Delaware Street in downtown Indianapolis. In campaigning from his porch, Harrison demonstrated that he was committed to remaining a local, accessible citizen, and throughout his public service, he was always a citizen first, public servant second.

In his *Reflections on the Revolution in France*, Edmund Burke observed the importance of being rooted in one's local community: "To be attached to the subdivision, to love the little platoon we belong to in society, is the first principle (the germ as it were) of public affections. It is the first link in the series by which we proceed toward a love to our country and to mankind." Burke reminds us that citizenship—for voters to elected officials alike—starts with how we live our lives each day. Citizenship begins our immediate community, including the people we live among and the neighborhood we live in.

Burke's insight reminds us that we might be citizens of a national idea, but our lived experience of citizenship is with our co-citizens in our community each day. We live out our civic duty as citizens by caring for our neighbors—for our little platoons—from our front porches.

Generative Generosity

We learned earlier in this chapter that philanthropy means "love of mankind." Being philanthropic and generous is an important part of creating and nurturing civic ecosystems today. But being philanthropic is not just for those with financial resources. We can each be generous—emotionally, intellectually, and in other ways—and cultivate a love of humanity. And our acts of generosity and philanthropy can rebuild civility, civil society, and also can be remarkably *generative*. The root of the word "generative" is *gen*, which means "birth" in both Greek and Latin. As you might expect, *gen* is the root of our words "genes," "genesis," "generate," "generation," "progeny," and more. *Gen* is also the root of our words "gentry," "gentlemen," and "generous."

Consider Joanna's generativity with her civic projects. Her porch is a civic incubator, generating momentum for community projects such as a masquerade ball or a Broadway musical. Joanna's civic work is part of a larger ecosystem comprising physical place, technology, social norms, civic innovators, and social organizations. Each of these interacts and reinforces the others.

The Harrison Center, the art consortium Joanna started, supports and helps generate local artistic talent. Herron High School was founded with the express purpose of cultivating a new generation of art patrons. Generativity and generosity—of resources but also of time and emotional energy—breeds more generativity and generosity and creates ecosystems that nurture civility, community, and our civic life.

Renewing Civil Society and Civility Starts with Us

In 176 AD, Roman emperor Marcus Aurelius, known to history as a "philosopher king," endowed four chairs of philosophy in the city of Athens. For the Epicureans, he endowed the Garden. For the Platonists, the Academy. For the Aristotelians, the Lyceum. And for the Stoics, the Porch—or the *Stoa*. The Stoics' porch was located at the ancient Agora, which for many years had been home to a variety of famous philosophical schools. And for the Stoics the porch represented an important idea: we can each realize our capacity for true freedom and flourishing when we choose to distinguish what we can control from what we can't, and decide to make the best of what is in our control.

The stoicism of Marcus Aurelius and that of his intellectual mentor, Epictetus, offers lessons in how to create a more civil future. In short, it starts with us. We can't change society, but we can change ourselves and how we operate in the world around us. And if enough of us decide to change ourselves, we might be able to change the world we live in, too.

Epictetus was a slave, and referred to himself as a cripple. Despite his disability and his lack of the political freedoms that many of us enjoy, he made the most of his circumstances, and ultimately became one of the most important philosophers in history.

Unlike Epictetus, Marcus Aurelius was born to freedom, privilege, and wealth. Yet as Roman emperor during a time of constant war and plague, he had his own struggles to bear. Like his teacher Epictetus before him, however, Marcus Aurelius strove to focus only on what he could control. He endeavored to treat those around him justly, and to live a life of personal virtue.

It's easy to look around us at the divided state of the world and blame our public leaders, the media, our education system, and more. But that's not a productive way to spend our time.

Instead, we should focus on what we *can* control.

Us.

The Stoic porch of Marcus Aurelius and Epictetus illuminates how each of us can do our part to restore civility to modern life. These philosophers remind us that change in society begins with ourselves. This chapter opened with my story of moving to Indianapolis after a frustrating season in Washington, DC. Soon after arriving, I saw how Joanna Taft sows seeds of friendship and community wherever she goes. She spreads and cultivates the garden of civilization in her wake by focusing on nurturing the individuals—the raw plots of soil—she encounters. The seeds she's sown have already flourished and been fruitful in her lifetime, and will continue to do so after it. She is a serial builder of social capital and a deployer of the timeless principles of civility, tools in her cache to create new institutions to make her community better.

Joanna's front porch—her *stoa*—is central to the relationships she forms and the institutions that she helps build. Like the Stoics, she focuses on controlling what she can, and on making the world around her better. In doing so, she embodies the ethos of the Stoic philosophers—the original "porchers."

The attitude of Stoic "porchers" shows how the disposition of civility is one we can all have anywhere, anytime—with a porch or without one. Anyone can be a part of healing their family life, their community, and even the world, one relationship, and one interaction, at a time.

Cultivating the disposition of civility in our personal garden—and the attitude of porching—means meeting people at a human level, cutting through tribes and superficial labels. Civility will enable us to build meaningful human connections whenever and wherever we can. This can take many forms, such as welcoming people into our home, initiating a conversation across political divides, or offering a simple smile and acknowledgment to a stranger on the street. We must resist the temptation to look around at the divided state of our world and feel stuck and helpless. Marcus Aurelius and Epictetus remind us that focusing on what we *can* do is the answer. And in truth, we can do a lot.

Our interactions with others can leave people better off, and restore faith and trust in society. These strengthened, trust-infused relationships, in turn, strengthen neighborhoods, cities, and countries.

The Joannas of the world are good stewards of the garden of civilization. They build and bind our social fabric. They lead their civility-rich lives to bridge divides and sow seeds of trust. We can choose to lead such lives, too.

We can do this whether or not we have a porch. We can each choose to adopt the disposition of civility, and the porching way of engaging the world. In a culture that is inclined to withdraw, we can reach out. In a moment of division, we can bridge the divide. In an era that excludes, we can include. In an era of tribalism, we can embrace difference. In a time that elevates self, we can elevate others.

In doing so, we can be part of healing the personal and social hurt caused by our tribal, toxic status quo, and of moderating the excesses of hostility and atomization and destructive politeness that define our public life today. In choosing to embody civility, we each have the chance to promote individual flourishing, civil society, and our free and democratic way of life.

Civility is the person-to-person phenomenon that helps each of us overcome our selfish nature so that our social nature might flourish. Civility helps promote integrity—*being* good as opposed to merely *seeming* good—which sustains our friendships, our social

When philosophers speak in exalted tones of "civic engagement" and "democratic deliberation," we are inclined to think of community associations and public life as the higher form of social involvement, but in everyday life, friendship and other informal types of sociability provide crucial social support.

—Robert Putnam, American political theorist

fabric, political institutions, and civil society. At micro and macro levels—in our neighborhoods, town meetings, and in the halls of Congress—civility builds the personal virtue that is essential to fostering trust between citizens.

Civility also facilitates the process of building and deploying social capital to meet needs and solve problems—and the relationships, intimate and occasional alike, that make our lives meaningful.

After the fall of the Soviet Union, British-Czech political philosopher Ernest Gellner explored a unique social and cultural phenomenon.[14] He realized that economic and political institutions—such as elections, democracy, and free markets—could not be air-dropped on post-Soviet nations that had been under oppressive and totalitarian communist regimes for decades. Why? Because those regimes promoted a culture of mistrust: they relied on neighbors spying on neighbors, and family members being willing to turn on one another for disloyalty to the Communist Party. People were constantly looking to turn one another in for "infractions."

This culture of mistrust depleted and virtually eradicated intermediary institutions of civil society—the sphere between the individual and the state, which includes church, family, social groups, and personal friendships. Front porches—or the Eastern European equivalent of quasi-public spaces for people to meet, relax, and convene—had been impoverished over years of peer-to-peer suspicion. This was problematic, because democratic and economic institutions rely on attitudes of cooperation. In order for them to take hold, a culture of trust had to be rebuilt. And the only way it could be rebuilt was by people choosing to sow seeds of trust in their everyday interactions with one another.

We've explored in this chapter the enduring tradition of writers and thinkers who have despaired at the state of civility, community, and civil society. The communal impulse exists in every era, as does the selfish one. This means that the state of civil society in every era will ebb and flow. There will be "civic churn": while social phenomena change, human nature doesn't. We'll still come together in relationship, and around shared causes, but it may look different. As previously noted, Robert Putnam's civic golden age was Robert Nisbet's low watermark for community; and when Tocqueville visited America, old civic institutions were dying, and new ones—including the National Benevolent Associations and temperance societies—being formed.

Throughout this civic churn, civility has an essential role. Civility helps build integrity, an idea we explored in Chapter 3. Integrity builds trust. Trust builds social capital. All of these, in turn, support our freedom, our democracy, our globalized market economy, and our civil society. None of these can be mandated by government policy. From civility and integrity flow norms and courtesies that build a truly civilized society—a society of people who trust one another because civil people are trustworthy. Cultivating the internal disposition of civility and integrity must be voluntary. Cultivating the internal disposition of civility must be voluntary. Its fruit must be organic. Civility is so important that it cannot be left to policy makers to "promote" or "create."

It's up to each of us to choose it.

How to Restore Trust, Civility, and Civil Society—and Save Democracy

1. Remember that our bonds are nourished by civility, and in turn build civil society and sustain our democracy. But our

bonds, like civil society and civilization itself, are fragile. We cannot take them for granted, but must be vigilant in nurturing them with our everyday actions and decisions. We can deploy the timeless principles of civility and re-build civil society in ways large and small. For example, we can get to know our neighbors, and keep in regular touch with them.

2. We can invite neighbors into our homes, or offer to help them when they're in need: water their plants while they travel, bring them groceries when they're ill, or have a meal delivered when they welcome a new child into the world.

3. Consider creating a "third space" that can be place of building relationship and community, and be a refuge from our divided world. This can be a front lawn, a liv-ing room, a park, or a front porch. If there's someone you'd like to know better in your community, consider having them over. Quasi-public spaces of healing, such as the porch, can elevate an interaction out of the trans-parently transactional and into the personal. This can be good for the soul and a recipe for fruitful new friendships.

4. Accept hospitality when it's offered. It's easy to make ex-cuses. Don't. Be there. Be willing to learn from the expe-riences and ideas of others. Remember that everyone has something to teach you. Very rarely will you regret it.

5. When interacting with strangers in the marketplace of life—such as public transit, travel, the grocery store, etc.—remember to look people in the eye whenever you can. Acknowledge and affirm their personhood, human dignity, value, and worth. Remember to smile, too—when you do so, you bring about greater comity in our world.

6. Don't assume the worst about others. Hold on to your emotional and mental energy by telling stories of exoneration, not condemnation.

7. When you meet someone new, try to nurture the connection, like Joanna did for me, and like my mother has done for innumerable others. Here are some ideas for how to do so:

- Discover their interests.
- Try to connect them with other people you know with similar interests.
- When you hear of an interesting event, take a few minutes to think of three people who might enjoy it, and invite them or simply share the information with them.
- If they say no, and even if they don't respond, choose not to close down or be offended. Choose to tell yourself a story that exonerates them—for example, that they had a scheduling or personal conflict.
- Resolve to invite them again. This is how virtuous cycles of community and hospitality begin. Resilience and persistent grace make the world go round.
- When you read an article that reminds you of someone, or of numerous people, share it with them. Every outreach and form of connection matters because it builds and maintains social trust.
- If others don't respond to your invitations or initiatives, don't stew on the sense of rejection. Resolve not to be offended. Tell stories of exoneration—"They're probably just busy!"—not stories of condemnation. Remember that you're only responsible for your own

actions: you cannot control their response, but you can control yours. The practice of thinking of others builds the empathy and trust so direly needed in our broken and isolated world.

6

Equality

When Thomas Jefferson was President of the United States, he had a zany idea for how to manifest the "all men are created equal" creed that he had penned a few decades earlier. Determined that British aristocratic norms of social deference would never take root in America, he resolved that under his presidency, all manners that acknowledged rank or status would be abolished.

Jefferson outlined his "pell-mell etiquette" in an 1803 "Memorandum on Official Etiquette" to his Cabinet.[1] Anyone who entered the White House had to leave all notions of superiority at the door.[2] Congressmen, judges, lords, foreign diplomats—all were equal in the Thomas Jefferson White House. A laudable attempt to align ideas and practice, the effort was something of a disaster. The unintended effects of his new

> *When brought together in society, all are perfectly equal, whether foreign or domestic, titled or untitled, in or out of office. . . . No title being admitted here, those of foreigners, give no precedence. Differences of grade among diplomatic members, give no precedence.*
>
> —Thomas Jefferson

code of etiquette—namely, offending the snobbish manners police of his day—were a *feature* of his system of manners, not a bug.

The Merry Affair

The night was December 2, 1803. The British ambassador to America, Anthony Merry, and his wife were—along with James and Dolley Madison—invited by Thomas Jefferson to the White House for dinner. Presuming himself to be the guest of honor, Merry dressed to impress. He donned a plumage-topped hat, a ceremonial sword, a gold braid, and shoes with buckles so gleaming he could see his reflection in them.[3]

Merry was first irked that Jefferson wasn't waiting eagerly to greet him in the reception hall. Little did Merry know that this was just the beginning of Jefferson's plot to puncture his pretense. Merry was dismayed that Jefferson was not so intent on polish and keeping up appearances. "Utter slovenliness," "negligence actually studied," "indifference to appearances," Merry later complained to a friend when describing the evening.

When it was time to move from the reception hall to dinner, Jefferson—horror of horrors!—overlooked Mrs. Merry entirely, and *escorted Dolley Madison to the dining room instead*. As if that were not bad enough, Mr. and Mrs. Merry were scandalized to see that the dinner table was round instead of rectangular. There would be no way for the room to know that they were guests of import! Worse, there was no seating arrangement. It was *pell-mell* seating—confused, disordered, chaotic. Merry was forced to fight with the masses—including some savage person who went by the title "Congressman"—to find a seat. Indignant and offended by the "omission of all distinction" in the White House, the Merrys resolved to never dine with Jefferson again.[4]

"This will be the cause of war," the wife of the Spanish minister whispered into the ear of Dolley Madison as the dinner ended.[5] After this fateful evening, Jefferson wrote out his *Canons of Etiquette*, which he hoped would "give force to the principle of equality, or pêle mêle, & prevent the growth of precedence out of courtesy."[6] Despite his egalitarian sentiments, Jefferson was an American aristocrat if there ever was one. He was wealthy and highly educated—he was fluent in Latin and French, and enjoyed reading Plato and Aristotle in the original Greek. He was a Renaissance man, a well-traveled sophisticate, and a citizen of the world. Having spent time as the US ambassador to France at the court of Louis XVI, he knew the rules better than anyone. He flouted them for the sport of deflating a pompous Anthony Merry, and to make a philosophical statement: our basic, equal moral worth as persons wasn't purely theoretical. It was practical, and should inform how we live our lives.

As we'll discuss further in our next chapter, it's ironic and hypocritical that Jefferson was so passionate about human equality while owning other human beings throughout his life. But his personal failure to live out his ideals does not negate the truth of the equal moral worth of persons, and the importance of our actions and social norms affirming our basic equality.

Equality and Precedence: A Timeless Tension

Human nature is marked by our desire for equality with others—but also for precedence above others. Our desire for superiority is an expression of our self-love, which, we've learned, is in tension with our foundational human need and desire for friendship and community with others. Our selfish human nature is why those who live in democracies—and those, such as Jefferson, who helped to create them—have struggled and failed to perfectly realize social and political equality for all people. Given humankind's selfish nature, and given America's democratic aspirations, what might a republican etiquette look like? Is it possible to live up to our ideals of being a place where, as Alexis de Tocqueville noted, "privileges of birth have never existed, and where wealth gives no particular right to the one who possesses it"?[7]

Equality and Utopia

America, a nation that intentionally threw off the monarchical yoke and the associated system of inherited honors, titles, and ranks, is yet a perpetually class-conscious nation. Still, each generation has the chance to create itself anew without being bound by the hierarchies of past generations.

At least, this is the theory.

The hope that we can rise up the ranks through hard work and grit, transcending the station of our birth, is the core of the American dream. A result of lacking strict, preset hierarchies, however, is that Americans are perpetually insecure and conscious of where they currently fall in the pecking order.

> *If you find an American who feels entirely class-secure, stuff and exhibit him. He's a rare specimen.*
>
> —Paul Fussell

In his book *Democratic Vistas*, Walt Whitman noted that in a classless society of equals there would still exist a constant struggle between individuals for self-respect and approval from others. No institutional or political arrangement—no matter how earnest, noble, or aspirational—will completely eliminate that struggle.

The vision of a perfectly equal, classless society is a "utopia"—a word invented by English statesman and philosopher Thomas More that literally means "no place." An impeccably equal society will never exist. Attempts to realize complete human equality are misguided, harmful, and, ironically, frequently create *more* inequality in the process. Attempts to erase social differences entirely are dehumanizing and dystopian.

Kurt Vonnegut's "Harrison Bergeron" memorably shows how this pursuit of equality means treating people terribly unequally. "The year was 2081, and everybody was finally equal," the short story begins. The world of Harrison Bergeron is a world where the "United States Handicapper General" is all powerful. This Cabinet-level role ensures that everyone is equal in every way—in appearance, capabilities, intellect, and all. For example, those with above-average intelligence must wear an earpiece that makes horrid noises every twenty seconds, which prevents them from "taking unfair advantage of their brains."

L. P. Hartley's novel *Facial Justice* explores the "prejudice of good looks" in a future world not unlike our own. Government plastic surgeons remedy inequalities of appearance. But instead of making everyone beautiful, they make everyone plain.

Though a perfectly equal society may be impossible, not to mention undesirable because of its invariably unjust consequences, we must not give up our efforts to

> *But as the distinctions of rank are obliterated [in America], as men differing in education and in birth meet and mingle in the same places of resort, it is almost impossible to agree upon the rules of good breeding . . . they grow less civil, but at the same time less quarrelsome.*
>
> —Alexis de Tocqueville

make our culture *more* socially equal. People naturally define social difference between them and others because differences—in taste and lifestyle choices—are an important part of expressing our personality and individuality. We often value our freedom of individual expression as much as, if not more than, equality with others. We will also be tempted to assign value to our difference, usually viewing our own position and preferences more favorably. We must resist the temptation to look down on others who are different from us, and refocus on norms that demonstrate the equal moral worth of persons and that reflect the value of human equality and dignity.

Inequality, Present and Past

Today, our democratic sensibilities are aggravated by flagrant displays of inequality. This may be one reason why many modern flyers find air travel so grating. Every aspect of the experience is meant to praise and reward those who can afford first-class and upgraded travel. From the moment you enter the airport, passengers with preferred airline status and premium tickets are whisked to rarefied concierge service instead of having to wait in line like everyone else. They are offered complimentary checked baggage, lounge access, the opportunity to board and deplane first, and much more. While those in first class are plied with beverages and snacks, those in coach are nickel-and-dimed for everything from snacks to headphones to, in some cases, water.

This differentiated treatment between the "haves" and the "have-nots" in air travel is no accident. Individuals in first class are given preferred treatment precisely so that the "have-nots" see it, long for it, and fork out for an upgrade. "People only pay to be in the first-class section because there is a coach section behind it," as one writer put it.[8] Those who can afford to pay for preferred tickets on airlines are rewarded not just materially, but also by the envious looks of their fellow passengers. We relish feeling superior to others, but resent it when we feel others are superior to us.

Customs that ingrain social inequality are nothing new. Across history, rules of politeness have frequently become tools for insiders to keep the outsiders out. I call these rules that divide "class markers." Knowledge and deployment of these norms declares one's elite status. Charles William Day, in his 1834 *Hints on Etiquette and the Usages of Society*, describes them as "the barrier which society draws around itself as a protection."[9]

The once-popular fish knife is illustrative of this. In the pre–stainless steel era, the alloys used to make knives ensured that those who enjoyed lemon with their fish were left with a metallic taste in their mouth. The pure-silver fish knife was the upper classes' invention, to enable them to relish the pairing without the taste of metal; but because not everyone could afford pure silver, the norm demanding the use of the fish knife wasn't exactly democratic. Another example of a historical class marker is high heels, which were all the rage for European men and women after Louis XIV of France made them fashionable—though only the *truly* privileged were permitted to wear red-colored footwear in his court.

Often, these fads in social norms began as benign matters of *taste* that were later imbued with *moral* significance. This means that people who practiced these norms were considered *good*, and those who did not—even if they simply had never had the opportunity to learn them—were dismissed as morally inferior. Relevant to our discussion in Chapter 3, these rules gave people the opportunity to assume the *appearance* of virtue without its substance.

The rules of etiquette often exist to keep people out, which is underscored by the frequency with which they change: as class markers become well-known, everyone starts to follow them, which makes it difficult for them to serve their distinguishing function, and it thus becomes necessary to adopt *new* rules, and so on. For example, it was for a time in the nineteenth century considered fashionable to eat soup with a fork, but as soon as the masses adopted the practice, it was quickly condemned as foolish, and the spoon resumed its place.[10] Switching forks from left hand to right was *en vogue* on the Continent, but when everyone started doing so—including "vulgar" Americans—Europeans reverted to *not* switching. (Americans have to this day generally kept the zigzag, or the "star-spangled fork flip," as some etiquette authorities have affectionately named it.)

Consider the pineapple. A ubiquitous symbol of hospitality today, this delicious fruit was once the symbol of ultimate luxury, available only in the rarefied realms of the sophisticated, wealthy, and elite. It was a coveted object in the homes of aristocrats across England, and at its height a single pineapple could cost upward of eleven thousand pounds sterling in today's currency.

That is, of course, until the sweet, tropical fruit was democratized. Enterprising individuals began renting the pineapple to families who couldn't afford to own one, suddenly making the luxury status symbol available to the masses. Other entrepreneurs began importing them en masse, flooding the market, decreasing their price—and deflating their cachet. As soon as the working classes were able to get their hands on pineapples, patricians immediately abandoned them. If everyone had a pineapple, how could the fruit possibly differentiate between the haves and have-nots? The sun had set on the English pineapple.

It's a rare American who doesn't secretly want to be upper-middle class.

—Paul Fussell

This story illustrates how social elites use the rules and matters of taste to mark divisions *within* a group—and then will change the standards of politeness and the rules as soon as the lower classes learn them. After all, when everyone knows the rules of politeness, one can no longer distinguish between aristocracy and parvenus.

Civility and Social Equality

By restraining our self-love so that our social natures can flourish, civility is how we keep the conflicting desires for precedence and equality with others in check. By building the social trust that in turn helps build civil society and maintains other democratic institutions, civility promotes social equality in the context of our everyday interactions.

When we act civilly, we respect others as beings with equal dignity and moral worth. Civility promotes equality by reframing how we view our interactions with others: each exchange with other people is a chance to recognize and affirm our equal status as members of the human community.

The rules of politeness have been, and continue to be, used to divide and oppress. They are often a means to maintain a position of power. But civility has long been a tool of promoting greater equality among persons.

Civility is . . . of more value than politeness. Politeness flatters the vices of others, and civility prevents ours from being brought to light. It is a barrier which men have placed within themselves to prevent the corruption of each other.

—Montesquieu, eighteenth-century French philosopher

William Penn, the Quakers, and Civil Equality

William Penn, the Quaker writer and founder of Pennsylvania, was a free-spirited youth prone to rebellion. When he turned eighteen his parents sent him off to the court of Louis XIV to become acquainted with the customs of the "civilized." Penn's parents hoped he would learn the importance of following the rules and deferring to superiors. His time with Louis's courtiers had precisely the opposite effect. What Penn saw was a despot who provided an almost comical example of how those in power use etiquette to preserve the status quo and solidify their positions of superiority over other, less powerful people.

> *In the courts of princes, in the drawing-rooms of the great, where success and preferment depend, not upon the esteem of intelligent and well-informed equals, but upon the fanciful and foolish favor of ignorant, presumptuous, and proud superiors; flattery and falsehood too often prevail over merit and abilities.*
>
> —Adam Smith

For example, Louis XIV built his magnificent Palace of Versailles thirty minutes outside of Paris, and moved his courtiers with him so that he could monitor and control their every move. He had meticulous rituals for each part of the day. He required that his courtiers maintain a fresh wardrobe of the finest and most expensive clothing. These rules ensured that his nobles were too preoccupied, busy, and indebted to plan a rebellion. It was difficult for courtiers to remember the ever-expanding, and ever-evolving, protocols that Louis XIV expected at Versailles. To assist them, Louis had signs, or *étiquets*, erected throughout

Versailles to remind his courtiers of his mandates. These *étiquets* are the origin of our word "etiquette," showing that those who criticize etiquette as a mode of social control and oppression are not entirely wrong.

The obsequious displays of deference in the court of Louis XIV—known as the "Sun King" because he ensured that life at Versailles revolved around him—disaffected Penn and made a lasting impression on him. The experience caused him to reflect on the pernicious effects of flattery and the deferential norms that inflate the ego, and in so doing, harm others. It may have been Penn's experience in France that prompted his conversion to Quakerism, a Christian sect that practiced radical egalitarianism and consciously disobeyed deferential social norms of the day.

In *No Cross, No Crown*, which he wrote while imprisoned in the Tower of London for his religious heterodoxy, Penn recounts a story that illustrates the perils of pro forma shows of deference. While wandering the streets of Paris late one evening, a man suddenly began yelling at him and angrily challenged him to a duel. What had caused this gentleman's rage? He thought that Penn had taken "no notice of him." In other words, he thought that Penn had snubbed him by not returning his "civil salute" to him with his hat. Penn had not meant to insult the man. He had not even noticed the polite gesture![11] But the man perceived Penn to have insulted him, and so was prepared to kill him for it. This is Penn's concern with the way that social norms work: they inflate people's pride, so much so that some will take another's life to defend them.

Penn reflected on the frivolity of his near-death experience. How could anyone be willing to take a life over such a *senseless, unintentional* slight? Was the whole ceremony of tipping a hat "worth the life of a man"? Clearly people's priorities were disordered, he thought.

I ask any man of understanding or conscience, if the whole ceremony [of being challenged to a duel] was worth the life of a man, considering the dignity of the nature, and the importance of the life of man, both with respect to God his Creator, himself, and the benefit of civil society.

—William Penn, seventeenth-century English aristocrat, Quaker, and founder of Pennsylvania

One afternoon in the mid-1660s, Penn decided to take a small break from his studies at Oxford, and return home. Young William offered his father, Admiral Penn, a warm greeting—"I am glad to see thee in good health!" This greeting is perfectly appropriate for us today. But the admiral was enraged. Young William had failed to comply with the customary practice of kneeling and removing his hat, and had offended his father with his informality. As Diderot and d'Alembert's entry on Quakerism in the famous enlightenment *Encyclopédie* notes: "The vice-admiral thought his son [Penn] had gone mad but he soon realized that he had simply become a Quaker."

Quakerism was a Protestant Christian sect that emphasized inner spiritual guidance over church hierarchy. Also known as Friends, the Quakers held a radical egalitarianism that was borne out of their belief in the fundamental dignity and equality of each person. Like other Quakers, Penn possessed a commitment to equality that caused him to reject norms and practices that enshrined hierarchy and rank. The admiral was worried. If he couldn't convince Penn to renounce Quakerism—if he couldn't persuade him to uphold the polite conventions of his day—what hope would William have of the social and political advancement that his father hoped for him? But Penn remained steadfast, even attempting (and failing) to convert his father to Quakerism. The exasperated admiral realized the futility of changing his son, and ultimately disowned him.

Quakers were rather infamous for their radical social equality. For example, they intentionally eschewed the practice of using deferential pronouns when addressing others, which especially irked their social superiors.

The King James version of the Lord's Prayer—*Our Father which art in heaven, hallowed be thy name . . .* —used the informal "thy," instead of the more formal "your," to signify the intimate relationship between Christ and God the Father, the prayer and the receiver.

English used to have two forms of address: "you" and "thou." "You" was the formal form of address. It was used when speaking to strangers and social superiors. "Thou" was informal and used for family and close friends. Penn and his fellow Quakers held that humankind's God-given dignity makes us all completely equal in the eyes of God. They were deeply suspicious of "empty gestures, puffing up vanity and empty of actual respect." Accordingly, the Quakers used the egalitarian "thou" toward everyone.

Quakers were widely imprisoned for failing to comply with this norm and other polite niceties of their day, such as tipping their hats to others. They refused to abide by these arbitrary (and harmful, in their view) man-made rules because they believed such rules unduly inflated the self-love that was the root of man's social suffering. Besides, the Quakers feared, honored, and "quaked" before no one but God alone.

For Penn, there "was no discovery of honor or respect" in the empty gestures of bowing, removing hats, addressing with titles, or using the more deferential "you" to social superiors. "It is rather eluding and equivocating it; cheating people of the honor and respect that is due to them; giving them nothing in the show of something," he wrote. Penn embodied true civility, and showed that it is grounded in fundamental respect for others. He opposed what Samuel Johnson defined in his 1755 *Dictionary* as "mouth-honour," a term used by Shakespeare's Macbeth: "civility outwardly expressed without sincerity."

Penn respected the dignity and fundamental equality of all people, including those perceived to be his social superiors, too much to patronize them. He would later go on to found Pennsylvania (he fought against the state's being named after him) on the principles of tolerance and equal respect for people of different religions.

Status Anxiety

William Penn knew that pride was central to the human condition, and would always cause us to look for ways to feel superior to those around us. He responded by taking himself out of the game of pride, flattery, and status entirely. Many people don't, and are imprisoned by it. Americans, for instance, are in a constant state of status anxiety. Focusing on the rules of politeness only adds to that anxiety. The people who are most insecure and status-conscious are the ones most likely to weaponize etiquette, using it to foster delusions of grandeur.

The British sitcom *Keeping Up Appearances* illustrates this truth—and also shows that status anxiety is hardly limited to Americans. Hyacinth Bucket is a middle-class snob. One day, her mailman arrives and greets her enthusiastically, "Hi, Mrs. Bucket!" Righteously indignant, she corrects him furiously—"It's pronounced *Bouquet (Boo-kay)*!"—a French affectation that she maintains throughout the show. Hyacinth's main quest in life is to prove her social standing, including her superiority over her neighbors, and to gain approval from those she considers to be "upper class." Fancying herself a member of England's smart set, she eagerly dispenses "kindnesses" to others to fulfill her *noblesse oblige*.

Only, Hyacinth is not the most self-aware or empathetic person. She does things that *she* would want done, but that those around her don't appreciate much at all. She'll also perform acts that make her *seem* generous, but that are nakedly self-interested. Her efforts often send others running in the other direction from her acts of supposed goodwill.

Punctilious about the rules of etiquette and social graces, there is nothing Hyacinth loves more than to see someone breaking the rules so that she can then correct them. She is completely unaware of how everyone fears and avoids her. Hyacinth is, in her own eyes, the epitome of taste and decorum. In the eyes of everyone else, she's an intolerable snob. Her favorite pastimes are throwing "candlelight suppers"—of course, only for worthy guests—and calling people "Philistine" for lacking the good taste that she has.

Ever the social climber, Hyacinth's lower-class family and roots embarrass her. She wants everyone in her life to accept the charade that she is desirable and popular—even going so far as to send herself Christmas cards just so she can tell her postman how many more she received this year compared to last. Confident of her own greatness, her life's mission is to ensure that everyone else recognizes it, too. When they fail to, she—like Mr. and Mrs. Merry from our opening story—is shocked, indignant, and offended.

In watching Hyacinth bumble her way through life, we glimpse the joy that Thomas Jefferson likely had in deflating the pride of the snobbish Mr. and Mrs. Merry. It's apparently a universal human quality to delight in puncturing the ego of snobs and to laugh at those who think they are better than others. Hyacinth represents the perpetual case of status panic that plagues the middle class and resonates with people the world over. *Keeping Up Appearances* was enormously popular not only in England but around the world: the show has been purchased for syndication over a thousand times, making it the BBC's most exported television program.

People often go to extraordinary lengths to assure themselves and others of their worth. Paul Fussell pokes fun at America's middle class for adopting "pseudo-upper-middle-class gestures" such as buying their own heirlooms, subscribing to *The New Yorker*, printing dinner invitations, or using English spellings of words to feel like they have achieved a higher station in life.

> *The desire to belong, and to belong by some mechanical act like purchasing something, is another sign of the middle class.*
>
> —Paul Fussell

It's tempting to make social status—measured by wealth, success, possessions, social tastes, and mores—the sole criterion of one's worth as a person. When people cling to these things, they transform themselves into *snobs* who are constantly worried about their own self-worth and whether their taste or possessions adequately confer and reflect their value to the world. Like Hyacinth and Anthony Merry, they become obsessed with "correctness." People who use the rules of politeness to divide are the most insecure of us about their own worth. This, too, is an expression of the tension in our nature and desires for both equality and precedence: people are eager to dwell on the mistakes of others so that, at least for a moment, they are assured of their own acceptance.

The snob insists that there is a "right" way and a "wrong" way for everything, and such status-conscious people are constantly monitoring themselves and others for breaches. They are quick to point out the flaws in the conduct or taste of others because it makes them, in comparison, superior. Excluding the outsider or newcomer makes the status-anxious snob feel like they belong. Mrs. Bucket shows a paradox: those most punctilious about polite manners can often be the rudest people.

True courtesy will instinctively check faddish manners at the door in the interest of kindness— which is the root from which the entire family tree of civil behavior springs.

—Tamar Adler, food writer

Recognizing Difference and Equality: The Myth of Republican Etiquette?

Jefferson's simplified diplomatic protocol was unpopular with foreign dignitaries, as Anthony Merry showed us. But domestic custodians of tradition and self-appointed etiquette experts also despised it. While serving as a confidant to Ulysses S. Grant during the Civil War, De Benneville Randolph Keim gained intimate familiarity with the inner workings, rituals, and ceremonies that governed the United States government. In 1889, he published the definitive work on the topic, *Hand-book of Official and Social Etiquette and Public Ceremonials at Washington.* In this work, Keim took direct aim at Jefferson's pell-mell etiquette, calling it "unjust and in bad taste." Keim praised James Madison, who finally "put an end to the Jeffersonian code, and restored the dignified social institution of the American school of the administrations of Washington and Adams."[12]

In his book, Keim left no aspect of life in America's capital untouched. Rules about state dinners, the use of diplomatic titles, the proper distribution of personal calling cards, the appropriate means of mounting and dismounting a horse, and how to be a good conversationalist are all covered. Knowing his

> *It is not empty gesticulations nor the blandishments of complimentary epithets that constitute good manners, but dignity tempered with freedom, reserve mingled with affability, and conversation softened with geniality and enlivened with wit.*
>
> —De Benneville Randolph Keim, nineteenth-century journalist and etiquette writer

audience would be skeptical of a list of fusty etiquette rules, Keim addressed the elephant in the room from the outset. "There are many who deride food manners as antagonistic to the spirit of liberty," he began. "And while it is not essential to imitate the forms of pageantry which invest royalty, it is possible to observe the recognized rules of decency, if not refinement and culture, without being aristocratic."[13]

Keim argued that treating others with basic respect and decency was the culmination of our nation's founding ideals of human equality. Our nation's highest offices were open to all, not merely those of wealth or noble lineage. Practicing a basic civility with everyone—or "genuine politeness" instead of mere "splendor of outward forms"—was a way that we could live up to our ideals, and ensure the general welfare of society. By reviving the timeless principles of civility and deploying them toward those we meet, we can each live out our founding ideal of equality, too.

Transcending Class, Embracing Equality

Once, at a state dinner, Queen Victoria broke the rules of politeness and did the unthinkable: *she lifted up her finger bowl to her lips and drank from it.*

Why?

Her guest, the Shah of Persia, had done so first.

This story is told elsewhere with different protagonists, including Eleanor Roosevelt, and is enduring because the message behind it rings true: civility places others—relationship and community—above blind compliance with rules that can divide us.

Sticklers for rules are often socially insecure people who are quick to dismiss people for not having the "correct" taste or social practices. People who conduct themselves with civility, by contrast, understand that civility and integrity sometimes require breaking the rules in order to live up to our inner values and to truly respect others by recognizing their equal moral worth.

Self-conscious, status-anxious people weaponize the rules of politeness. They are also the first to display gracelessness with others and to lash out at people for not recognizing their status. These people delight in ordering around people at restaurants or in stores because they feel powerless in life, and enjoy the feeling of power and superiority over others—if only fleetingly.

This impulse to compare and measure ourselves against others—and to exert dominance over them—can manifest itself in any person, with any level of wealth, from any place in the world and of any social class. This is because we each have self-love and *libido dominandi* within us, waiting beneath the surface of our souls to be unleashed. As we learned from St. Augustine in Chapter 1, the *libido dominandi*—the lust to dominate others—is part of human nature. It is an expression of our foundational selfishness as human beings—a facet of our nature that transcends social class.

> *There is nothing noble in being superior to your fellow man; true nobility is being superior to your former self.*
>
> —Ernest Hemingway, twentieth-century American writer

Yet the capacity to resist the *libido dominandi* also exists within all of us.

There are a few things we can do to ensure that our everyday interactions promote greater equality, not division, and shed status anxiety for good. First, we can remind ourselves of our own dignity and equal moral worth. This reminder can help us become more content in our own skin. This can help us resist comparing our status with that of others. Fostering contentment with who we are can also mitigate internal self-esteem deficits, and help diminish the need to exert power in our relationships with others.

Second, we can defy the urge to allow the rules of politeness to divide us from others. We can refuse to let the rules make us feel superior to those around us. We can reject artificial divisions between groups. We can choose to transcend class and work to create a more civil, and more equal, world.

We can become people who, like William Penn, transcend social class. We can remove ourselves from prevailing social hierarchies entirely and reject the rules and games and angling that define the status-conscious of the world. We can free ourselves from the need to compensate for our own insecurities by diminishing others. We can be liberated from the opinions of others and be free to be original, innovative, and curious.

People like William Penn transcend social class by adopting a particular frame of mind—the disposition of civility that sees others as beings with equal moral worth. Members of the classless class see people as they really are: as human beings, similar to themselves in the way that matters most—sharing the imprint of the divine, infused with irreducible dignity and worth—yet also infinitely and beautifully different. They see people as beings to be cherished and respected, not flattered and patronized. This allows them to see past the arbitrary distinctions, matters of taste, and trivial norms of politeness that divide us.

We can remember that status-conscious people like Anthony Merry and Hyacinth Bucket are never completely happy, nor completely their own. They are instead at the mercy of the mercurial impressions of others. They are always scanning the room looking for where they and you fit into the social hierarchy. We can free ourselves of this. In a world of Merrys and Buckets, we can choose to be William Penns.

The promise and fulfillment that comes with being a member of the classless class is open to us all. A life free of social anxiety, angling, and insecurity is available to anyone with the motivation to pursue it.

Though we—like Thomas Jefferson, whose life of contradiction we'll explore further in our next chapter—will never perfectly live up to our own ideals of equality, we can keep trying. Instead of feeling annoyed or indignant toward the snobs in the world, we can have sympathy for them, knowing that they are not their own, and that their self-contentment will always be elusive. We can also show grace for others who, like us, fail along the way.

Creating a world of greater social equality—and welcoming a classless class—begins with cultivating our humanity and our humaneness toward others. It begins with changing ourselves—in cultivating the disposition of civility that sees others as beings inherently worthy of our respect—and extends into our small, everyday exchanges. It ends with a more civil—and equal—world.

How to create a more equal and civil world:

1. Resolve to recognize the basic equal moral worth of those around you. As Dr. King reminded us, we must see each other as we really are: beings with equal dignity and moral worth. Feeling superior to others hurts us by giving us a false sense of superiority, and hurts others by giving them a false sense of inferiority. Recall that when we hurt others—by

demeaning them with our snobbish, self-satisified actions—
we also hurt ourselves.

2. As you stay mindful of your own dignity and equal moral
worth as a person—as you let this truth permeate your
mind—allow it to help heal any inner wounds and deficits
that might tempt you to compare yourself to, or look down
on and abuse, others. When lured into looking down on
others, or exerting power over someone, consider what
inner deficiency is manifesting, and return to the recom-
mendation in point one: remember that being a human
means that you have dignity and worth. You are a remarkable work of art, capable of creating more beauty in the
world around you. Resolve not to derive cheapened, short-
lived feelings of significance by looking down on others.

3. Resist the urge to disparage others for breaking rules of
propriety. Don't allow the rules of politeness to divide you
from them. Reject artificial divisions between groups.

4. Stay mindful of your ongoing inner battle—between self-
love and love of others, between our desire for precedence
over others and our equality with them. Even just being
aware of it is a step toward victory, and toward reinforcing
our collective project to affirm and protect the equal dignity of persons.

5. In a world of Anthony Merrys and Hyacinth Buckets,
choose to be a William Penn. Strive to transcend social
class—liberating yourself from the mercurial opinions of
others, becoming free to enjoy the beauty in relationship
and the world around us for its own sake, liberated from
the worry of having to impress anyone else, and working
to create a more civil, and more equal, world.

7

Civil Disobedience

Edward Coles isn't a well-known figure in American history, but he should be.

Our last chapter began with a story about Thomas Jefferson when he, out of a resolve to embody his ideals of basic human equality, purged all Old World protocols of deference to rank and status from the official etiquette of the United States government. He dedicated his life to the ideals of human equality, yet still found a way to justify to himself his ownership of slaves, which he held even to his death.

Unironically, Jefferson once noted that slavery transforms slaveholders into "despots" and destroys their morals.[1] He knew that slavery was both objectively wrong, and toxic to his beloved American democratic project because it deformed the souls of slave owners. It cultivated their selfish nature, their *libido dominandi*, which rendered them unfit for self-governance in a republican regime. Jefferson wanted egalitarianism for himself and others when it came to manners while he was president, but apparently not when it came to owning other human beings—an institution that he understood was antithetical to American democracy.

Edward Coles, a contemporary of Jefferson, also believed in basic human equality. Unlike Jefferson, however, he made personal sacrifices to live out the ideal of the equal moral worth of persons: Coles freed his slaves as soon as he inherited them. Coles shows how the disposition of civility has been a tool of pursuing justice and equality for all in our past, and how civility can help us do so now. He shows us how disobeying prevailing norms—norms that require us to be silent in the face of injustice—is a duty of civility and integral to promoting justice in our world.

Coles, born to a wealthy founding Virginian family, was a generation behind the founding fathers. He was a young neighbor to Thomas Jefferson and a political aide to James Madison when he was president. In 1807, at the age of twenty-one, Coles became convinced that slavery was not only morally wrong but detrimental to the republic. He decided to do something about it. After his father died, Coles inherited his family's estate, which included nineteen slaves. Coles put his farm up for sale, freed his slaves, and immediately left Virginia for a nonslaveholding territory, Illinois. There, he ran for governor on an abolitionist platform and won, serving from 1822 to 1826.

In 1814, while an aide to President James Madison, Coles wrote Thomas Jefferson, his famous neighbor, a rather pointed letter. How, Coles asked, could Jefferson claim to believe that all persons were fundamentally equal while simultaneously owning persons as property?[2]

Coles was terrified. This was not only a former US president, but also one of the world's most powerful, important, and influential men, and a veritable genius—and Coles was calling him a hypocrite. Jefferson was the "Architect of American Liberty," someone who had done a tremendous amount of good for the project of human equality—and Coles was saying that for all of Jefferson's achievements, his moral failings in owning slaves was inexcusable. At the time he wrote the letter to Jefferson, Coles was a political aide to James Madison, the sitting president.

Coles was writing in a nonofficial capacity to a past president about the highly sensitive political issue of slavery. Surely this was a fireable offense!

But Coles couldn't wait. Jefferson's obvious hypocrisy was precisely why Coles had to write. Coles began his missive, "I never took up my pen with more hesitation or felt more embarrassment than I now do in addressing you on the subject of this letter."

Coles knew that calling out someone in Jefferson's position of power could be costly. It could mean the loss of his job and possibly any prospect of ever working in American politics again. But Coles boldly questioned Jefferson anyway. He asked him about the tension between his ideals and his practices. He pleaded with Jefferson to not only emancipate his slaves, but to join him in the abolitionist cause and help see the end of slavery throughout the nation.

Coles thought that Jefferson's power and influence required him to help those less fortunate than himself, and that his responsibility extended to the cause of emancipation. How could Jefferson sit idly by and be contented with his ideas of equality while half the population was in servitude to the other half? He urged Jefferson to "put into complete practice those hallowed principles contained in that renowned Declaration, of which you were the immortal author. . . ."

> *Permit me then, my dear sir, again to entreat you to exert your great powers of mind and influence, and to employ some of your present leisure, in devising a mode to liberate one half of our fellow beings from an ignominious bondage to the other.*
>
> —Edward Coles, in a letter to Thomas Jefferson, July 31, 1814

Somewhat surprisingly, Jefferson responded. He didn't have

to. Coles was not calling Jefferson out publicly. No one knew about the line of questioning and implicit accusations of hypocrisy. It would have been more comfortable for Jefferson to ignore Coles's letter altogether and go back to his charmed life of a retired statesman defined by reading good books, inventing, and enjoying fine French wine. But Jefferson wrote back.

Maybe he responded because he was fond of, or amused by, the young, idealistic, upstart politico. Maybe he felt internally conflicted. He was the Architect of American Liberty publicly, and a slave owner privately. Perhaps he wrote back because he felt the need to justify his actions not to Coles, but to *himself.* Whatever the reason, Jefferson wrote back. His example reminds us how easy it is to shirk our obligations—or to fail to live up to our morals—when they are inconvenient.

The love of justice and the love of country plead equally the cause of these people [slaves] and it is a moral reproach to us that they should have pleaded it so long in vain. . . .

—Thomas Jefferson, unironically condemning the injustice of slavery in a letter to Edward Coles, August 25, 1814

Jefferson began his reply by acknowledging Coles's concern. He agreed that justice was on the side of abolitionists, and lamented that slavery still existed. Surely disappointingly to Coles, Jefferson evaded any acknowledgment of wrongdoing, or commitment to action. He mentioned his past efforts at emancipation. He referenced the bloody Haitian revolution, noting that—through violence or political means—abolition was clearly in the near future. He expressed support for gradual emancipation, freeing those slaves born after a certain day. But he concluded that he was too old for the task. Jefferson quoted from Virgil's epic poem *The Aeneid,* which describes the elderly Priam, the King of Troy, putting on long-unused armor to face a pointless and ignoble death in a futile attempt to defend his city from Greek invasion.[3] Abolishing slavery was a challenge best left to younger men, Jefferson said to Coles before signing off and offering "all [his] prayers" for the abolitionist cause. Prayers, Jefferson claimed, were the only resources a man of his advanced years had left.

Coles, undeterred, wrote one more letter imploring Jefferson to change his mind. Jefferson, he started his letter (and I'm paraphrasing), do you think I'd be writing to you for help if I thought for a moment that I and other young, aspiring politicians were capable of abolishing slavery ourselves? Obviously not. This is a big, serious issue. Your prayers are not enough. We need your action, too.

Coles pulled out every argument he could think of. He appealed to Jefferson's conscience. He tried to reframe Jefferson's old age as an advantage—what could he have to lose at this point? He even prodded Jefferson's pride: Benjamin Franklin—in *his* old age!—had seen it fit to fight for the cause of

I am sensible of the partialities with which you have looked toward me as the person who should undertake this salutary but arduous work [of abolition]. But this, my dear sir, is like bidding old Priam to buckle the armor of Hector "trementibus aequo humeris et inutile ferruncingi" [*This is a slightly inaccurate quote from* The Aeneid, *which translates,* "He wrapped a shield around his shaking shoulders and put on useless iron."] *No, I have overlived the generation with which mutual labors & perils begat mutual confidence and influence. This enterprise [of freeing slaves] is for the young....*

—Thomas Jefferson, in a letter to Edward Coles, August 25, 1814 ending American slavery. Couldn't Jefferson, too? Pleasantries had fallen to the wayside. Coles pulled no punches in his attempt to motivate Jefferson to action.

Jefferson never replied.

This exchange is a rare instance in which Jefferson was directly confronted about his lived contradiction—the disparity between the principles of human equality and freedom that he spent his life advocating for, and his practice of owning human beings. Jefferson did not even attempt to justify retaining his slaves. He couldn't.

> *Doctor Franklin, to whom, by the way, Pennsylvania owes her early riddance of the evils of Slavery, was as actively and as usefully employed on as arduous duties after he had past your age as he had ever been at any period of his life.*
>
> —Edward Coles, in a letter to Thomas Jefferson, September 26, 1814

Speaking Truth to Power: The Hallmark of Citizenship, Justice, and Civility

Was Coles out of line to confront Jefferson with his hypocrisy? Not at all. His letters showed how much he respected Jefferson, because he was telling the elderly statesman an important truth—albeit an uncomfortable one. Some might have thought Coles was rude in doing so. Some might have called Coles's letters offensive. Jefferson himself may have been offended at Coles's obvious suggestion that Jefferson was a walking contradiction, and that his accomplishments—for all the good they did—were not enough. Coles's letters may have been rude and offensive. But in choosing this path, Coles was being deeply civil.

This is where the difference between civility and politeness becomes practically important. When we are tempted to hold back discussing important topics or speaking difficult truths—especially to people in authority—for fear of impropriety, causing offense, or reprisal, politeness has become a tool of silence and suppression.

Coles, by contrast, spoke truth to power, which is what civility demands. Coles was living out fully the *civil* part of civil disobedience: the duties of a citizen to defy prevailing norms for a higher principle, such as justice and equality for all.

Civility, not politeness, is indispensable to our progress toward political equality because, as Coles showed, it enables us to take action and confront injustice head-on. The *polite* thing for Coles to have done would have been to show obeisance to Jefferson and stay quiet about his hypocrisy—to sweep the uglier aspects of our history under the rug, and maintain an unruffled and polished appearance. It goes without saying that flattering and ingratiating himself to Jefferson—rather than calling him a hypocrite—would have been the savvier career move for a young, civic-minded person. But Coles took the road less traveled: he took the difficult, civil path.

Civility, not politeness, affirms that the inherent equality and dignity of each person is essential, which is why it speaks truth to power in word and deed. Coles's example can encourage us to recommit our own lives to living out ideals of equality and respect, ideals that are indispensable to democracy and human flourishing, and which civility both embodies and enables. George Bernard Shaw reminded us that improving the world depends on unreasonable men and women who are willing to take action, and that there is no truly just social progress—no true justice for the downtrodden, the oppressed, or society writ large—without civility. As he wrote in *Man and Superman*, "The reasonable man adapts himself to the world: the unreasonable one persists in trying to adapt the world to himself. Therefore all progress depends on the unreasonable man."

Civility and Civil Disobedience

When confronted with an evil injustice such as slavery, what can be done? Can civility be reconciled with disobeying the law passed and enacted by *civis*? Can it be civil to defy prevailing norms of social decorum that protect an unjust status quo?

In the introduction to this book we explored insights from Dr. Martin Luther King, Jr.'s "Letter from Birmingham Jail" about why civility supports civil disobedience, or the principled, intentional breaking of laws and norms. Sometimes people break individual laws and norms that undermine the overall rule of law and basic human equality. On December 1, 1955, Rosa Parks broke Chapter 6, Section 11 of the Montgomery City Code in protest of a specific Jim Crow law that discriminated against persons of color, and was subsequently arrested.

Counterintuitively, her lawbreaking action manifested respect for the rule of law, because the law she broke violated the rule of law in the first place. The paradox of civility is that sometimes breaking laws and norms is an important way of respecting the equality of all persons, supporting the rule of law, and promoting the democratic project. Parks broke *a* law with the intent of making *the* law more just for Americans.

In democratic republics like America, where all citizens are equal under the law, the right to protest is a duty of citizenship when the right to equal justice under the law is withheld from certain members of the population. When the equality of some citizens is not recognized, civil disobedience is necessary. Indeed, civility—the duties of citizenship—sometimes requires disobedience.

America's right to disobey and protest is enshrined in its founding documents. Members of the American *civis* are entitled to certain rights, and with those rights come the responsibilities of citizenship. Sometimes, as Edward Coles taught us, protest against unjust laws or norms is a duty of citizenship.

As we learned in Chapter 1, a truly civilized *civis* is one where legal institutions, and the habits of citizens, are oriented toward respecting the inherent dignity and equality of all. A civilized society depends on the character—the civility—of its citizens. Recognizing equality means recognizing inherent human dignity. It is what promotes *humaneness* in human communities.

The ideal of character is to be without any marked character; to maim by compression, like a Chinese lady's foot, every part of human nature which stands out prominently, and tends to make the person markedly dissimilar in outline to commonplace humanity.

—John Stuart Mill, nineteenth-century English philosopher

When certain members of the *civis* are deprived of basic rights—either through formal, legal institutions or through informal norms—it is the responsibility of other members of the *civis* to protest that unjust deprivation.

As Dr. King wrote in his "Letter from Birmingham Jail," throughout history people have challenged prevailing laws in loyalty to a higher, moral law. From Shadrach, Meshach, and Abednego's rejection of the laws of King Nebuchadnezzar, to early Christians who were willing to face the lions rather than renounce their faith, to those who participated in the Boston Tea Party, protest and civil disobedience have been shown to illuminate the soul of civility.

How do we determine when such action is warranted?

Dr. King offers us a framework for understanding when the duties of the *civis* require disobedience of prevailing norms and laws. He wrote in his letter, "How does one determine whether a law is just or unjust? A just law is a man-made code that squares with the moral law or the law of God. An unjust law or norm contradicts moral law." He continues, "An unjust law is a human law that is not rooted in eternal law and natural law. Any law that uplifts human personality is just. Any law that degrades human personality is unjust." It is at times our duty as citizens to disobey immoral laws and norms that deprive—that violate the rights of other citizens and degrade the human personality.[4]

Civility obligates conduct befitting a citizen of the *civitas*. Civility at times requires being impolite or rude, or even offending people, as Edward Coles taught us. But civility always respects the basic personhood and dignity of others. When advocates for justice and equality take to the streets, lead protests, and write editorials or public letters against people in power hiding behind an unjust status quo, as long as they do so with the end of respecting the human dignity of those they criticize—and do not intentionally harm them—they are being civil. The disobedient are living up to the duties of civility and citizenship, because those duties require standing against injustice. Protest is civil, because it is an effective—and, when used well, respectful—tool for demanding and achieving the equal recognition of all persons under the law and in society. Unlike politeness, civility in all its forms has been, and is, essential to achieving and maintaining equality.

Many commentators criticize the use of civil norms to repress, control, and keep people in positions of powerlessness. As we saw in the last chapter, the rules of politeness can often separate those who have wealth, education, and prestige from those who do not, and have been used by entire groups to justify their superiority. John Stuart Mill, for example, condemned people's obsession over general rules of conduct. He observed that his compatriots wanted a single agreed-upon standard, when in fact expressions of the human personality are and should be allowed to be infinite in their variety.[5]

That monster, custom, who all sense doth eat,

Of habits devil, is angel yet in this,

That to the use of actions fair and good

He likewise gives a frock or livery

That aptly is put on.

—Shakespeare

Mill would have disagreed with Shakespeare's Coriolanus—who stated, "What custom wills, in all things we should do't." Mill believed that blindly following custom simply because it is custom is wrong. In so doing, we are prevented from exercising our moral faculties—and our freedom.[6]

Our love and respect for others will sometimes require us to put aside the rules. Jesus Christ, for example, was not one to mince words when it came to criticizing the unjust status quo that surrounded him. He spoke truth to power and exposed the idolatry, hypocrisy, and pretense of others. Without a doubt, it seems impolite and offensive to call people out. "You brood of vipers," Christ said. "How can you who are evil say anything good?" This hardly seems like polite speech. But Christ knew that telling the truth was a means of respecting and loving people. And that coddling them in their misguided beliefs, selfishness, and sin harmed them.

Civil Disobedience and *Satyagraha*

America was founded on protest. What is a revolution if not forceful protestation and dissent? Americans have two important legal groundings—the Declaration of Independence and the First Amendment of the United States Constitution—for the rights and duties of citizens to protest and petition their government. Americans can and should protest unjust laws that discriminate against and oppress certain portions of the population. Sometimes, moral rights and duties precede the law.

We've explored throughout this chapter how civil disobedience is an important part of our duties to the *civis*. It requires loyalty to principles and values—such as the moral equality and dignity of human beings—that existed prior to the *civis*. Dr. King argued that "an unjust law is no law at all." When positive law contradicts natural law, we are bound by morality to disobey it.

The life stories and works of three thought leaders and political dissidents further refine the philosophical, legal, and political justification for civil disobedience, and foster clarity on the relationship between civility and civil disobedience today.

American transcendentalist Henry David Thoreau wrote "Resistance to Civil Government," also called "Civil Disobedience." Mahatma Gandhi developed the concept of *satyagraha* (pronounced suh-tee-AH-gruh-huh). Martin Luther King, Jr.'s "Letter from Birmingham Jail" is a work we've explored at length in this book. All of them have much to teach us about how to think more clearly about remedying injustice in our own era.

In his "Civil Disobedience," Thoreau explores the duties that citizens have to protest and resist their government when it acts, or calls on them to act, unjustly. Thoreau's views on civil disobedience—as well as Gandhi's, as we'll explore shortly—were formed by the *Bhagavad Gita*, the Hindu sacred text we learned about in Chapter 2. Thoreau even took a copy of the *Gita* to Walden Pond! He was specifically concerned with the evils of American slavery and the country's war with Mexico (1846–1848) following America's annexation of Texas. We should be men first, Thoreau argues, and subjects—or citizens—second. By this, he means that our duty is to honor our fellow man first and foremost, and to pursue peace, equality, and justice.

Thoreau thought that the best government is one that can rely on the conscience of individual citizens, and as a result can stay limited in nature—a theme we explored earlier. He opens his essay, "I heartily accept the motto, 'That government is best which governs least.'"

In Thoreau's ideal world, we wouldn't need government to interfere with our interactions with one another, because we would act with grace and justice toward our fellow citizens on our own accord. Because human self-love is an indelible part of human nature, it will always be a part of our lived experience, and some governance is necessary. Too much government, however, dehumanizes us and promotes injustice—an idea we explored in our chapter on civility and freedom. Individuals can ensure that government is kept limited and remains a tool of justice, not injustice. This is where the duty of the citizen to engage in civil disobedience comes in.

A corporation—or nation—with a conscience is built by the individual consciences of persons. Thoreau wrote, "The mass of men serve the state thus, not as men mainly, but as machines, with their bodies." People serving the state with their bodies but not their minds is a recipe for mass complicity in evil. Instead, it is necessary that individuals bring their consciences—their minds to engage critically, and their hearts to engage morally—to bear on their citizenship and service to the state.

This requires thinking critically and sometimes *refusing* to do what is asked of us as citizens—especially when what is asked of us goes against basic laws of morality.

There are thousands who are in opinion opposed to slavery and to the war, who yet in effect do nothing to put an end to them; who, esteeming themselves children of Washington and Franklin, sit down with their hands in their pockets, and say that they know not what to do, and do nothing; who even postpone the question of freedom to the question of free trade, and quietly read the prices-current along with the latest advices from Mexico, after dinner, and, it may be, fall asleep over them both.

—Henry David Thoreau, nineteenth-century American philosopher

For Thoreau, this was the case with slavery. He wrote, "I cannot for an instant recognize that political organization as my government which is the slave's government also." Thoreau knew that his audience would willingly justify protest and revolution in the face of tyranny, given America's separation from Britain in 1776. Thoreau anticipated his readers claiming, "Everything is fine! No need for protest or rebellion here." But Thoreau disagreed: "When a sixth of the population of a nation which has undertaken to be the refuge of liberty are slaves, and a whole country is unjustly overrun and conquered by a foreign army, and subjected to military law, I think that it is not too soon for honest men to rebel and revolutionize."

At times, protest against government is not just a *right* we possess as citizens in a democracy, but a *duty* we hold as members of the *civitas*.

"What is the price-current of an honest man and patriot today?" Thoreau laments. "They hesitate, and they regret, and sometimes they petition; but they do nothing in earnest and with effect. They will wait, well disposed, for others to remedy the evil, that they may no longer have it to regret." The duties of citizenship—of civility—require us to act in the face of injustice instead of waiting passively for others to act on our behalf. Thoreau's arguments in "Civil Disobedience" influenced the thinking of both Mahatma Gandhi and Martin Luther King, Jr.

Unjust laws exist: Shall we be content to obey them, or shall we endeavor to amend them, and obey them until we have succeeded, or shall we transgress them at once?

—Henry David Thoreau

Mahatma Gandhi, known as one of the greatest political and spiritual leaders of the twentieth century, led the nonviolent protest that helped put an end to British colonial rule in India. Gandhi developed the concept of *satyagraha*—a notion of civil, nonviolent resistance—as part of his efforts to lead India's independence from the British Empire. *Satyagraha* is derived from the Sanskrit words *satya*, or "truth," and *āgraha*, or "holding firmly to." Gandhi believed that "truth [*satya*] implies love, and firmness [*āgraha*] engenders and therefore serves as a synonym for force."[7] He understood that truly loving someone does not mean coddling them in their wrongness or smoothing over important differences, as politeness does.

Speaking the truth firmly and out of love and respect for others is also how we have come to understand civility throughout this book. In contrast to politeness, which "smooths over" differences, civility instead respects someone enough to tell them a hard truth, yet in a way that does not devolve into a malicious, ad hominem attack or violence. "I thus began to call the Indian movement *satyagraha*, that is to say, the force which is born of truth and love or nonviolence," he said.

Some of Gandhi's contemporaries argued for harsher measures, even violence, to win independence. But for Gandhi, it was impossible to separate means from ends. Respecting others in and of themselves—and not instrumentalizing them, or disregarding their equal moral worth, even if they stood in the way of his achieving his goals of Indian independence—was imperative. Injustice only enshrined and begot further injustice.

Gandhi shows us why civility can support our political equality. Committing injustice in the pursuit of justice—or using people as disposable means to ends, even if the ends are just—is not justice at all. Civility, like Gandhi's vision of civil disobedience, helps us keep in clear sight ultimate goals and values—such as the moral equality of all persons, even those we disagree with—as we pursue equality and justice today.

Gandhi said it well: "They say, 'means are, after all, means.' I would say, 'means are, after all, everything.'"[8]

Martin Luther King, Jr., was a student of the work of both Thoreau and Gandhi. He recounts in his autobiography how he was changed by his study of Gandhi's use of fasts and nonviolent resistance, as well as Gandhi's idea of *satyagraha*.[9]

Dr. King was convinced that there was a time and a place for action in the face of injustice, but never for violence. He understood that

As I delved deeper into the philosophy of Gandhi ... I came to see for the first time its potency in the area of social reform. ... It was in this Gandhian emphasis on love and nonviolence that I discovered the method for social reform that I had been seeking.

—Martin Luther King, Jr.

nonviolent resistance was an expression of love and respect for those who disagreed with him on the issue of racial segregation. In his "Letter from Birmingham Jail," Dr. King rejected the two extremes of passivity and violence, the "'do nothingism' of the complacent" and "the hatred and despair of the black nationalist."

For Dr. King, standing against those who supported racial segregation through nonviolent protest was the most loving—and civil—thing he could do. He was taking action to show them the flaws in their belief that African Americans were not equal to white Americans. But he communicated his opposition to them in a way that respected and upheld their dignity. Dr. King sought a better way: "the more excellent way of love and nonviolent protest."[10]

Dr. King describes the process of "self-purification" that he and others underwent prior to their social protests. This process was grounded in love for those against whom they were protesting, seeking their opponents' good and appealing to their consciences and hearts in persuading them to abandon their intolerant and racist views. He understood that it was essential to adopt a disposition of fundamental respect and affection for others if he had any hope of changing their minds through his protest and activism. This disposition was both useful for persuasion and a personal obligation.

Civility is both an *instrumental* good—a useful tool to achieve important goals—and an *inherent* good, because respecting the dignity of others is good for its own sake. Thoreau, Gandhi, and Dr. King chose the disposition of civility—the duties of citizens in the *civitas*, but also the duties of persons to a higher moral order—in the face of the gross injustice of war, the caste system, and the dehumanizing practice of slavery. In each case, civility was their tool of choice, and helped each of them make the world a more equal and just place.

How to Decide When Civil Protest Is Warranted: Abolition and the Third Reich

Twentieth-century liberal philosopher John Rawls argued that civil disobedience had to have a goal beyond the act of disobedience itself. It must be designed to communicate and appeal to the broader community. He thought that acts of violence or actions that were disproportionate and vindictive would undermine that goal. To protect the power of civil disobedience, he called for those engaged in disobedience to respect private property, submit willingly to arrest, and generally avoid violence and other conduct that would undermine the stability of the rule of law.

When it comes to engaging in civil protest and disobedience, respect for human dignity has been the litmus test for leaders of successful campaigns of social change, including Gandhi and Dr. King, in the past. It can be our litmus test, too. We have a duty to respect the equal moral worth of others, which means that we cannot temporarily discard civility when it gets in the way of our achieving our goals.

Still, we must ask: Are there instances when we should be willing to overlook the fundamental respect we owe to others in the name of a greater good?

There are important lessons we might learn from America's abolitionists, those who followed in the principled footsteps of Edward Coles, and who saw the moral evil of slavery and chose to act when others in their society chose to turn a blind eye.

If there was any time in history when it was morally justified to depart from civility, it was in the fight to abolish slavery. Abolitionists had every reason to consider violence as a tool to achieve their just ends; some, such as John Brown, did.[11] But the most prominent leaders in the early battle to end slavery on both sides of the Atlantic did not, because they knew that justice at any cost is not justice at all.

English abolitionist William Wilberforce wrote, "God Almighty has set before me two great objects, the suppression of the slave trade and the reformation of manners." In essence, opposing slavery and promoting true civility are cut from the same cloth: both respect the fundamental dignity of others, and consider others as oneself. In so doing, both abolition and civility curb the impulse to dominate and discriminate against broad swaths of humanity. Respect for others, especially when they hold views different from our own, begins with appreciating the value inherent in each human being.

William Lloyd Garrison, the founder of the American Anti-Slavery Society, was a pacifist for whom even *voting* for the abolition of slavery was too coercive. Yet he was no shrinking violet: "As harsh as truth, and as uncompromising as justice," Garrison once scandalized supporters and opponents alike when he burned the Constitution, claiming it was complicit in slavery.[12] He knew that *true* civility is more than trivial courtesy or naïve "niceness." Civility requires taking our opponents' dignity seriously, which means taking their ideas seriously, and that sometimes requires forceful and robust argumentation. But for Garrison, that never meant disregarding the dignity of his opponents. He was committed to the proposition that equality applies to everyone—friend *and* foe.

Frederick Douglass was an escaped slave, antislavery writer, and orator who had more faith than Garrison in the value of the Constitution to the abolitionist cause. But the two men were united in their belief that *persuading* one's opponents, not bullying them, was the more effective tool. He understood that "if there is no struggle, there is no progress."[13] But for Douglass, "struggle" did not mean winning at any cost. He knew that if he was to ensure that *all* enjoyed the advantages of the rule of law, he could not undermine the rule of law in the process. Douglass would have agreed with Gandhi: means are everything.

The tendency to dehumanize those with different views of justice is still with us. We can resist this temptation by deciding in advance what our personal boundaries are for pursuing justice. What line are we unwilling to cross? What is beyond the pale? Once that line is drawn, and once we have decided what conduct is out of bounds, we must hold to that conviction regardless of what the other side does, and regardless of how appealing the potential political payoff is.

The inverse of military theorist Carl von Clausewitz's famous formulation, "War is politics by other means," is that *politics is war by other means.* The political realm exists so that disagreements can be resolved without violence. Normal political disagreements can and should be resolved through normal political means. In deciding in advance what is out of bounds, what tools and means must never be resorted to—for example, violence—the temptation to act irresponsibly is removed from the calculation.

None of the challenges we face in our world presently come close to the mass horrors of Hitler's Third Reich. Twentieth-century German theologian Dietrich Bonhoeffer had been a pacifist all his life before returning to his native Germany from America to help in the struggle against the Third Reich. He was ultimately executed for being complicit in a plot to assassinate Hitler. Yet Bonhoeffer was never certain that violence, even against a genocidal dictator, was right in the first place.

Dietrich Bonhoeffer was hesitant to engage in violence in assassinating Hitler, the leader of arguably the most inhumane regime in human history. If Bonhoeffer was unsure about engaging in political violence against his enemies, even when he was assuredly in the right, we should be skeptical of attempts to justify violence in our own moment, too. If Garrison, Douglass, and Wilberforce could be civil while criticizing slaveholders—people who *owned* other persons—we can be civil in disagreements in our modern political realm.

Though violence has sometimes led to liberty, such as in the Haitian Revolution[14] and even the American Revolution itself, dispensing with civility and the fundamental respect we owe to others can be a rapid path to gross injustice. Many rightly condemn America's founders for failing to recognize the dignity of all persons in the past. But nor must we justify negating the value of some people today for a greater end. Though it required a civil war to end the institution of slavery, leading abolitionists refused to ignore the humanity of their opponents.

Twentieth-century German-Jewish philosopher Hannah Arendt escaped a German detention camp in France in 1941 and came to America. She adored the American way of life, because she appreciated the freedom and tolerance that she had seen dissipate in her native Germany. She was adamant, however, that the American project required constant and vigilant protection by its citizens.

The state is a great and noble steed who is tardy in his motions owing to his very size, and requires to be stirred into life. I am that gadfly which God has attached to the state, and all day long and in all places am always fastening upon you, arousing and persuading and reproaching you. You will not easily find another like me, and therefore I would advise you to spare me.

—Socrates, in Plato's "Apology," referring to himself as a gadfly for confronting Athens with unwelcome truths

For Arendt, political dissent was an important part of protecting American political ideas. She held that civil disobedience was important to highlighting injustice, but was also required to make a given law better. In engaging in protest and dissent, we are both exercising our rights and fulfilling our duty as citizens. In doing this, we are making America better, as disobedience and protest are necessary for social and political change. Arendt understood that societies needed gadflies such as Socrates, who lost his life by telling his fellow Athenians truths they did not wish to hear. Social progress depended on the bold leadership of people like Gandhi and Martin Luther King, Jr.—people who were not polite, but were *proactive*. Figures such as these and other courageous leaders in history are essential in pushing a society to confront its shortcomings and make itself better.

Great human rights advocates in America's past, and in world history more generally, illuminate a path to a more just and civil future—one that respects the equality and dignity and liberty of *everyone* we encounter—one that embraces civility, not politeness.

Living Out Civility, Not Politeness

Our desire for precedence over others produces injustice and inequality, as we've explored. But it does much more than that. This expression of our selfish nature also empowers people to erect political structures, institutions, and cultures that ingrain inequality as well. Most cultures in human history have not thought to question institutions that subjugated women, cultural and ethnic minorities, people with disabilities, and anyone else in the "out-group." Many in history were unbothered by the systematic degradation and oppression of other human beings. Liberal democracy is an innovation in the historical record, unique in its aim of recognizing the personhood of all human beings, and in seeking to achieve social and political equality for its citizens. Despite the fact that modern democracies have yet to perfectly realize social and political equality for all human beings—and likely never will—civility, and the civil disobedience that it supports, can provide, has provided, and will continue to provide a path toward a more just and equal future. Across history, civility has empowered many advocates in achieving justice and equality for all. It can help us in this noble goal, too. After he manumitted his slaves and moved to Illinois, Edward Coles ran for governor of the Prairie State on an abolitionist platform, living out his philosophical commitments to equality. During the campaign, he leaked his letters to Jefferson, which we explored earlier, to the press. This move fueled his campaign and led him to victory. Coles became the second governor of Illinois, serving from 1822 to 1826. During that time Coles led the abolitionist movement that ultimately ensured Illinois did not become a slave state. When Abraham Lincoln was elected President, and they met, Lincoln was alit with respect for Coles, whom he warmly thanked for all that he had done for the abolitionist movement in Illinois.

Coles lived to see the Emancipation Proclamation issued by Abraham Lincoln on September 22, 1862, and enacted the following year. He lived to see the ratification of the Thirteenth Amendment. His lifelong dream was realized: the end of slavery in America.[15]

We need latter-day versions of Edward Coles to pick up the mantle of civility and the pursuit of justice as we continue to realize human equality in our own moment.

Edward Coles's life is a powerful response to those who claim that we should not judge the past by the standards of the present. Coles embodies the reality that across history, there have been people who understood the immorality of slavery and racism. He understood that we are all equal in the ways that matter most. He took risks and sacrificed to live out that ideal in his life. He knew that citizenship called us to disobey prevailing norms and laws at times. He knew that citizenship required civility—not politeness.

We can aspire to the same ideal.

How Civil Disobedience is A Duty of Civility and Citizenship and Can Create A More Just World

1. Remember that civil disobedience gets to the heart of true civility—the disposition that respects the equal moral worth of persons. At times, the duties of citizenship require breaking prevailing laws and norms if they promote inequality and injustice. Civility sometimes demands that we speak truth to power, even when it might be costly to ourselves.

2. Recall the importance of speaking the truth as a means of respecting and loving others, recall Gandhi's concept of *satyagraha*—derived from the Sanskrit words *satya,* "truth," and *āgraha,* or "holding firmly to"—and the idea of civil, nonviolent resistance that was central to his campaign for India's independence from the British Empire.

3. When tempted to cut corners and harm others in the name of a higher moral goal, stay mindful of Dr. King's insight, and Gandhi's words: means are everything. One cannot pursue equality and justice while committing violence and injustice along the way.

4. Recollect that civility is both an *instrumental* good—a useful tool to achieve important goals—and an *inherent* good, because respecting the dignity of others is good for

its own sake. Thoreau, Gandhi, and Dr. King chose the disposition of civility—the duties of citizens in the *civitas,* but also the duties of persons to a higher moral order—in the face of the gross injustices of war, the caste system, and the dehumanizing practice of segregation.

5. When tempted to stay silent instead of telling someone an important truth, remember that truth-telling and civility are ways of respecting them.

6. If trying to discern when to speak up and act and when to be silent, take inspiration from Edward Coles, Frederick Douglass, Dr. Martin Luther King, Jr., and the many others who provide us with incredible examples of people who spoke the truth forcefully, but in and out of love for others, in history.

8

Polarization and Tolerance

The year was 1995, and by all accounts, it was the peak of the most uncivil era in American history.

At least, enough people felt that way that something rather remarkable happened. An unprecedented amount of political will and philanthropic capital was harnessed to send nearly half of Congress on retreat to restore the bonds of civic friendship that the political battles of recent years had strained.

The Pew Charitable Trusts spent $700,000 on a series of civility summits known as Bipartisan Congressional Retreats, in Hershey, Pennsylvania.[1] We learned in Chapter 1 that wherever two or more people are gathered, there will be incivility. This is because the challenges to civility are grounded in our shared, innate human nature, and are therefore timeless and faced by all people in all places. Virtually all human communities, and each generation, have had contingents that insisted that their moment was the most uncivil. People from Ptahhotep to Erasmus of Rotterdam wielded their pens, revived the timeless principles of civility, and saved society. America is no exception to this trend. But America in 1995 must have been in a pretty dire state, as an effort of this scale had never been tried before.

Congressional leaders on both ends of the political spectrum committed to ensuring the retreats' success. Aims for the first retreat, which was planned for 1997, were aspirational, but tempered. The goal was not to erase differences, but for both sides to recover a fundamental affection and empathy for their colleagues across the political aisle. Cultivating an inner disposition of fundamental respect for others—in other words, fostering civility—would allow them to work together despite differences of political opinion.

Statesmen . . . ought to know the different departments of things; what belongs to laws, and what manners alone can regulate. To these, great politicians may give a leaning, but they cannot give a law.

—Edmund Burke, eighteenth-century Anglo-Irish statesman

There was a sense that politicians' personal contempt for one another had prevented them from doing their jobs—a familiar sentiment in our own era. There was an unprecedented collective resolve to reverse that trend.

People speculated about why personal animosity had increased. Some said a cultural shift in Congress in the early 1990s was to blame. In prior decades, when a member was elected to Congress, they would move their family to Washington permanently, and set up a new life and community there. The benefit of this was that members of Congress saw one another socially on a regular basis: they walked the same streets of Capitol Hill, their children went to the same schools, and they ate at the same restaurants. They might have debated the merits of a bill on the House floor during the day, but at night they and their families would get together for dinner.

Novel pressure for congresspeople to stay rooted in their home districts changed things: fewer members made permanent moves to Washington, and often their families stayed in their home state. When members of Congress began to commute to the Capitol three days a week, this meant that they no longer knew one another as intimately. Nineteenth-century English statesman Sir William Harcourt wrote that a functioning *polis* depends on "constant dining with the opposition." Personal familiarity makes democratic political life possible. It allows vigorous, reasoned disagreement to end at the issues, and not be carried over into the personal realm.

> *Liberty lies in the hearts of men and women; when it dies there, no constitution, no law, no court can save it; no constitution, no law, no court can even do much to help it.*
>
> —Judge Learned Hand, twentieth-century American jurist

Some saw that, in the wake of members electing to keep their families at home, all-important personal relationships and trust were diminished.

Another theory as to why congressional tensions had become so strained was that it was the product of a toxic media culture. Bombast was rewarded. Those who controlled themselves and stayed at the level of the issues were ignored. This incentive structure prevented members from seeing those they disagreed with as their *colleagues*—even friends—inherently deserving of respect. It encouraged them to instrumentalize their political opponents and to see them as tools that could be used to gain public attention.

Congresspeople didn't know, respect, or trust one another anymore. To remedy this, members of Congress were invited to the civility retreats, and encouraged to bring their spouses and children with them. The goal was to remind our public leaders that they are more *alike* than *unlike*, with a shared moral status as members of the human community. The hope was to recover the civility necessary to see American democratic institutions function.

The retreats explored the personal and institutional obstacles to comity in Congress. Members discussed these questions in formal sessions together, but that took up only half the time. The other half was unstructured, when members and their families were invited to enjoy meals and games together, and to spend time on nonpolitical activities to help rebuild trust.

Historian David McCullough reminded attendees that personal incivility had always been a problem in American history. Partisan passions had been overcome in the past, and could be overcome now.[2] John Adams, for instance, in a letter to his wife, Abigail, lamented the rancor of the Third Continental Congress: "There are deep jealousies. Ill-natured observations and incriminations take the place of reason and argument." He had given up hope on the American project. A few months later, that very same Congress approved the Declaration of Independence. Upon hearing McCullough's observation, the collective mood of attendees at the retreat seemed to shift; maybe there was hope for America in the late twentieth century, too.

A theme of this book is that history is both cautionary and comforting. Failure to appreciate the personhood of our fellow citizens has brought us to the brink before. Yet we've overcome

Difference is the essence of humanity. Difference is an accident of birth and it should therefore never be the source of hatred or conflict. The answer to difference is to respect it. Therein lies a most fundamental principle of peace—respect for diversity.

—John Hume, twentieth-century Irish statesman and Nobel laureate these eras of deep division. We can learn from divided days in our past and do so again.

The success of the first retreat exceeded all expectations. Of the more than two hundred congresspeople who attended with their families, all were outspoken about their hope for the change their time away from work would bring. Then-speaker Newt Gingrich suggested doing a civility retreat every year to nurture the fragile bonds of civic trust built over the weekend retreat.

The zeitgeist had been elevated. There was a new resolve to find areas of agreement. When the congresspeople did disagree, they committed to doing so respectfully. Being with their colleagues and their families made it easier for them to "unbundle" one another from their political beliefs. They were people—husbands and wives, mothers and fathers—*before* they were politicians. Knowing one another's families led to greater accountability: disparaging a political opponent didn't just hurt one person; the family behind them had a face now, too.

Since Eve ate apples, much depends on dinner.

—Lord Byron, nineteenth-century English Romantic poet

Members also resolved to do their part to elevate our national conversation.[3] Washington said in unison, "Maybe we really could achieve that elusive ideal of civility."

The Problem of Tolerance

In *The Spirit of the Laws*, a book that was highly influential among the American founding fathers, Montesquieu observed that *too much* freedom had the same adverse consequences as *not enough* freedom. In totalitarian regimes, he wrote, people lack the *freedom* to speak their truths and their minds. In a society of complete freedom, people lack the *will* to speak the truth. They aren't enslaved to a despot; they are enslaved to their own biases and prejudices. As the story of the congressional civility summit illustrates, our current moment resembles Montesquieu's latter scenario, where our personal biases and prejudices—exacerbated by social media and modern news culture—cloud our will and ability to see other perspectives and engage with ideas we may disagree with, but which may nonetheless hold at least partial truths.

As human beings, we are drawn to people who are similar to ourselves. We like people who look and think and act like we do. In our globalized and cosmopolitan world, we are increasingly dependent on people who are apparently different from us, and difference can be difficult. How do we peacefully coexist with people who hold views that we vehemently disagree with?

In extremely absolute monarchies, historians betray the truth because they do not have the liberty to tell it; in extremely free states, they betray the truth because of their very liberty for, as it always produces divisions, each one becomes as much a slave of the prejudice of his faction as he would be of a despot.

—Montesquieu

The test of civility is how we treat people who are different from us. Tolerance requires a basic respect of others even if we are appalled by their words, beliefs, or conduct. Why? Because of our shared status of citizens in a democracy—and, more fundamentally, because of our shared status as members of the human community.

Tolerance and civility require humility. They ask us to appreciate the limits of our own knowledge and beliefs. They

Everyone brings to public discourse values that they cannot prove. The real test is how tolerant, humble, patient one is toward those with whom they disagree.

—Tim Keller, contemporary pastor and theologian

demand that we recognize that we might not have all the answers, and that everyone we encounter might have something to teach us—if we have the eyes to see and the ears to hear it. Civil people know that there is something we can learn from every person and in every setting. They understand that engaging across difference starts with listening and attempting to meet others on their own terms. There will always be difference and disagreement in human communities. Civility, which enables us to subvert our selfishness for the social project, is the only way we can peacefully live together in spite of—and in light of—these inevitable differences.

Reasonable minds will disagree on important subjects. Civility means that even *unreasonable* minds deserve some level of respect. This is because our disagreement does not negate our irreducible value as persons. In fact, it's when we differ from, or disagree with, others—especially on topics of great weight—that we need civility most.

It's Time to Unbundle People

One reason for the success of the civility summit was that America's public leaders were able to see one another once more as people first, more like them than unlike them. Outside of the office, off the congressional floor and away from Capitol Hill, and in their natural element with their families, they were enabled to see beyond their political beliefs, their party, or their voting record. This ability to perceive people in their fullness and complexity seems a lost art form in our moment.

Often, we reduce people to one aspect of who they are. We define them by their worst trait or mistake—something they said or did, which they probably regret, but which, thanks to the internet and social media, has been immortalized and widely circulated.

It is time that we start "unbundling" people.

In our chapter on civility, freedom, democracy, and human flourishing, we talked about "unbundling" experiences, a mental framework that can help us view an unpleasant experience or exchange in isolation—and not as part of a story of the universe conspiring against us. We explored how this can help us avoid "kicking the cat"—displacing our frustration and negative emotions onto others, or making assumptions about society and the world based on one experience. In addition to unbundling experiences, we need to unbundle people, too.

Our current culture views the world and people through a cheapened simplicity. Everything, and everyone, is either right or wrong, good or evil. We define people based on one thing they've done or said, sometimes even if it occurred years or decades ago, and "cancel" them for it. This view of the world and people is reductive, essentializing, and degrading to the diversity and beauty of the human personality.

We've adopted a strange perfectionism, intolerant of anything less than flawlessness. As we've learned, self-love and the *libido dominandi* are endemic to our nature. This ensures that we will, from time to time, make decisions for our own benefit and to the detriment of others. Each of us is

> *To err is human, to forgive, divine.*
>
> —Alexander Pope, eighteenth-century English poet

a little bit good and a little bit bad. Each of us, as we learned in Chapter 1, has a bit of Gilgamesh, and a bit of Enkidu; a bit of Dr. Jekyll and a bit of Mr. Hyde; a bit of the evil wolf from the Cherokee legend, and a bit of the good wolf.

Unbundling people can help us reclaim a full, nuanced, and rich view of the human person. It can help us see the *part* in light of the *whole,* mistakes in light of virtues, Gilgamesh in light of Enkidu. It can help us see our selfish, domineering nature in light of our dignity as human beings and our irreducible worth as persons.

Human beings are a contradiction—a chimera, as Pascal wrote. We're caught between our social and our selfish natures, and more often than we'd like, our self-love wins out. This means that we are each imperfect and always will be.

Can we outgrow our sterile, static view of others, and challenge ourselves to hold in mind multiple traits and characteristics of others—both virtues and vices—at once? Can we recognize the mistakes of others while at the same time remaining mindful of the irreducible human dignity of our fellow human beings—and the basic respect they are owed in light of that?

Practical Unbundling: Socrates and Jean Vanier

I've had practice unbundling in my own life. I've had to grapple with balancing the good and the bad of two of my seminal intellectual influences, Socrates and Jean Vanier. Socrates enchanted me with the rewards of the philosophic life, the world of ideas, the life of the mind, and the nobility of a life of embodied beauty, goodness, and truth. Socrates said that virtue is health of the soul, and vice is sickness of the soul. Virtue is its own reward, he said, because it promotes a healthy soul. Vice is its own punishment, because it reflects a soul's ill health. A life detached from the temptations of the world, Socrates said, allows us to more freely pursue the philosophic life—the highest and best life. These ideas captivated my mind and enlarged my soul.

So did the writings of Jean Vanier. He helped me understand the dignity of the human person in a more intimate way. He helped me appreciate the beautiful ways that we can learn about the human experience through encounters and friendships with people with disabilities. He taught me that true community begins with being vulnerable, embracing our fears and weakness, and humbly offering who we are to others. He helped me see the courage in allowing ourselves to be seen, known, and loved by others, and why the beauty of community is worth the risk of rejection. I was inspired by his creation of L'Arche, communities for people with intellectual and physical disabilities, and by his life itself, dedicated to proclaiming the dignity of human existence in all of its manifestations.

I am grateful for the way they formed me, but I disagree with many of Socrates' views, and with Jean Vanier's toxic life decisions.

As his student Plato describes him, Socrates was a proponent of eugenics.

> *Each person is sacred, no matter what his or her culture, religion, handicap, or fragility. Each person is created in God's image; each one has a heart, a capacity to love and to be loved.*
>
> —Jean Vanier, Catholic philosopher and theologian

Socrates wanted to abolish the family, art, poetry, and music. As a humanist, mother, and artist, I vehemently disagree with these ideas. Jean Vanier was an important advocate for the disability community and helped me appreciate why human dignity mattered, but after his death, it was revealed that throughout his leadership of L'Arche he serially abused, exploited, and mistreated women under his authority. I was disappointed to learn that Vanier had allowed his inner Gilgamesh, and his *libido dominandi,* to reign within his soul, hiding it from the world until his death. He did not lead a life of integrity, in alignment with his purported value of cherishing the dignity of the human person.

Do Socrates' bad opinions on eugenics or banning the family or art in society undermine his thoughts on why virtue is good for its own sake, or on the rewards of the philosophic life? Does Jean Vanier's secret life as a serial abuser of women undermine his ideas about the dignity of the human person, or the impact of his work for the disability community?

Absolutely not.

Am I guilty by association because I've been influenced by people with bad views, and who committed bad deeds? Or can I continue to appreciate the good in their thoughts and lives—the humanizing aspects of the works—while condemning that which is bad and dehumanizing in their legacy?

> *Forgiveness flounders because I exclude my enemy from the community of humans, and exclude myself from the community of sinners.*
>
> —Miroslav Volf, Croatian Protestant theologian

I've chosen the latter path.

Can we as a society be mature enough to condemn the bad in people, ancient and modern, while accepting, admiring, and benefiting from the good?

I hope so. This is what respecting human dignity, the hallmark of civility, requires.

Many of us have likely felt firsthand the pain of being misunderstood, essentialized, and cut off based on a mistake, or on one aspect of who we are. We should avoid doing that to others. We must stay mindful of the complex, multidimensional nature of humanity. Though we are tempted to oversimplify others, we each come to our beliefs, attitudes, emotions, and actions for many reasons. Can we stay curious about the reasons and stories behind the beliefs of those with whom we disagree?

Braver Angels: Rehumanizing Our Politics, and Promoting Tolerance Through Curiosity

Creating a culture of curiosity is the bread and butter of Braver Angels, which emerged from the ashes of a divisive 2016 presidential election.[4] Nearly a hundred thousand people have enjoyed their workshops, events, and debates, which aim to heal a deeply divided nation by putting people of different political stripes in contact with one another.

Like Lincoln, Braver Angels seeks to heal a broken America by improving how we view one another. Its aim is to help us see the basic humanity and commonalities we share across difference. The organization has two core programs: workshops and debates. The workshops allow participants to practice skills of human connection—such as paraphrasing, listening, asking questions of understanding—instead of conversion.

> *We must not be enemies. Though passion may have strained, it must not break our bonds of affection. The mystic chords of memory will swell when again touched, as surely they will be, by the better angels of our nature.*
>
> —Abraham Lincoln, First Inaugural Address

Braver Angels Debate, the group's second core program, is premised on the idea of civility as we've defined and explored it throughout this book. Respecting others involves candid, robust, and truthful dialogue uninhibited by the rules of politeness. Braver Angels Debate promotes viewpoint diversity by offering people a chance to hash out their differences of opinion head-on. It is a venue for structured disagreement about controversial questions of the day, with an eye to helping Americans build the habits of robust debate, reconciliation, and citizenship in their daily lives. The goal, once again, is not to *convert,* but to bring people who disagree in proximity together, to humanize them to one another, and to promote understanding and empathy across differing viewpoints.

As Braver Angels Debate founder April Lawson notes, civility is "taking the other side's worldview head-on and listening for what you might have to learn."[5] Braver Angels Debate cares about more than conversational tone. It encourages people to be civil—though not necessarily *polite*—as they hash out their opinions, and teaches that relationships need not degrade in the face of those differences. In creating a space for people to be uncertain, to change their minds, to be curious, to learn together, to bounce ideas off one another, and to grow through dialogue, Braver Angels Debate is unique—and much needed—in our modern era.

Braver Angels promotes civility by encouraging people to see the dignity of the person on the other side of the political aisle or computer screen. We learned in our chapter on civility and civil society that civic associations such as Braver Angels are the lifeblood of American

> *The health of a democratic society may be measured by the quality of functions performed by private citizens.*
>
> —Alexis de Tocqueville

society, important not only for helping cultivate habits of citizenship—such as engaging across difference and debate—but for simply existing. Alexis de Tocqueville noted that living in a free society required certain "habits of the heart." These habits, or practices, were a way of looking at the world and others, a frame of mind that saw others as allies in this project of self-governance.

If liberty means anything at all it means the right to tell people what they do not want to hear.

—George Orwell, twentieth-century English novelist and writer

We've already explored the importance of civic associations to social trust and the social fabric in our chapter on civil society, but Tocqueville reminds us that, for people across geographic, political, and cultural differences, civic associations cultivate tolerance and fellow-feeling around a shared cause. Civic associations have fostered Americans' ability to work together across differences of background and opinion to solve problems and improve our quality of life. In our deeply divided moment—defined by extremes that either shout down dissent or silence it in the name of political correctness—their approach is refreshing, and also what our country needs most in order to navigate our rifts.

Social Pressure and Free Speech

Social vigilantes such as Larry David, as we explored in our chapter on civility and freedom, are important tools of accountability. They comprise the informal institutions that regulate our actions.

But peer-to-peer accountability can at times devolve into a tyranny of its own.

The Greek concept of *parrhesia*, which literally means "to speak everything," entailed candid communication that spoke truth to power. One who used *parrhesia* would speak their mind without caring how their audience would react, or about the repercussions.

> *He who knows only his own side of the case knows little of that.*
>
> —John Stuart Mill, nineteenth-century English philosopher

To have free speech, one needs legal liberty. But one also needs the social and cultural liberty to speak freely without repercussions. Free speech requires that a speaker can trust listeners to endure hearing ideas they may not agree with.

John Stuart Mill worried about social barriers to free expression, which he explored in *On Liberty*. According to Mill, the gravest threat to free speech was social "tyranny of the majority," or the tendency of an audience to economically and socially punish speech and speakers it did not like. Legal freedoms alone were not enough to protect free expression. More important was a society that was open to dialogue even on topics that engendered disagreement.

Mill condemned the repressive nature of "class markers"—the aristocratic manners and the stuffy norms of politeness—in a democratic and tolerant society. He argued that "despotism of custom" encouraged individuals to moderate their tastes and needs, prompting them to "desire nothing too strongly," and, in practice, become like everyone else.

He criticized the social expectation that the middle and working classes accept their lot in life. In his time, when people resisted social hierarchies, or questioned those in a higher position, they were dismissed as "rude" and socially punished by aristocrats and their peers. Mill disdained this—and would have applauded Edward Coles, who stood up to Thomas Jefferson in critiquing his hypocrisy of owning slaves, a story we explored in our chapter on civil disobedience. Mill thought that criticism and conflict played an important role in a marketplace of ideas.

Mill said that when we encounter a new idea, there are three options: it's either wrong, partially right, or entirely true. Discerning between these possibilities can help us. Edmund Burke agreed: encountering opinions that we disagree with challenges us to think more deeply about why we hold the beliefs we do, and helps to refine our thinking.

> *He that wrestles with us strengthens our nerves and sharpens our skill. Our antagonist is our helper.*
>
> —Edmund Burke, eighteenth-century Anglo-Irish statesman, *Reflections on the Revolution in France* (1790)

When we see people fired, publicly shamed, or maligned for saying things that a vocal few on social media find distasteful, we should all be concerned. Such abuse promotes a conformity that disproportionately harms those without the social, cultural, and political power to survive it. Getting away with publicly abusing others—exerting power over them while they are defenseless—inflames our *libido dominandi* and deforms our soul. Bludgeoning and silencing people into such conformity is a tool of politeness. Civility instead empowers diversity of expression—and, crucially, cultural tolerance of diverse views. As psychiatrist Scott Alexander has written, derived from the works of philosophers Willard Van Orman Quine and Donald Davidson, we need tolerance, and the principle of charity. Alexander put it succinctly: "If you don't understand how someone could possibly believe something as stupid as they do, this is more likely a failure of understanding on your part than a failure of reason on theirs."

It's not just our public life that has become polarized and less tolerant. Academia, civic organizations, and even businesses are also generally more political and monolithic in their views on social and cultural issues. In his *Philosophical Letters*, Voltaire observed that in the London Stock Exchange—the symbol of commerce—people didn't care about differences in religion or belief, but only whether a person was solvent or bankrupt.

> Go into the London Stock Exchange ... and you will see representatives from all nations gathered together for the utility of men. Here Jew, Mohammedan, and Christian deal with each other as though they were all of the same faith, and only apply the word "infidel" to people who go bankrupt.
>
> —Voltaire, eighteenth-century French philosopher

The intolerance of difference in modern political and cultural life has bled into the business realm. Corporate activism has exacerbated political, social, and cultural differences within their ranks. When a company takes a unified, public, political stance—an increasingly popular business move—employees who may disagree with that unified stance feel marginalized. Democracy, and the human social project itself, is premised on the idea that while citizens *will* disagree, we can find compromise through reasoned and rigorous discourse. But today, we tend to characterize people we disagree with as "irrational" and "immoral." We refuse to compromise with them. How can civility be an answer to our intolerant and divided moment?

The Fragility of Toleration

By all accounts, the 1997 congressional civility summit was a smashing success. Congress had been rescued from the recesses of intolerance and polarization. The goal of perfect civility was in reach.

And then, the Monica Lewinsky scandal broke.

All bets were off. Once again, passions were strained. Bonds of affection were broken. The "mystic chords of memory" were crushed. The "better angels of our nature" that Abraham Lincoln once called upon in a time of great division had vacated Congress.

> *If all mankind minus one were of one opinion, and only one person were of the contrary opinion, mankind would be no more justified in silencing that one person, than he, if he had the power, would be justified in silencing mankind.*
>
> —John Stuart Mill

The political stakes were high. This was once again war.

President Bill Clinton was impeached—a vote decided directly along party lines. The House Democrats were bitter. When, in a fleeting moment of bipartisanship, House minority leader Dick Gephardt mentioned to his caucus the idea of another civility retreat to heal Congress's frayed bonds, he was booed by his party. He quickly changed the subject. The appetite for civility in Congress had been crushed.

Amazingly, there were two subsequent civility retreats, in 1999 and in the early 2000s.[6] But there was much less enthusiasm for them, and they were not well-attended. The golden age of civility was over. The 1997 retreat was a high watermark that would never be repeated.[7]

For those interested in reviving civility in our modern time, there are several things we can learn from the story of the congressional civility summits. First, trust and personal relationships matter when it comes to interacting with people we disagree with. This trust can be easily lost—but, just as important, it can be earned and regained, as we saw in the case of the 1997 summit. Second, because it can be so easily lost, trust and relationship and fundamental respect must be defended vigilantly. It is when trust is tested—perhaps in a moment of profound political disagreement, such as an impeachment—that we need it most. Third, there is an important role for civil society—voluntary associations and philanthropy, such as the Pew Charitable Trusts and the Aspen Institute, which facilitated the bipartisan retreats—in creating momentum around these ideas.

> *The worst offense of this kind which can be committed by a polemic is to stigmatize those who hold the contrary opinion as bad and immoral men.*
>
> —John Stuart Mill

Nothing New Under the Sun: History as Caution and Comfort

Even the greatest champions of the congressional civility summits of the late 1990s knew that the problem of incivility was nothing new. One long-forgotten story of incivility in Congress was told to illuminate that, while incivility was bad in their current moment, it could always be worse.

It was a crisp winter Friday afternoon in America's capitol, one like many before it and like many after it. No one expected February 28, 1890, to be so perilous. Congressman William Taulbee, a Democrat from Kentucky, had recently resigned from office, but was still furious that Charles Kincaid of *The Louisville Times* had published a story about his extramarital affair with a congressional staffer in 1887.[8] The scandal meant the end of Taulbee's ambitious political career, and he held Kincaid personally responsible. While no longer a congressman, Taulbee was often still around Capitol Hill, where Kincaid reported.

Taulbee tormented Kincaid every chance he could, sometimes even lying in wait while Kincaid tried to avoid him. Taulbee stepped on Kincaid's foot in an elevator and held it there while Kincaid groaned in pain. He threatened Kincaid's life, rammed him against the door of a streetcar, and shoved him into a metal railing. The relentless harassment soon became too much for Kincaid.

As the clock struck twelve on that fateful Friday afternoon, Kincaid was in the halls of Congress waiting for an interview when Taulbee appeared for his now-ritualized abuse of the exhausted reporter. Taulbee shouted at his target, pushed him, violently pulled his ear, and threatened Kincaid's life yet again. Kincaid decided that enough was enough.

Two hours later, on the steps of Congress, a shot rang out. Kincaid had shot Taulbee in the head, and made no attempt to hide. This was the first time that a member of Congress had been murdered in the Capitol. Some say that William Taulbee's blood can still be seen on the steps of Congress. Kincaid was later acquitted.

This low watermark of civility in public life gives us both caution and comfort. Comfort because, contrary to what many might think, we are not, in fact, living in the most uncivil era. But violence has indeed revisited the halls of Congress in our own day, which is why caution is merited. The fact that abuse and murderous violence has happened before in our nation's history—and this is but one of *many* such examples—shows its constant threat in our present. Society, and our free and flourishing way of life, is fragile. Civility, and the basic respect for personhood that it requires, is what makes it possible. When we forget civility, we put our society at risk.

It is a commonplace remark that older people invariably feel that the younger generation is speeding swiftly on the road to perdition. But whether the present younger generation is really any nearer to that frightful end than any previous one, is a question that we, of the present older generation, are scarcely qualified to answer.

—Emily Post, twentieth-century American etiquette expert

Despite the fact that incivility has always been with us—in America and beyond—every few decades, a flurry of "civility declinists" argue that we are living through an era of exceptional incivility and that we need to get our act together to see our democracy survive.

We looked at the "civility declinist" genre from a historical perspective in Chapter 2, where we also discovered why certain principles of civility tend to stand across time and culture.

On the one hand, we saw that these writers in the "civility declinist" genre are wrong: we don't live in the worst, most uncivil era.

On the other hand, they direct us to an important truth: a lack of civility leads to social dysfunction and decay, especially in modern democracy. This is something of a paradox, though, as democracies pose a particular challenge to the imposition of tight social norms. Having a healthy respect for personal autonomy and individual freedom means that we must sometimes allow people the freedom not to follow social norms, too.

Some argue that a lack of civility has negative consequences for our democratic institutions. Others argue that incivility corrodes civil society. Still others note that deteriorating civility means that our relationships will fail and society will suffer. The bottom line is that the challenges to—and the risks of not having—civility are multifaceted and complex because civility is a social virtue and humanity is multifaceted and complex. No single person or event is to blame for our current predicament.

Donald Trump's ascendance to the pinnacle of American public life was a stressor to our nation's, and our world's, problem with incivility. But, as the story between Taulbee and Kincaid taught us, and as this book argues, incivility among public officials, or in human affairs in general, is nothing new. Trump's crass behavior exposed problems and heightened divisions that have long existed both in our nature and in contemporary culture. Though Trump unquestionably coarsened American public life, it's a mistake to think that he was the origin of the problem. We must remember this, because if we misidentify the source of the problem of incivility today, we will miss the opportunity to think clearly about, and act on, solutions.

Why Civic Friendship Matters

The problem of incivility is timeless. But, as we learned in Chapter 2, so are the principles of civility. Man is a social animal. Friendship is what makes life worth living. It is fragile, because the self-love endemic to our nature will always be a threat to it. Friendship enriches our lives personally, but it is also essential to a thriving *civis* of human community. Friendship is an essential building block of society because it helps us build trust and affection across differences.

The congressional civility summits, and the divisions in our own moment, remind us of the fragility of friendship and the high cost to our democracy when civic bonds are strained. The summits also tell us that friendship can be restored: the retreats seemed to do some good in building friendships and trust, at least temporarily. Yet as we now know, these bonds— friendship across difference, among citizens, and between our public leaders—are fragile. Investing in them day by day can help restore the civic fabric and culture of American life, and renew our democracy for future generations.

The most fruitful and natural play of the mind is conversation. I find it sweeter than any other action in life; and if I were forced to choose, I think I would rather lose my sight than my hearing and voice.

—Michel de Montaigne, sixteenth-century French essayist

Friendship—like virtue, as we learned in our chapter on integrity—is a habit. Aristotle said that a city is a partnership for living well. He understood that friendship was the building block of the city, and that civil habits were the building blocks of friendship. He claimed there are three kinds of friendship:[9] there are friendships of utility, friendships of pleasure, and also "perfect friendship."

In friendships of *utility*, individuals come together in relationship because of some benefit they stand to gain. Think of business contacts forging deals over a power lunch. Once the two people no longer stand to benefit from each other, the relationship ends. The friendship of *pleasure* exists only as long as the two parties gain some sort of pleasure from interaction. Think of a "friends with benefits" sort of relationship. Once the mutual pleasure ends, the relationship also ends. Finally, there is the *perfect friendship*, which Aristotle says is "made up of men [or women] who are good and alike in virtue; for each alike wish well to each other . . . they are good in themselves." A perfect friendship is a friendship not of usefulness, pleasure, or benefit. It is good for its own sake, and is also the building block of society.

Cicero said that selfishness and greed are primary enemies of friendship. He writes, "The most fatal blow to friendship in the majority of cases was the lust of gold, in the case of the best men it was a rivalry for office and reputation, by which it had often happened that the most violent enmity had arisen between the closest friends."

Remember the friendship between Gilgamesh and Enkidu in Chapter 1? The two primordial beings were diametrically opposed, and amid a fight to the death, when Enkidu harnessed the transformative power of friendship to turn his foe into his friend. Enkidu's kindness to Gilgamesh transformed the latter from a monstrous tyrant into an ideal hero, king, and friend. Aristotle and Cicero wrote that true friendship occurs only between two virtuous people. As the story about the friendship between Gilgamesh and Enkidu shows, we are not born virtuous, but friendships can make us into better people, and in turn elevate our interactions with society in general. Gilgamesh and Enkidu discovered eudemonic friendship—a friendship that deepened both of their souls, made them more humane, and contributed to their personal and social flourishing.

> *Let us have the courage to give advice with candor. In friendship, let the influence of friends who give good advice be paramount; and let this influence be used to enforce advice not only in plainspoken terms, but sometimes, if the case demands it, with sharpness; and when so used, let it be obeyed.*
>
> —Cicero, first-century BC Roman statesman

This is where civility comes in. As we've learned, civility motivates us to overcome our self-love so that our social natures can flourish. That is why, in all times and places, all groups and cultures have had norms and expectations of social conduct that support this project of community, and of friendship: to help the social triumph over the selfish aspects of our nature. Cicero reminds us that true friends are also honest with one another. They are willing to tell one another hard truths, but do so tempered with affection. Telling someone the truth is what it means to truly love and respect them. Their basic affection and respect for one another allows friends to stay friends across difference.

We're also more likely to extend grace to, forgive, befriend—and less likely to vilify—people we know personally. This is true among our public leaders, and for us, too. Life with others ennobles and adds meaning to our lives. It's often difficult, but as more of us allow ourselves to be formed, motivated, and inspired by relationships with others—as Gilgamesh allowed himself to be transformed by his relationship with Enkidu—we may find that the elusive goal of a more civil future is within reach after all.

> *What shall we do with laws without manners?*
>
> —Horace, first-century BC Roman poet

Civility is the stuff that makes a free society—especially a democracy—work. This is because it promotes reasoned, tempered dialogue and interactions between citizens, a virtue of civility that is especially important for our lawmakers. Civility promotes basic decency while also taking certain modes of action off the table.

Why Polarization Subverts Democracy

Hyper-partisanship and political divisiveness subvert democracy. When Congress isn't working, it's often a sign that trust and personal relationships have broken down. Polarization in Congress can lead to gridlock. This is problematic, because there is so much pressure to respond to politically charged issues—

such as climate change—that if Congress *doesn't* address these challenges, other branches of government will. In recent years, as Congress has become more and more dysfunctional, we've seen political temperatures rise because the executive branch and the courts have been making an increasing number of important policy decisions that Congress—as the people's representatives in Washington—*should* be dealing with, but can't. The result is less democratic accountability—where important decisions are made by unelected civil servants and judges—and a more controversial and acrimonious public square.

Civility and Tolerance

Civility tempers and elevates the interactions between citizens, whether or not those citizens are public leaders. Civility begins with recognizing our shared humanity. It starts with seeing that we are more alike than unlike, and viewing our difference in light of our likeness. It starts in the small ways, sowing seeds of the friendships and trust that ensure our *civitas* survives.

Deliberative democracy depends on the premise that people of goodwill can negotiate differences and work together in a productive way through rational—and civil—debate. Civility builds an active willingness to listen to others, to consider their point of view alongside our own, and to evaluate varying conceptions of "the good." The civil citizen accepts that others have genuinely held moral positions, and that reasonable minds can disagree. These traits are equally essential for all positions along the political spectrum, and for our democracy, public leaders, and citizens alike.

We've learned that the lack of civility is a timeless problem for human communities, yet there are several challenges that are particular to our current moment. First, we have lost

> *Democracy is essentially a*
> *means, a utilitarian device for*
> *safeguarding internal peace and*
> *individual freedom. As such*
> *it is by no means infallible or*
> *certain.*
>
> —Friedrich Hayek, twentieth-
> century Austrian-British
> economist and social
> philosopher

a shared vision of the common good. We no longer share the same *ends* of public life. This has led to a tone of moralism and demands for purity on the political left and right alike. Instead of focusing on the fact that we are more *alike* than *unlike,* united in our shared humanity, this moralistic tendency makes it easy to dehumanize those who disagree with us. What may be purely an intellectual difference is now seen as a *moral* difference—a war of good versus evil. And what's the point of having a conversation with, or being decent to, an evil person?

Second, given that we differ on ends, social peace is only possible if we agree on how to live together in light of those differences. We have lost a shared appreciation of the *means* to achieving and pursuing the common good in the presence of deep differences. We've lost faith in our political process. The political institutions meant to promote our social bonds and mitigate our selfish impulses are instead seen as barriers to pursuing our vision of the good. Democracy doesn't require that we agree on the ends of public life. It's premised on the fact that we often won't agree. But it does require us to agree to certain means, methods, processes, and protocols—and when those means are threatened, our democratic way of life is in peril.

Institutions and institutional constraints matter. But they will only survive when a quorum of citizens and public leaders understand and appreciate *why* they matter. As the stakes of our public life increase, it is problematic when leaders on the polit-

ical left and right—and the
voters who support them—
fail to respect the role of
our institutions in keeping
our society free.[10]

*And do as adversaries do in
law, strive mightily, but eat and
drink as friends.*

—Shakespeare

The Role of Public Leaders and Citizens in Fostering Tolerance, Comity, and Civility

Thoughtful people have long reflected about which was more important when it came to elevating a civic culture: public leaders or citizens? The answer is both. There's no question that public leaders have a central role to play in decreasing partisanship and promoting tolerance and civility. Their conduct, tone, and the use of their platforms set a tone that ripples throughout broader society. Public leaders reflect what they think voters want. Citizens mirror what they imbibe from their leaders on social media, radio, and television. To depolarize our society, and promote tolerance and civility, public leaders and citizens must both play important roles.

Socrates argued that a just person has an excellent and healthy soul. Harming others is an act of injustice. It harms both the person being harmed and the one doing the harming. A just person will not harm others, but will instead seek justice and health for them, friends and enemies alike. Reminiscent of an appropriate sentiment from Abraham Lincoln—"Do I not defeat my enemy when I make him my friend?"—the just person will neutralize enemies by converting them to a life of justice. Political leaders should use their platforms to promote justice and sow healing. Citizens can choose not to reward leaders who scapegoat or call for violence and harm to political enemies.

Socrates sought to speak for the benefit of others—to

promote justice in their souls. Sophists, or paid teachers of rhetoric in ancient Greece, however, speak to win, to feel smart, and to impress others.

Aristotle made the same point in his *Politics*. He distinguishes between a *prince* and a *tyrant*. The former is concerned with the well-being of the state and its citizens. The latter pursues only his own ends. The prince focuses on one question: Is this to the advantage of all my subjects? Leaders should use their platforms to benefit their citizens, not for personal gain. Erasmus said that a leader who uses people only for personal benefit degrades them, desecrates them, and relegates them to the status of workhorses that do his bidding.

> *I believe, when statesmen forsake their own private conscience for the sake of their public duties . . . they lead their country by a short route to chaos.*

Public leaders should respect their citizens by ennobling them with their speech. They should not use them as pawns for self-gain. Leaders should remember that when they forsake their conscience, they hurt their country, they disrespect their citizens, and they also hurt themselves. Citizens must not allow themselves to be used. They must see through naked ambition and spurn leaders who debase and inflame with their rhetoric.

Our national motto is *e pluribus unum*. "Out of many, *one*." We must see one another as persons first—connected and unified by our common humanity—and care more about common decency and kindness than about which fork to use. This is what allows us to coexist amidst deep difference. It is also what allows for reasoned, spirited debate—the lifeblood of democracy. Discourse on topics of the first order—religion, philosophy, politics—is only possible when we recognize that differences are not problems to be *fixed* but resources to be *mined*. Remembering this is central to our free and democratic society. A path toward a depolarized, more tolerant, and more civil future begins with each of us—public leaders and citizens alike—choosing to see, love, and respect the dignity and diversity of one another.

How To Promote Tolerance and Diminish Partisanship

1. Reasonable minds will disagree on important subjects. Civility means that even unreasonable minds deserve some level of respect. This is because our disagreement does not negate our irreducible value as persons. In fact, it's when we differ from, or disagree with, others—especially on topics of great weight—that we need civility most. Civility requires that we owe a bare minimum of respect to others, even when we vehemently disagree.

2. Unbundle people. Resist the temptation to define people by one aspect of who they are or by their worst trait or decision. Unbundling people can help us reclaim a full, nuanced, and rich view of the human person. It can help us see the part in light of the whole, mistakes in light of virtues, Gilgamesh in light of Enkidu. Each of us is a little bit good and a little bit bad. Let's recognize and embrace this aspect of our humanity and not view the world and others through a cheapened, static simplicity.

3. When you get into a disagreement with a friend or family member, remember context—the entirety of the history and relationship you have with them. Keep that front of mind when you get into disagreements. Don't let disagreements—even disagreements on big, important

issues—be the focal point of your relationship. There's more to life than politics. Having relationships is the life well-lived.

4. Remember the transformative power of friendship. Allowing ourselves to be shaped, inspired, and motivated to surrender self-love enables us to discover eudemonic friendship that deepens our soul, makes us more human and humane, and helps us thrive personally and socially.

5. Stay curious about the many reasons people come to their beliefs about the world. Remember that everyone has something to teach us.

6. Don't publicly shame and abuse others—don't exert power over them while they are defenseless. To do so inflames our *libido dominandi* and deforms our soul. Bludgeoning and silencing people into conformity is a tool of politeness. Civility instead empowers diversity of expression—and, crucially, cultural tolerance of diverse views.

7. Form friendships across difference, and then strive to be taught and formed by friendship. Basic trust, affection, and friendship makes navigating difference with others easier. Trust and friendship can be cultivated—as we learned from the United States congressional civility summits. But—like civilization itself—they are fragile and can easily be broken. They must be vigilantly nurtured in order for them to prevail.

8. Remember the difference between civility and politeness, and that true friendship requires civil truth-telling in love, not patronizing politeness.

   a. Reminders for public figures: Say what you mean. Don't lie.

   b. Ennoble, don't debase. The test of a true leader is whether their words bring out the best in their audience or the worst. Tyrants inflame. Princes guide.

c. Don't use audiences for self-aggrandizement.

d. Don't say something just because you think it is what your audience wants to hear. That's patronizing to them, and not respectful.

e. Remember you don't have to have an opinion and speak out on every issue all the time. Embrace silence, and heed Marcus Aurelius' words: "You always own the option of having no opinion."

9

Citizenship in a Digital Age

Genesis 11 in the Hebrew Bible recounts the story of the Tower of Babel.

There once was a time when all of humankind spoke a single, unified language. They decided to build a tower that would reach up to the heavens and earn for them eternal glory. Dismayed by this display of hubris, God confused human language so that they could no longer understand one another, and scattered human beings across the Earth.

The story of the Tower of Babel reveals important truths about the human condition. It affirms the unity of the human race. Despite our differences in language, geography, or religion, we are the same in the most important way: we are members of the human community.

The Babel narrative confirms our social nature. We are drawn to other people and to doing things together that we cannot accomplish alone—such as building a tower that reaches the heavens, or creating civilization itself. The story also shows that, in addition to being social, we are selfish and prideful by nature—attributes that have divided human community in all times and places.

Lastly, as an origin story of human language, Babel illuminates how words can unite or divide us. It reveals the duality of the tongue: it can bring us together and help us achieve great things, or it can divide us. It shows that we're bound to miscommunicate or weaponize words. When our use of language is governed by civility, which requires us to sacrifice self for the good of the communal project, we will flourish together.

The Babel narrative offers several truths about what it means to be human, which may explain why versions of this story are found across history and culture. From Sumerian and Greek mythology to the narrative traditions in Mexican and Cherokee cultures, from Nepal and Botswana to the Lozi people of Zambia, the Tower of Babel story has audiences in all times and places.[1]

As we learned in Chapter 1, and as Babel shows us, there is cross-cultural recognition of the threat that human self-love poses to human community. The Tower of Babel account demonstrates that our selfishness isolates us. It explains why we're fated to endure social discord and miscommunication, and how our language can be a weapon of social division. The challenges to civility are inherent in human nature, and those challenges are exacerbated by new technologies.

As we've learned, the problem is timeless.

So is the solution.

Civility as Language

Civility is a language. It is the "grammar of conduct," as C. S. Lewis wrote. People in all times and places have had languages of civility to display and communicate respect for those around them. The language of civility is embedded in our verbal languages, but also in our rituals and behavior. Spoken languages are codified in dictionaries; the language of civility is codified in rituals and norms—or in books by authors from Ptahhotep in 2350 BC ancient Egypt to Emily Post in twentieth-century America. Each culture has cultivated a common language of civility, shared social norms that embody shared moral understandings, to govern how people act—mitigating the selfish for the social—and to sustain the human social project. Civility is communicative moral conduct.[2]

> *Jane Austen's principles [of civility and manners] might be described as the grammar of conduct. Now grammar is something anyone can learn; it is also something that everyone must learn.*
>
> —C. S. Lewis, twentieth-century English literature professor and author

Language is inherently a social enterprise. Civility is, too. There is no need for any sort of language—verbal or otherwise—in isolation.

There's a conceptual and etymological link between the words "communication" and "community." They share the same root: both words derive from the Latin word *communis*, which loosely means "doing things together." Communication—and technologies that amplify and expedite it—is a double-edged sword for the project of human community. Communication can foster community, or be the death of it. There is a duality to language because there is duality to our nature. The story of Babel showed us that language can unite us and enable us to achieve incredible things. But because of our selfishness and pride, language—verbal and behavioral—can also divide us.

"What Has Been Done Will Be Done Again"

Virtually all technological developments in human history have been attempts to bridge gaps between persons, to bring us closer and connect us physically or relationally. It's paradoxical that our human efforts to bridge our divides through technology have, in fact, frequently divided us. Our current era is no exception.

We've explored throughout this book the timelessness of challenges to civility. People have long worried that new social and cultural changes—such as mass anonymous society, commerce, novel technologies, and other epiphenomena—would undermine the social spirit. As we explored in our chapter on civil society, it seems that every society has a villain to blame for the decline of civility and community. But humankind's communal impulse is resilient.

People have been worried before about technology's toll on relationships

In very many English homes the radio is literally never turned off, though it is manipulated from time to time so as to make sure that only light music will come out of it. I know people who will keep the radio playing all through a meal and at the same time continue talking just loudly enough for the voices and the music to cancel out. This is done with a definite purpose. The music prevents the conversation from becoming serious or even coherent, while the chatter of voices stops one from listening attentively to the music and thus prevents the onset of that dreaded thing, thought.

—George Orwell, twentieth-century English novelist and writer and conversation—such as George Orwell's concern about the radio. The internet and social media are often portrayed as contemporary villains to community. While such worries are as old as human community itself, our media landscape today presents some unique challenges to civility.

Challenges to Civility Unique to Our Digital Age

New technologies have made communication easier, cheaper, and ubiquitous. They mediate and depersonalize our exchanges in ways that can obscure the humanity of the person on the other end of our emails, tweets, and texts—all of which makes it easier to express our selfishness.

The Greek word *logos* overlaps both "reason" and "speech," two attributes that only humans possess. Our communication today undermines the historical connection between speech and reason: new technologies often deploy communication to inflame passions instead of nurturing our reason.

Modern technologies pose novel hazards to human well-being. Violating our privacy, spreading misinformation, undermining free speech and our democratic institutions, platforming people with hateful views, impoverishing our conversation and friendships, and promoting a culture that values spectacle and appearance over reality—modern skeptics of technology have sound cause for concern.

In her books *Alone Together* and *Reclaiming Conversation*, Sherry Turkle of

> *All of humanity's problems stem from man's inability to sit quietly in a room alone.*
>
> —Blaise Pascal, seventeenth-century French polymath

MIT reveals how our technological and digital age compromises our humanity, and impoverishes the relationships that help us become human. Keeping us distracted and superficial, technology erodes our ability to empathize and reflect. The immediacy of our communication encourages us to exchange quantity for quality in our interactions.

Remember the exchange between Edward Coles and Thomas Jefferson? Coles, the son of a wealthy Virginian landowner, wrote to Jefferson and asked him to help the abolitionist effort. Jefferson wrote back and demurred, saying he was too old and the fight against slavery was best left to younger men. In their exchange, they each took a month to respond to the other's letters. Their correspondence was thoughtful and provocative on the most important issue of the day—slavery. The letters were also beautifully written.

Such an exchange is difficult to imagine today, but not impossible. More emails, followers, and friends—but fewer meaningful connections and discussions on subjects of import, topics whose contemplation would make the world richer and nourish the soul.

Anonymous and digitally mediated communication reduces our ability to see the human being on the other side of the interaction, making it easier to dehumanize and depersonalize them. And when we dehumanize others, we dehumanize ourselves.

The way we use technology has powerful con-

> *The fault, dear Brutus, is not in our stars / But in ourselves.*
>
> —Shakespeare

sequences. It can be a tool for good or for ill. Our use of technology is an extension of the human condition, which, as Pascal said, is defined by greatness and wretchedness.

Technology and the Human Condition: The Challenge of Digital Anonymity

In Book II of Plato's *Republic*, Plato's brother Glaucon tells the story of the Ring of Gyges. Gyges was a shepherd in the ancient city of Lydia who discovered a cave while tending to his flock. In the cave he discovered the body of a man who wore a golden ring. Gyges took the ring, and determined that when he wore it, it made him invisible. Gyges then used his newfound power of invisibility to murder the king of Lydia, seduce the queen, and take the king's throne for himself.

Glaucon suggests that this is precisely what any person in Gyges' situation would do, as man's heart tends toward injustice. Fear of consequences, Glaucon maintains, is the only thing that prevents him from acting unjustly. "No man would keep his hands off what was not his own when he could safely take what he liked out of the market," Glaucon says, "or go into houses and lie with any one at his pleasure, or kill or release from prison whom he would, and in all respects be like a god among men."

We learned in our chapter on civility, freedom, democracy, and human flourishing that social shame is a powerful means of promoting pro-social behavior: Paris's politeness campaign taught us that appealing to people's social conscience is more effective in promoting civility than

The surest way to work up a crusade in favor of some good cause is to promise people they will have a chance of maltreating someone. To be able to destroy with good conscience—this is the height of psychological luxury, the most delicious of moral treats.

—Aldous Huxley, twentieth-century English novelist

top-down laws. Incivility thrives in situations where we are most anonymous and unaccountable to others. This includes social media, but also extends to road rage, gossip, off-the-record comments, and other instances where we think our anonymity will save us from the consequences of our actions. Without our identity being attached to our actions, without the fear of repercussions and consequences, we're capable of great evil.

Technological platforms enable anonymity, but even when our identity is attached to them, technologically mediated interaction makes depersonalization and dehumanization easier. We must each make a concerted effort to *re-personalize* our digital interactions. We must be vigilant to stay mindful of the humanity of others, and the basic respect they are owed.

The Problem of Depersonalization: Civility, Call Centers, and Customer Service

There are few things that I take greater delight in than finding a good deal. I think it's genetic. My paternal grandmother, an Irish lass from Portland, Maine, loved to regale us with her latest conquests. She was always hunting for a "BAH-gen."

One time, however, my passion for treasure hunting went too far. Recently married, I was excited to purchase a blender from an upscale home goods store: because we had registered there, we were eligible for 15 percent off any purchase. When the customer service representative told me that my blender of choice was exempt from the discount, I didn't respond well. My face flushed with frustration. *Exempt?* I was adamant about getting that discount—not because money was tight, but because it was "a matter of justice." Arbitrary policy and bureaucracy were taking precedence over the human and customer experience! I asked to speak with the customer service agent's manager. I threatened to never shop there again.

In the end, the poor customer service representative gave me the discount.

I won! I had triumphed over the bureaucracy.

But immediately, I felt like I had lost.

I felt miserable and ugly inside. I had been unkind to the customer service agent because, for a moment, nothing seemed more important to me than achieving my end of getting the paltry discount. She didn't make the rules. She was just doing her job. Yet, in my righteous quest for the coupon, I had failed to treat her as she deserved, and I felt miserable for it.

I apologized to her for letting my baser, selfish nature get the better of me.

Graciously, she forgave me.

We often think of the internet or social media as the platforms and technologies that invite the worst expressions of our human nature. But it's not just social media that can bring out the worst in us. The depersonalizing nature of other technologically mediated interactions—from phone calls to emails—makes it easier for us to do and say things we wouldn't do or say in person.

Often when people call in to customer service lines, it's because something is amiss. Our consumerist culture has conditioned us to have the expectation that the customer is always right. This mentality of entitlement can inflame the inner tyrant—the selfishness and *libido dominandi* within each of us—when things don't go our way. When people don't get what they want, or don't get it quickly enough, they lash out, berate, and throw temper tantrums.

Customer service representatives report shocking treatment when they are not able to indulge their customers. Representatives have told me stories of enduring traumatizing verbal abuse from customers. "Burn in acid," one customer hurled at a customer service representative. "You should kill yourself," said another. Call center employees shared with me recurring threats made by customers toward them, such as "Let me talk to your manager" and "I'm going to make sure you lose your job."

Communicating over the phone is a form of technologically mediated interaction with others. Not seeing people face-to-face, we are more likely to depersonalize, dehumanize, and instrumentalize them, especially when we don't get what we want. We forget that a human being is at the other end of the phone line. Even if we do remember that we're talking to a person—and not just a machine—it's easy to justify treating the representative poorly if it means a chance to vent our frustration and resolve our issue rapidly. As I learned, there are costs associated with exploiting the power imbalance inherent to these interactions—to others, but also to ourselves. We are deeply connected with those around us, and we wound our souls in treating our fellow human beings poorly.

Though not anonymous, our interactions with customer service representatives are depersonalized. Without faces, names, or reputations attached to the interaction, customers frequently feel they can get away with treating representatives poorly without being held accountable. Not seeing people face-to-face allows us to turn off "psychological filters" such as civility, along with the empathy and basic respect for others that civility demands.[3] This is why otherwise decent people—people who would never be abusive in any other context—can walk away from an interaction with no remorse or understanding of the emotional distress their bullying behavior caused.

Several times in this book we've explored the theme of emotional displacement, or "kicking the cat": people are frustrated by one thing, but take it out on something or someone else. They have a deficit in their lives, and they try to compensate for that deficit by exerting power over others consequence-free, as Gyges did in Plato's parable.

We know that hurt people hurt people. When people have an inadequate appreciation of the amazing gift of being human, when they insufficiently comprehend their own human dignity, they are more likely to lash out and dehumanize others. But abusing others hurts the abused and the abuser alike. When we berate an anonymous customer service representative over the phone, it hurts not only them, but our own psyche.

As a society that claims to respect the dignity and equality of all persons, we must not tolerate treating anyone from any walk of life as an emotional punching bag. If each of us decides to be more respectful and civil in our interactions with others—in person, on social media, and with anonymous customer service representatives—our society can become more civil and humane, too.

Affirming Humanity in a Technologically Mediated World

[Eye contact] is part of being a citizen and a responsible member of society. It is also a way to stay in touch with your surroundings, break down social barriers, and understand whom you should and should not trust.

—Timothy D. Snyder, contemporary American historian

In our technologically and digitally mediated age, it's essential to recognize and affirm our humanity and that of others wherever and whenever we can. In his book *On Tyranny: Twenty Lessons from the Twentieth Century*, Timothy D. Snyder writes that making eye contact as often as possible is an important prevention against totalitarianism. Eye contact—along with a firm handshake—is a way to communicate trust, to help those you meet feel seen and respected.

Moral virtue comes about as a result of habit.

—Aristotle

Increasingly, dining establishments are choosing to promote presence and connection between guests. Shirking the "customer is always right" mentality, restaurants are banning phones, forcing patrons to be less connected to the digital world but more connected to one another. The famed New York French restaurant Le Cirque, prior to its closure, required patrons to check phones at the door. Chez Panisse, a well-known restaurant in Berkeley, California, bans cell phones completely. Le Petit Jardin in Saint-Guilhem-le-Désert, France, enforces its cell phone ban in a rather innovative way: following the referee-card system, waiters use social shame to its highest and best by blowing whistles at customers when they are caught red-handed violating the restaurant's no-phone rule. On the second offense, they're asked to leave.

As human beings, we tend to blame technology platforms, politicians, and other people for our problems. But what is our role in creating a more civil and connected future in our digital age?

Making eye contact is one way of rehumanizing our technological age. Allowing technology to help us cultivate habits of treating others well—especially important for our children—is another. Only people—not machines, not gadgets—inherently deserve respect. People have dignity and are endowed with intrinsic moral worth. But being kind and courteous to artificial intelligence, such as Alexa, Siri, or Google Home, can help us cultivate habits of civility that can transfer over to our interactions with people.

We shouldn't be continually calculating the level of respect we owe those we interact with. We shouldn't practice treating our boss one way and a customer service representative or our Uber driver another. It's especially important that we model basic respect in our interactions, because even before children appreciate concepts such as human dignity and the worth of persons, their characters are formed by how they see the adults in their lives conduct themselves.

Cultivate Your Digital Garden

Technology, soulless gadgets, and faceless corporations are easy scapegoats for our problems today. Yet blaming social media as the cause of the many contemporary problems we face takes away our power to make important changes in our world. We each have an opportunity—and duty—to improve the tenor, and alleviate the toxicity, of our public discourse.

Our general tendency is to accept it [a new technology] at once without question as a good thing, not considering that its whole value is to be measured by its effect upon the spirit and quality of life, and that until this effect be ascertained our estimate of it is worthless and misleading.

—Albert Jay Nock, twentieth-century American writer

When I left Washington, DC, I withdrew from public life. Overwhelmed by the problems I saw firsthand, I resolved to better invest my time and energy in my own little corner of the world. I started a newsletter and intellectual community, Civic Renaissance, as an attempt to cultivate my digital garden. I couldn't snap my fingers and improve the state of civility in our country or world, but I could change myself and do what I could to make my own sphere of influence a small part of the solution.

Online groups can create their own guidelines for engagement, and enforce them. Norms should be geared toward fundamentally respecting others and facilitating respectful, reasoned, robust conversation, keeping the dignity of the human person front of mind. For the Civic Renaissance Facebook community that I curate (and which you should join!), here are the guidelines:

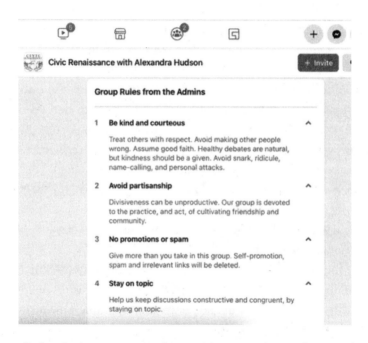

Individuals can create their own personal set of principles to follow in their own lives, too. At the end of this chapter, I'll share some practices that I've benefited from in my online interactions.

It's easy for people to despair at the state of our national conversation and to conclude, based on what they read on Twitter or watch on cable news, that no one is interested in pursuing the truth and no one is worth engaging with seriously. Thoughtful

> *You always own the option of having no opinion.*
>
> —Marcus Aurelius, second-century Roman emperor

people across the political spectrum think that these and other problems related to our digital age are so severe, legislation is required.

These are important ideas that reasonable minds disagree on, and that we must continue to have conversations about in the days to come. While policy makers debate macro-level solutions, we each have a role to play in creating community and civility in our digital era.

As I've worked on this book, I've discovered many people who are interested in pursuing truth and having real conversations. These people are out there; it's up to us to find one another. My hope is that people who read this book come away with a sense of optimism, encouragement, and a renewed commitment to find and engage like minds who are equally dissatisfied with our status quo, and equally enthusiastic to be part of a solution. By each of us deciding to be different in how we engage with others, we can make a difference in elevating our national conversation.

Incivility in all its dehumanizing forms—from bullying, slandering, online shaming, spreading lies and misinformation, and more—flourishes in anonymity and isolation. Our technologically mediated modes of communication enable us to depersonalize and dehumanize others. We must resist that temptation. When we forget that there is a human being on the other end of a digital interaction, when our interactions are depersonalized, we become part of the problem.

In elevating our technological practices and how we interact with others—in making eye contact and being present with people personally, in cultivating our digital garden—we can be part of the solution.

Unity Out of Division?

The story of Pentecost found in the New Testament has spiritual value to me as a Christian. It also has symbolic significance to non-Christian audiences, as it offers a response to the problem of the inevitable miscommunication and division among human communities that the Tower of Babel narrative presents. After Christ's death, resurrection, and ascension, a wind from heaven descended on Christ's apostles, bringing "tongues of fire" upon each person's head. Every apostle began to speak in other languages—languages that they had never studied or spoken before. They preached the Gospel in Jerusalem, and people were astounded to hear them speaking *in their own language.*

The story of Pentecost answers the problem of Babel, and of the duality of language—verbal, as well as the unspoken language of our social norms. Language can foster unity or promote division and discord, an expression of a fallen human condition and self-love. The digital interconnectedness of our modern era means that one individual's decision to weaponize language can now harm countless others on heretofore unknown scales.

Pentecost shows how we can redeem and harness the power of

> *Parthians, Medes, and Elamites; residents of Mesopotamia, Judea, and Cappadocia, Pontus and Asia, Phrygia and Pamphylia, Egypt and the parts of Libya near Cyrene; visitors from Rome (both Jews and converts to Judaism); Cretans and Arabs—we hear them declaring the wonders of God in our own tongues! Amazed and perplexed, they asked one another, "What does this mean?"*
>
> —Acts 2:9–12

language, verbal and nonverbal alike. The story offers a model for how we can see our differences in light of our commonalities. We can reject the pride that caused the linguistic divides in the first place, and the self-love that nourished sentiments of linguistic or cultural superiority after the people of Babel were scattered across the Earth. The people of Babel allowed their miscommunication to fortify their differences and permanently separate them.

Like the apostles who spoke new languages to new people at Pentecost, we can choose to speak the universal language of the timeless principles of civility, both online and in real life. As we learned in Chapter 2, many of these principles transcend culture and place, and embody a language that respects our shared dignity and affirms our humanity. In recovering this language of the soul of civility, we can be instruments of healing and reconciliation in our broken world.

How to Cultivate our Digital Garden and Promote Civility in Our Digital, Technologically Mediated Age

1. Remember the power and duality of language, which reflects the duality of the human condition: it can be used to unite or divide, to heal our world or make it a worse place to live. Choose to use your words to heal and elevate others and our world.
2. When you interact with people in a digitally mediated way—either online or over the phone with customer service representatives—remember the human on the other side. Digital interaction makes it easy to forget another's personhood. Don't.
3. No matter whom you interact with, remember that they are not an emotional punching bag. Technology, by dif-

fusing the humanity of the person on the other end of a digital interaction, can often cloud this fact. Fight the urge to take your frustrations out on others, and avoid emotional displacement, or "kicking the cat."

4. When interacting with angry strangers online, try to save your emotional energy for more worthy endeavors. Here is a set of guidelines I try to follow.

    a. Don't tweet, text, message, or email while anxious, angry, or frustrated. Come back to it the next day.

    b. When possible, try to shift online conversations about sensitive topics to phone, video, or in-person conversations. These modes of communication are more personal and humanizing, and remind us that there is a person on the other side of our digital interactions.

    c. Don't tweet something about someone you wouldn't say to them in person.

    d. Remember that persuasion is preferable to "winning."

    e. Don't argue in the comments section.

    f. Avoid wasting your emotional energy arguing with strangers on the internet.

    g. Start a discussion by acknowledging areas of agreement.

Here are some other suggestions, some of which you might find useful.

1. Read something before sharing it. Fight the urge to share on the basis of a headline (or perhaps even worse, someone *else's* summary).

2. Remember the old advertisement for Tootsie Pops? It takes *three licks* to get to the center (the last one being a

bite, of course!). If it takes more than *three clicks* to get to the original source for an article, don't share it. (Thanks, Abdul Shabazz, for this one!)

3. Never, ever "hate-click"—you'll likely reward incendiary commentary and you'll certainly not find yourself edified.
4. Be critical of what you read—don't unquestioningly accept the content you consume.

Here are additional ideas for best practices that I've benefited from:

5. Cross-reference the facts of a given story against three sources of reporting from three different ideological backgrounds. Chances are, the common points of reporting are the facts of a story, and the rest is ideological trappings that you might well do without.
6. When possible, read entire, original sources—reports, full interviews, press releases, legal opinions, and more—before reading secondary reporting *about* them.
7. Remember: *you do not need to have an opinion on everything.* No one can be completely informed on all issues. And though our media culture rewards rapidity and certainty, it's helpful to keep this in mind. Resist the urge to respond to "breaking news" as it's happening. In our fast-paced world, stories develop quickly, and often the truth emerges over time.
8. We can consider taking a page from Thomas Jefferson's playbook on how to curb "fake news." He once proposed that editors divide and expressly label news into four categories: truth, probability, possibility, and lies. "The third and fourth," he said, "should be professedly for those readers who would rather have lies for their money than the blank paper they would occupy."

Part III

CIVILITY IN PRACTICE

10

Hospitality

Few stories better explore the duties of hospitality, and the timeless principles of civility that govern the guest-host relationship, than Homer's *The Odyssey*. Among my favorite vignettes in the ancient Greek epic is the story of Eumaeus, a slave who lived on the island of Ithaca in the Ionian Sea. Eumaeus had little in the way of material possessions, but when he saw a poor, aged, dirty beggar, someone who appeared to have even less than he did, he immediately invited the stranger into his home, fed him, offered him clothes, and shared an evening of conversation with his downtrodden guest. Eumaeus showed this kindness to the stranger without knowing that the stranger was really his beloved master Odysseus in disguise.

The story of Eumaeus illuminates the duty of hospitality, and of welcoming strangers and those in need into our lives and our homes—*The Odyssey*'s cen-

One must honor guests and foreigners and strangers, even those much poorer than oneself. Zeus watches over beggars and guests and strangers. What I have to give is small, but I will give it gladly.

—Homer, *The Odyssey,* translated by Emily Wilson

tral theme. The Greek word for hospitality is *xenia,* which means both "stranger" and "friend," reflecting the way in which showing openness and warmth to others can transform a stranger into a friend. As we will explore, this duty of hospitality to strangers is an ideal found in many ancient cultures.

The Duality of Hospitality

The basic principles of hospitality, like the principles of civility, are remarkably timeless; people the world over have discovered the richness of friendship, and at some point, every friend was once a stranger. Hospitality, though, also invites risk that is endemic to every interaction with strangers. This duality of hospitality—the rewards and risks involved in opening our hearts, hearths, and homes to strangers—is captured in the Latin root of hospitality, *hospes.* Just as the Greek word *xenia* means both "stranger" and "friend," the Latin *hospes* means "guest," "host," and "stranger."

In Old French, *hoste* meant both "guest" and "host": a relationship in which both participants are united by mutual vulnerability. In the same way that it is vulnerable to be a guest—to be at the mercy of someone else's kindness—it is vulnerable to be a host.

Hospes is the root of the word "hospitality," but also of our word "hostility," an emotion bred from dysfunctional guest-host relationships—when the stranger becomes our enemy rather than our friend.

The Danish word *hygge* (pronounced HYOO-guh) literally means "to cozy around together." *Hygge* embodies a near-universal cultural value of prioritizing life in friendship, intimacy, and community with others.

The Same, Yet Different: Hospitality Today

The duality of hospitality has caused many people to play it safe. They elect to care for themselves and their own instead of choosing the gamble of taking a stranger in. Eumaeus' response to the stranger at his doorstep may seem foreign to us. Today, if a stranger in need appeared on our doorstep, many likely would refer them to a local homeless shelter or government social services agency before welcoming them into their home.

Our culture is not less hospitable and more *xenophobic*—a term meaning "fearful of the stranger" that derives from *xenia*—than it was in past eras. Nor were people then any more *xenophilic*—a word meaning "loving of the stranger" that I think is due for a revival. A theme throughout this book is that human nature hasn't changed. We're just as capable of selfishness or generous hospitality now as we've been in any other era.

> *We no longer know this beautiful bond of hospitality, and we must admit that the times have produced such great changes among peoples and especially among us, that we are much less obligated by the sacred and respectable laws of this duty than the ancients were.*
>
> —Denis Diderot and Jean le Rond d'Alembert's eighteenth-century *Encyclopédie*

Still, there are important differences between our current moment and the past that explain the differences in hospitality customs. For most of human history, traveling far and wide was the exception, and staying put the rule. Now the reverse is true. In the past, travel was expensive, dangerous, and difficult, and travelers were entirely dependent on the kindness of strangers for their basic needs. Today we rely on hotels and credit cards for accommodations and depend less on one another.

Ours is not the only era in which people have suspected that social and economic changes have made our own era less hospitable than in prior periods. In our chapter on civil society, we learned of people, from fourteenth-century Tunisian Islamic thinker Ibn Khaldun to twentieth-century writer Robert Nisbett, who worried that wealth or war would dislocate our communities and make us less welcoming to our neighbors. The entry on hospitality in Diderot and d'Alembert's 1765 *Encyclopédie* laments that hospitality was on the decline, and that their own era was less likely to show kindness to the stranger the way the ancient cultures that came before them had.

The Roman poet Horace sardonically referred to people who viewed the past through sepia-toned spectacles as *audatores temporis acti*—"praisers of time past." Horace's words affirm a recurring theme of this book: circumstances may change, but human nature remains fundamentally the same. The risks and rewards of hospitality are just as powerful today as they were three centuries or three millennia ago. We are no less likely to be, or no less capable of being, kind to the stranger than were the ancient Greeks—or any other culture, for that matter. As we have seen throughout this book, the tensions in our nature—between our love of others and our love of self, and between our duties to our tribe and our general obligations to the rest of humanity—are the same today. But are we less hospitable today than in past eras? I don't think so.

Dublin with an Italian Flair

When I was in graduate school in London on a scholarship with the Rotary Foundation, I was reluctant to let my student's budget interfere with my wanderlust. My now-husband and I had planned a trip to Ireland, but I had waited too long to reserve accommodations. Everything was booked or beyond our means.

With our flights already scheduled, I decided to throw myself at the mercy of complete strangers. I emailed one of my fellow Rotary Scholars in Dublin and explained my situation. He sent me a name and an address. The next thing we knew, we arrived at the doorstep of an old brick town house in Dublin. Beyond their affiliation with the Dublin Rotary Club, we had no idea who they were or what to expect. We took a deep breath, knocked, and waited to meet complete strangers who had agreed to take us in.

When Paolo opened the door, he quickly ushered us in to another world. Paolo's mother-in-law was hand-rolling fresh pasta in the kitchen. His wife, Elisabetta, offered us a glass of Lambrusco, a wine from their hometown of Modena, Italy. The scent of a softly simmering ragu tickled our noses. They had re-created their entire northern Italian life—complete with a prosciutto slicer, a wine cellar, and authentic homemade Modenese balsamic vinegar—right in the heart of Dublin.

An Arab admonished his son: "My son, if on a journey with a fellow traveler, love him as yourself, and think not to deceive a person, lest you, too, be deceived."

—Petrus Alfonsi, twelfth-century writer and Jewish convert to Christianity from Islamic Spain, *Disciplina Clericalis*

We adored getting to know them that weekend, but more than anything, we were humbled by their graciousness in taking us in. In offering to host complete strangers, they had taken as much of a risk as we had taken in showing up on their doorstep. Looking back, we laugh that, after our having been hosted by Italians, no one in Ireland has ever eaten as well as we have. Paolo and Elisabetta clarified for me that while we are generally less dependent on strangers today than in the past, we're no less capable of generous hospitality now.

Civility and Hospitality

Hospitality is a noble expression of civility. Civility and hospitality go hand in hand: the more one cultivates the disposition of civility, the more hospitable one becomes. The more one practices hospitality, the more one appreciates the beauty and dignity of the human person, and the more civil one becomes to all one meets. Hospitality confronts us with the beauty of personhood and community, which makes it easier to overcome our selfishness so our social nature can thrive. The more hospitable we are, the more we manifest civility in other spheres.

Civility is the obligation we have to treat the "other"—

The Stoics regarded [hospitality] as a duty inspired by God himself. One must, they said, do good to people who come to our countries, less for their sake than for our own interest, for the sake of virtue and in order to perfect in our souls human sentiments, which must not be limited to the ties of blood and friendship, but extended to all mortals.

—Denis Diderot and Jean le Rond d'Alembert, *Encyclopédie*

including the stranger—with the decency we accord to those closest to us. This high standard of conduct is, as we'll recall from
earlier in this book, *kindness*
in its literal sense: treating
strangers and visitors with the
benevolence with which we
would treat our *kin*, the etymological root of kindness.
Being kind means treating a
person with the benevolence
one would if they were family
even if they aren't.

Eumaeus had next to
nothing, yet shared what
little he had with someone

*Nature knows no difference
between Europe and Americans
in blood, birth, bodies, etc. . . .
God having of one blood made
all mankind.*

—Roger Williams, religious
dissident and founder of Rhode
Island

more needy than himself. Time and time again, *The Odyssey* val-
orizes kindness to the stranger. According to Homer, welcoming
the newcomer is the stuff of good manners and civility, while bad
manners, incivility, and "barbarism" are hostility and cruelty.

People across time and place have celebrated kindness to the
stranger.

When Roger Williams, founder of Rhode Island, was kicked
out of Massachusetts for his stubbornly heterodox religious views,
the Narragansett Native Americans welcomed him into their
community. In his work *A Key into the Language of America*, Williams praised the ways in which the Native Americans he lived
with were more civilized, and civil, than his fellow Englishmen.

Why? Because they were more compassionate, benevolent,
and kind. They cared for those in need in their own society.
They had no underhoused persons. Few fatherless children went
unprovided for. Robbery, murder, and adultery were much less
common. More than that, the Native Americans cared for those
outside of their society—including by accepting Williams into

their community. Williams claimed that they were more civilized because they were more *humane*. They had shown him hospitality, tolerance, and kindness—they had acted with civility—when his fellow Englishmen had not.

[Hospitality is] the virtue of a great soul that cares for the whole universe through the ties of humanity.

—Louis de Jaucourt, eighteenth-century French scholar and author of the entry on hospitality in the *Encyclopédie*

As we learned in Chapter 2, a central idea in Stoic thought is *oikeiosis*, which involves a duty to show civil welcoming to the stranger, and kindness to those who can do nothing for us in return. This is reminiscent of the idea of *ren* in Confucianism, also explored in Chapter 2. *Ren* means "benevolence" or "common humanity," and pertains to what we owe to one another in light of our equal moral worth as persons.

Homeric Hospitality: The Timeless Principles of Civility in Practice

Norms that facilitate human connection and community are remarkably universal. Homer's *The Odyssey* offers us civil and hospitable norms that are important reminders to this day.

TIMELESS PRINCIPLES OF HOMERIC HOSTING:

1. *Be proactively generous.* In *The Odyssey*, good hosts immediately invite strangers into their home, and offer them a bath, a comfortable place to rest, food, and drink.
2. *Give without knowledge of who you are giving to.* In *The Odyssey*, good hosts offer unqualified hospitality—helping

someone just because of their personhood, not making the gesture contingent on who a person is or whether they repay the kindness.

3. *Let your guests leave when they want to.* In *The Odyssey*, the goddess Calypso keeps Odysseus on her island against his will for seven years until the Greek god Zeus forces her to let him go. Holding one's guest captive was in poor taste 2,800 years ago when *The Odyssey* was composed, and continues to be today.

4. *When guests leave, send them on their way with gifts and practical assistance for their journey ahead.* Ensure your guests leave better off than when they arrived. The ancient Greeks called this *pompe,* or "sending," and it is a beautiful example of "above and beyond" civility and hospitality.

HOMER'S TIMELESS GUIDELINES FOR GOOD GUESTING

1. *Do not take from your hosts until first offered.* Just as good hosts should promptly offer food, drink, and shelter to guests, guests should not take without first being offered. When Odysseus and his men landed on the island of the Cyclops hungry and thirsty, they were eager to devour the cheese and other food that they found in a cave. Odysseus prohibited it, reminding his men that good guests do not take without first being offered.

2. *Don't insult your host.* Be flexible, adapt to the customs of your hosts and surroundings, and be thankful for what's offered. "A man who challenges those who have welcomed him in a strange land is worthless and a fool; he spites himself," says Odysseus.

3. *Thank your hosts.* In *The Odyssey,* failure to properly thank a host is punished, while thanking a host profusely is rewarded.

4. *Don't overstay your welcome.* Benjamin Franklin quipped that guests, like fish, begin to smell after three days. Homer would have agreed. As a host should not keep a guest against their will, a guest should not exhaust the generosity of their host. The villains in *The Odyssey* are the suitors who come to Ithaca to win the hand of Odysseus' wife, Penelope, as Odysseus is thought to be dead. The suitors become the guests who never leave! They come without being invited, stay despite being asked to leave, and drink and eat Odysseus' home into near poverty.

These principles are just as valuable for us today as they were in ancient Greece. Daniel of Beccles, the Emily Post of the thirteenth century whom we met in Chapter 2, also offers us some remarkably timeless principles of hospitality. Arrive on time and avoid the tavern en route, lest you never make it to dinner at all. A courteous guest should show restraint in speech, and use moderation while drinking and eating. Beccles knew a glutton wasn't likely to receive a repeat invitation! "Listen, learn the manner of dining if you wish to be prosperous, distinguished, and thriving with wealth," he advises. (He also saw the wisdom in a nice catnap after a meal—a ritual I think is well worth reviving.)[1]

Guidelines such as these have stood the test of time because they are grounded in the disposition of civility—of basic respect for our fellow persons. Human nature doesn't change. We are just as capable of fracturing the fragile bonds of human relationships as we were in past millennia. We're also just as in need of companionship and community as we've ever been. For this reason, it's worth refreshing ourselves from the well of ancient wisdom about the timeless principles of hospitality and applied civility.

Hospitality and Generative Generosity

Hospitality is a form of generative generosity, a concept we explored in our chapter on civility and civil society. When we receive hospitality, we desire to show it to others.

I was raised in a home that valued showing hospitality to newcomers. My mother's example of hospitality as I grew up was a formidable teacher, and hosting has always come naturally to me. That, combined with the feeling of gratitude for the hospitality Paolo, Elisabetta, and many others had shown me throughout my life and when I was in need, made me want to show hospitality to others.

A few weeks after our visit to Ireland, I attempted something I'd never done before: hosting my own Canadian Thanksgiving dinner. I was born in Los Angeles, but raised in Vancouver, Canada. We celebrated both Thanksgivings each year as I grew up, because why would one pass up an opportunity to gather with family and friends and show gratitude for life's many blessings?

This was my first Thanksgiving—Canadian or otherwise—on my own, and my ambitious, twenty-two-year-old self succumbed to my unfortunate tendency to wildly overestimate my capabilities. The first problem I encountered was finding the cornerstone to any Thanksgiving dinner: the turkey. I did not anticipate it being such a challenge to find a turkey in London in the first half of October, but there apparently is not a sufficiently robust Canadian expatriate community to warrant widely available turkey in the early fall.

I instead made do with roasting several rotund chickens—which, if I'm being honest, was more scrumptious than turkey would have been anyway; there's a reason we normally eat turkey only once a year. I then invited my guests to bring their favorite celebratory dish from their culture, dispersing both the cost and burden of preparation. It was the most multicultural Thanksgiving of any kind that I had ever been to—all the major continents were covered, with guests from the Middle East, all across Asia, Latin America, Africa, and elsewhere.

My aim in hosting was not to impress. It couldn't have been: my faux-turkey chicken was not terribly impressive. I instead hoped to use the meal to build friendship with my international London community, who might not have experienced the exotic tradition of Canadian Thanksgiving before. In a moment of an astounding lack of self-awareness, a month later, I volunteered to host an American Thanksgiving. This time, thankfully, I had the aid of other expats—and turkey was also easier to come by.

In *The Rituals of Dinner*, Margaret Visser notes the dark side of hospitality. She argues that hosting others can be a power play. The host has the opportunity to be the guest of honor, the center of all praise and attention in the comfort of their own home. Guests must fawn and thank them whether or not the hospitality or food is any good, and often feel obligated to reciprocate whether they want to or not. While cynical, I've come to see some wisdom in her insight. In my years of hosting, there have been times when I've felt depleted by hospitality instead of rejuvenated by it. During these seasons, I find myself inordinately dwelling on the trivial matters of who reciprocated invitations, who sent thank-you notes, who was an enjoyable guest, who responded favorably to invitations, and who did not.

There's nothing wrong with being selective about whom one invites into the intimacy of one's home, and when. But I've realized that when I've found myself caught up in the trite and petty aspects of hospitality, I've fulfilled Margaret Visser's fear and allowed hosting to become too much about me, and not enough about others. Recognizing that my hospitality has become too much about me allows me to see the reason behind my seasons of sensitive pride, woundedness, and general fatigue—and has helped me avoid these feelings. When I realize that my "fat, relentless ego," to borrow Iris Murdoch's memorable phrase once more, has, yet again, begun to detract from my ability to care for others well, I'll correct my disordered passions by refocusing on the true reason hospitality matters: as an aid to building togetherness, trust, gratitude, friendship, and the joint project of living well together. The Latin word from which we get "companion" literally means "a person with whom one shares bread." To dine is to celebrate life and togetherness. To cease dining is to cease to communicate, which is in turn to stop understanding one another.

Most often, what people remember at the end of a shared meal isn't the fine wine or gourmet cuisine—although these things certainly don't hurt. In the post-pandemic world, for many people it can be difficult to muster the energy to get dressed just for an evening dinner party—especially with Netflix and cozy loungewear beckoning. Sometimes, accepting hospitality can feel like going to the gym—difficult, but never regretted afterward. Few people regret an evening spent in good conversation and in good company.

Eating nourishes us physically, but eating with others nourishes us psychologically, socially, and emotionally. All cultures have norms and rituals around shared meals: communal dining is essential to human flourishing, but also fragile. The family dinner table is the hearth of society. It's where our primary social bonds, and habits of communal living, are born and nurtured. Sharing a meal with a friend or as a family requires effort. Like the cultivation of community, and civilization itself, shared meals require choices and effort.

The Chinese *Book of Rites*, compiled in the first
century BC, warns that "the ruin of states, the
distraction of families, and the perishing of individuals
are always preceded by their abandonment of rules
of propriety."

The customs around hospitality and communal dining have
endured because they promote trust and community. For example, the custom of toasting originated with the host's pouring
wine from his own glass into his guests' and then back again,
thereby demonstrating that the wine was free of poison. Our
clink, santé!—in which the edges of our glasses touch (though
usually without exchanging their contents)—pays homage to
that tradition.

Shared meals promote not only trust, but gratitude. The
Thanksgiving dinner tradition is only one example. The Greek
noun *eucharistia*, the name for the Christian ritual commemorat-
ing Christ's last supper with his disciples—is literally translated
as "thanksgiving." It's no coincidence that the cornerstones of the
largest world religions are rituals of communal meals. Passover is
the Jewish tradition of sharing a meal to give thanks to Yahweh
for delivering the Jewish people from slavery in Egypt. In the
Islamic tradition, Iftar is the feast that breaks the Ramadan fast.

We're all familiar with the reasons that we do not host or dine
with others. We're busy, tired, and can't afford it. And what if we
make a mistake and embarrass ourselves? What if people say no?
But—as recent increases in friendlessness, loneliness, suicide,
and other "deaths of despair" suggest—the stakes in closing our
hearts and our homes to new friendships are high. Life is worth
celebrating. Sharing a meal affirms this. Intimate venues to exchange stories and ideas are what empower us to engage, listen,

synthesize, and learn, and are indispensable to building trust, friendship, and community. Shared meals and hospitality motivate us to continue this joint project of life together. The rituals of hospitality buttress our society—one dinner, one conversation, one shared meal at a time.

Justice and Beneficence, Omission and Commission

Many of the civility manuals we have explored throughout this book are composed of both dos and don'ts. This is because acting with civility toward others consists both in the things we *do* and the things we do *not* do. Civility can be minimal. There is a "negative" civility that, like negative rights, follows a principle of "do no harm." We restrain our self-interest by choosing not to cut someone off in traffic or jump the line because we are in a hurry. Here, our inaction promotes peaceful coexistence with others.

Civility can also be maximal, and impose "positive" obligations on us to go above and beyond to help others. Hospitality and welcoming people into our homes are examples of *positive civility*. They are beautiful, supererogatory acts that go above and beyond ordinary norms.

Supererogation is a concept in Catholic theology that refers to extravagant kindness beyond what is required. It derives from the Latin *super*, meaning "beyond," and *erogare*, meaning "to pay out," suggesting a payment beyond what we owe.

Christian theology makes a distinction between acts of "commission" and acts of "omission." Acts, or sins, of *commission* are those things that were done that shouldn't have been done, and for which we are responsible. Sins of *omission* are those things that we didn't do but should have done, and we are morally responsible for having not done them. In the eyes of God, we are culpable for both. John Stuart Mill agreed. He wrote, "A person may cause evil to others not only by his actions but by his inaction, and in either case he is justly accountable to them for the injury."

Our self-love enables us to find reasons to avoid our obligations to others. Our selfishness makes it easier to be mindful of our duties to our family and our "tribe" than to humanity in general. But our duties—of positive and negative civility to our family and friends, as well as to strangers—still exist. Complying with these duties helps us not just survive, but thrive as human communities.

> *Society . . . cannot subsist among those who are at all times ready to hurt and injure one another. . . . If there is any society among robbers and murderers, they must at least, according to the trite observation, abstain from robbing and murdering one another.*
>
> —Adam Smith, eighteenth-century Scottish moral philosopher, *Theory of Moral Sentiments* (1759)

In his *Theory of Moral Sentiments*, Adam Smith distinguished between "justice" and "beneficence." Justice is the *minimum* we owe to others, and refers to our negative duties to "do no harm." It's what allows a community or a group to simply coexist in peace. Beneficence is an old word for "active goodness"—a sort of "above and beyond" maximal civility. The word describes the things we do for others that help us thrive as a species. It encompasses the actions that go above and beyond the ordinary morality of not harming others, the "positive" or active things we do to improve others' situations. It is the "second mile" ethic called for in the Christian Gospels, or the hospitality that *The Odyssey* celebrates—a theme that we will explore in greater depth later in this chapter. Justice is necessary for a human community to *survive*. It can subsist without voluntary acts of generosity, hospitality, civility, and kindness. Beneficence is essential for it to *flourish*.

> *Beneficence is always free, it cannot be extorted by force, the mere want of it exposes to no punishment; because the mere want of beneficence tends to do no real positive evil.*
>
> —Adam Smith

Smith understood that, because of the basic self-interestedness of man, it was unreasonable to expect people to act beneficently toward others in all situations. But Smith also knew that unfettered pursuit of our self-interest would undermine human flourishing. Governmental institutions alone are not enough to limit the negative consequences of human selfishness. For this reason, Smith encouraged each of us to impose checks on our self-interest by cultivating what he called "sympathy," or the "fellow-feeling" we share with others. Hospitality is an expression of duties of justice and beneficence to our fellow human beings, and by extension, of civility.

Hospitality Across Time and Place

There is a reason that the major thinkers in world history—Confucius, Buddha, Jesus Christ, and Mohammed—all cite human selfishness and excessive self-love as the root of suffering and social discord.

Human beings are inherently reliant on one another. We sometimes find ourselves dependent on supererogatory, above-and-beyond acts of kindness from strangers. Civility, as we've learned throughout this book, is about our duties to one another as members of the human community. Hospitality, like civility, is about what we owe to our fellow persons— especially those whom we do not like, those who are not like us, and those who cannot do anything for us in return.

Our selfish natures cause us to downplay our duties to others. For this reason, across millennia of history and countless cultures, benevolence to the stranger and the person in need has been actively taught, and consistently been a foundational value.

As we've learned, hospitality and civility date back to the ancient Greek world. Zeus was known as Xenios, or "god of strangers," and was often invoked to defend the rights of beggars, strangers, foreigners, and visitors when people failed to adhere to the norms of *xenia*. Zeus was also the god of justice— *dike*—and those who did not care for strangers risked Zeus's reprisal and divine justice.

Yet hospitality, benevolence, and civility toward the stranger—the one who can do nothing for us in return—is not only a Western ideal. It is praised in cultures across time and place. *One Thousand and One Nights*, for example, lauds the hospitality Sinbad receives from many of the kings he encounters on his adventures. The Hindu *Vedas* describe hospitality as a sacred duty owed to all other beings. People who go above and beyond to make those around them feel welcome, comfortable, and at home are praised as being the lifeblood of a healthy human community. A main principle of Pashtunwali, the code of honor of Afghanistan's Pashtun people, is *melmastia*. This involves showing respect and hospitality to all visitors, irrespective of race, religion, national affiliation, or economic status— and without any hope of being repaid in return.

Focusing on the timeless principles that these ancient texts articulate allows us to more easily see the solutions to the challenges we face today. It allows us to sift through the trappings, the folkways, the matters of cultural taste that so many have used to justify feelings of superiority, and to avoid a fastidious fixation on the rules that divide us. It helps us identify such "class markers" for what they are, and thereby avoid weaponizing manners in our own lives.

In some cultures people eat with chopsticks, in others with forks, in others with their hands. Some greet new people with a bow, others with a smile and a handshake. Some eat at a table, others on the floor. There is nothing *inherently* good about these acts; one is not categorically correct or ethically "better" than the other. These norms are "social lubricators," rules that suit the needs of a society's particular cultural context, tastes, and preferences, rules that a visitor to a given culture should adopt in order to support the project of community and relationship across difference.

The norms of *xenia* remind us that complying with the social lubricators in a particular culture is the morally right thing to do, not because these rules are intrinsically or universally good but because, in that particular setting, people have decided to do things a certain way to resolve a social problem. As a guest, it's kind to adopt the cultural norms and standards of your host—barring overtly harmful or destructive norms, of course.

Strangers in Disguise

Consider a remarkably ubiquitous scene: a visiting foreigner of great importance (perhaps even a god) appears disguised as someone poor and in need.

One who is hospitable to his guests, and when they leave awaits his next guests, will be a welcome guest in the heavens.

—*Tirukkural*, a treasured ancient Indian text on ethics and morality

We observe this in the story of Eumaeus, who shows kindness to Odysseus when he appears as a beggar. The suitors, by contrast, ridicule and berate Odysseus while he is disguised. Instead of being kind, they add to his harm. In the end, they are slaughtered; Homer ensures they ultimately get their comeuppance for their contempt for society's needy and vulnerable.

Cultures and religious traditions across the globe affirm the virtue of kindness to strangers. The Hebrew Bible tells the story of Abraham welcoming three strangers into his home—strangers who turn out to be angels. In Hebrew, this long-standing practice is called *hachnasat orchim*, or "welcoming guests." Similarly, Jesus Christ admonishes his followers to do kindness unto "the least of these" as though they were doing kindness directly to him. In India and Nepal, meanwhile, the ethic of hospitality is grounded in *Atithi Devo Bhava*, a principle that means "the guest is God." There are numerous traditional stories, from East to West, that embody this principle, where a guest reveals themselves to be a god and repays the host for their kindness. This principle informs the warm hospitality of modern India and Nepal, which emphasizes graciousness toward guests at home and in all social situations, and affirms the timeless principles of hospitality—civility

All foreigners and beggars come from Zeus, and any act of kindness is a blessing.

—Homer

in practice. Civility and hospitality cross-cut class because they are fundamentally about kindness. It is benevolence—not cruelty—to our fellow man that makes one truly noble.

Becoming Hospitals of the Social Spirit: Reviving Civility and Hospitality Today

The Latin word *hospes* is the root for our words "guest," "host," "stranger," "hostile," and "hospitality," as we've already learned.

It is also the root of our modern word "hospital." Hospitality, both practical and emotional, transforms our homes and our lives into hospitals of the social spirit.

Our homes can be hospitals for our social fabric, repairing and healing our body politic bit by bit. We can reclaim the power of hospitality, ordinary yet profound, and know that we are transforming our personal spheres into places of spiritual, emotional, and relational healing.

As my husband and I have built our life together in our marriage, we've reflected on how the different homes we've lived in can embody the ideas we care about. How can we bring to life the conversation, community, comfort, rest, dialogue, debate, and healing so needed in our moment?

We pursued this purpose when we lived in tiny, modern apartments in Milwaukee, Wisconsin, and Washington, DC. We've grown our family, and moved to larger, historic homes in Indianapolis—homes that have great big front porches of the sort that Richard H. Thomas eulogizes in his essay "From Porch to Patio." We are constantly evaluating how the space we have can be put to greater use to serve others. We are always eager to open our home to others so as to build connection, community, and relationships, and to use the property to build bridges in our time of division.

One rule of thumb I've had is to not own anything—a piece of furniture, décor, tableware, or any other household good—that I care more about than I do people. I've found this helps me keep my priorities in check and never be tempted to resent a guest, friend, or one of my own children for damaging a beloved possession. We've created a beautiful, comfortable, welcoming home, but we also strive to focus on friendship and connection more than on the trappings of elegant hospitality. With whatever resources or space we've had at our disposal, we've stewarded our homes to bring healing to our broken and isolated era.

Invariably, we will overlook opportunities to be hospitable to others. Our selfish nature will at times win out. Our busyness, fear of rejection, or insecurities will prevent us from reaching out to the stranger in need. We may be tempted to allow our attachment to our pride, things, and possessions to take precedence over our love of our children, guests, or friends. When we fall short, we can reflect on how, when next given the chance, we can act with civility and hospitality, and in so doing, help to heal our broken, despairing, and lonely world. Hospitality begins by reclaiming a sense of what we owe to one another by virtue of our shared humanity.

> *I hate a man, even as I hate hell fire, who lets his poverty tempt him into lying.*
>
> —Homer, *The Odyssey*, explaining that being poor or in need is not an excuse for being immoral or unkind

In a surprising show of egalitarianism, Homer reminds us that decency to the downtrodden is open to all people. Civility and hospitality are fundamentally about kindness, which is why they transcend differences of class, education, ethnicity, and race. Throughout this book, we've explored how cruelty to others harms the harmed, but also the soul of the harmer. The converse is true. When we are benevolent to our fellow persons, we ennoble them, but also ourselves.

In recovering common hospitality—in making our homes social hospitals—we can transform strangers into neighbors, the "other" into a friend, and help heal our broken world. In resisting our tribal and self-interested natures, and reaching across the divide and showing kindness, we find an essential building block of human friendship and flourishing, and enter into a more humane, hospitable—and civil—future.

How to Create a More Hospitable and Civil World

Hospitality to the stranger—the person we don't know, and who cannot do anything for us in return—is a risky proposition. Hence, *hospes* is the root of "hospitality" but also "hostile," representing the two possible outcomes of hospitality. But remember that kindness to the other is valued across history, cultures, and ethical traditions—and illuminates the soul of civility.

1. Resolve to make your heart and home a *hospital*—a word that shares the same etymological root as "hospitality"—of our social fabric. Invite someone to enjoy a meal with you at a restaurant. It's okay to start small—especially if you're out of practice. If people decline, don't take the rejection to heart. You've ennobled them with your invitation—and also enlarged your own soul with the generous gesture. Be open to being surprised by how many people welcome the invitation.

2. It may feel like a stretch, but try inviting someone into your home. Again, start small and build. The home is an intimate, beautiful, fertile ground for friendship.

3. When and if you host others, focus on what matters most. Remember that you don't need an immaculate home or elegant tablescape to show hospitality. People remember the conversation and friendship more than the trappings.

4. While eating with others:
    a. Put phones away.
    b. Be present.
    c. Look people in the eye.
    d. Really listen and respond. Don't merely think about the next thing you'll say.

5. If you find yourself getting mired in pettiness—"This person didn't respond to my last invitation, so I'm not inviting them again"; "That person did not write a thank-you note"; "This person never invites us back"—check that your self-love is held at bay. Remember the reason for hospitality: it's not about you—or the self-satisfaction of being an exceptional host—but to bless others. Self-love is an unstable foundation for true hospitality—and for society in general, as we've learned throughout this book—and is a recipe for disappointing social interactions.

6. Accept hospitality when it is offered. You might be ready to make excuses—and *Frasier* reruns never disappoint. But don't. Be there. Be willing to learn from the experiences and ideas of others. Remember that everyone has something to teach you. If you go into a new social environment with that attitude, you'll rarely regret it.

7. Hospitality can be beautiful when it happens in our homes, but it's beautiful wherever it happens. Exercise empathy muscles wherever possible—at work, at home, running errands, driving, shopping, and anyplace else. Try to see the needs around you—in your neighborhood and your community—and meet them if you can.

11

Education

In her role as Judi the Manners Lady, my mother has always known that, when it comes to creating a more civil future, investing in children is the most important effort imaginable. Reaching children means the hope of changing our future for the better. In 1997, she founded The Manners Club, a place for children and their parents to learn manners and character, out of our home in Quincy, Massachusetts.

The logo of The Manners Club.

Parents had the option to drop their children off at class and leave, but my mother encouraged them to stay so that they could continue to reinforce what the children had learned after the class ended. When parents began bringing recording devices to class so that they could remember what had been taught, my mother recorded an album with sixteen original songs that parents could take home with them. (I recorded two of the songs on the album.)

Manners begin in the home. They have to. But they don't end there. Teachers, government, police officers are important reinforcements for the principles of character and self-control that manners embody, but parents are a child's first and best teacher.

—Judi the Manners Lady, also known as my lovely mother

Amid growing concerns about the lack of civility in modern public life—remember the congressional civility summits from our chapter on polarization?—the 1990s and early 2000s were good years to be in the manners industry. Politicians and parents alike hungered for the character education my mother offered. She made empowering parents and the teachers at the schools she visited a priority, knowing that home and school are where cultures of civility begin. Her visits to schools for assemblies lasted only one day; it was up to teachers and parents to help form students' character day in and day out. She readily reminded both parents and teachers of their important responsibility: creating a civil future depended on their work cultivating civility in the next generation.

Civility and Education

Believing in education requires us to accept that human beings are not born perfect or complete. We are born with self-love, which, as we have seen throughout this book, is the root of personal and social ills across human history. For individual and communal harmony, we must first be *taught* to think of others before ourselves, and then *reminded* to do so consistently throughout our lives. Education should aim to help us lead better lives of personal flourishing in friendship and community by countering the indelible, baser aspects of our nature: the *incurvatus in se,* or the "inward curve to the self," and the *libido dominandi.* This can and should happen both in the home and within our mainstream educational institutions. Families, communities, and schools all have roles to play in combating the innate inward curve to the self within our society's young. It is important that educational environments create cultures of civility that promote the pro-human, pro-social norms and habits of a free and flourishing society.

> *Good manners is the art of making those people easy with whom we converse. Whoever makes the fewest persons uneasy is the best bred in the company.*
>
> —Jonathan Swift, eighteenth-century Anglo-Irish writer

Civility helps us displace our love of self with love of others. This process is necessary in order to help make us suitable for life in community. Civility, and surrendering our desires for the social project, isn't natural or spontaneous. It must be taught to the young, modeled by adults, and practiced continually throughout an individual's life.

Because civility—and civilization itself, as we learned in Chapter 1—is not effortlessly natural, education is central to sustaining it. Such an education also prepares a person to be a citizen in the *civis,* for the *civis,* like civility, is also unnatural: it is created and sustained only with continued efforts. And because civility can be learned, it is open to anyone. It is not dictated by the lottery of one's birth.

Knowing how civility can look in practice—in our daily interactions—is one thing. But how can we get more of it? How can it be taught to, and learned by, the next generation? Are there any places where civility is being taught in a way that promotes integrity, freedom, social and political equality, tolerance across difference, and fundamental respect for humanity?

This chapter will explore these questions. It will also investigate how education has historically been linked to cultivating civility, and will consider modern-day examples of institutions forging that link.

The History of Civility in Education

The mind is not a vessel that needs filling, but wood that needs igniting.

—Plutarch, first-century Greek philosopher

In ancient Greece and Rome, education was understood as "soul craft." It was a process of ordering our loves and priorities. It was not merely a process of memorizing and regurgitating facts for a test. Education aimed to instill in students a wonder and curiosity about others and the world around them. It was a given that education should provide students with the social and practical tools to continue learning, growing, adapting, and thriving in community throughout their lives.

Our modern word "ethics" derives from the Greek word *ethos*—which means "character." This supports the reason why, across history, education has been viewed as the process by which *ethics* are taught and *character* is formed.

Education was the formation of a student's character. Story-telling, history, and ideas offered moral instruction and gave students ideals to strive for. Education exposed students to a variety of disciplines—geometry, rhetoric, philosophy, poetry, and more—providing them with a baseline of knowledge that could help them continue to adapt, problem-solve, and live abundantly. The educational project of the ancient world was unapologetically value-laden: there was a good life, and certain decisions and life habits helped us get there. Other decisions and habits deterred us in this quest. Achieving the good life required orienting a student's loves and priorities toward the good, virtue, and the well-being of family, community, and the *polis*, or city.

The liberal arts curriculum, which exposed students to different disciplines—literally the *liberating* arts—liberated us from our baser desires, and freed us from the uglier aspects of human nature. Today, "liberal arts" is often used interchangeably with "humanities." The "liberal arts" is an apt term: in liberating us from our ignoble instincts, liberal arts enable us to become more fully human, and more humane. The liberal arts and the humanities were the modes of education that made a person free and fit for citizenship. They did this by cultivating love of virtue and the *polis*, and by promoting the reason and self-governance that allowed people to move beyond being dominated by their own passions.

Our word "education" comes from the Latin wood *educere*, which means "bring out, lead forth." True to the original meaning of education, the humanities and liberal arts aimed to cultivate—or bring out—a student's humanity to the fullest. The right education could help bring our best selves to bear in our relationships with one another and our communities in order to help solve the problems of the day.

The ancient Greeks had a word for this vision of education: *paideia*.

Paideia was the Greeks' all-encompassing approach to religion, politics, history, and literature, a word that meant "education" and "culture." *Paideia* shaped a Greek citizen's character, to the end of bringing forth a student's human potential.

The Greek *paideia* found expression in ancient Roman culture in the term *humanitas,* a word that meant "education" and "culture" as well as "benevolence" and "love of humanity." The Latin *humanitas* is at the root of our concept of the "humanities." This etymology underscores how Greeks and Romans understood education: the practice of developing our humanity to the fullest, cultivating within us a love for our fellow human beings.

Cruelty—or in Latin, *acerbitas*—toward others is innate to us, an expression of human selfishness. When we are cruel, we are in a sense *closer* to our uncultivated, unrefined, barbaric nature. But through the study of philosophy and literature, which exposes us to beauty, goodness, and truth, our humanity and humanness is, to continue our garden metaphor from Chapter 1, tilled. This process helps us learn to appreciate our own humanity, and that of others.

Such a curriculum softened the rougher edges of our human nature, teaching those who studied it ways to pursue peace and harmony with others, and to avoid cruelty, violence, and conflict. It also made its students *free,* and able to govern themselves and enjoy the fruits of life in a republic.

Civility and Love of Mankind: Paideia, Philanthropia, Humanitas, Civility

Humanitas is the communal fellow-feeling that acts as a brake on the natural impulse to advance our purely private interests.[1] As noted, *paideia* was often rendered as *humanitas* in Latin. *Humanitas* was also used to translate the Greek word *philanthropia*, which literally means "love of humanity." That is because *paideia*, *philanthropia*, and *humanitas* all have a common aim: to restrain the base aspects of our nature, and to help cultivate in us a love of our fellow humans, a trait we are not born with, so that we might flourish personally and communally.

Education today should be geared toward cultivating *philanthropia*, which derives from the Greek words *philos*, or "love," and *anthrōpos*, or "human beings." The romanized word for this concept is *humanitas*. Education today should aim to foster love of our fellow man, and avert misanthropy—from the Greek meaning "hatred of man," and *immanitas*, which connotes cruelty to our fellow persons.

This should sound familiar. Civility describes precisely this same disposition: the willingness to curb our immediate desires, to mitigate our self-love, for the sake of those around us. *Philanthropia* and *humanitas* connote sympathy and compassion for others, kindness toward our fellow human beings based on our shared humanity. And respecting the fundamental dignity of our fellow persons is, as we explored in Chapter 1, the basis of civility, as well as of civilization itself.

When the humanists of the European Renaissance of the fifteenth century recovered the ancient notion of *humanitas*, they linked the concept with civility.[2] Renaissance humanists thought that cultivating the disposition of *humanitas*, or civility, was the very purpose of education. The humanists sought to reform their society through the study of art, history, philosophy, and literature: they instructed members of the ruling class in these subjects with the goal of cultivating a sense in them of what conduct was praiseworthy, what was blameworthy, and what was worth emulating in their own lives and in their leadership. The humanists' theory of civility correlated benevolent conduct with benevolent character, something that all people could attain.

They concluded that true nobility was not found in wealth or power, but in kindness and generosity to our fellow man.

For the "prince of the humanists," Erasmus of Rotterdam—whom we met in Chapter 2 and have encountered throughout this book—the educational project was explicitly social. His *Colloquia*—a word that means "dialogue"—was the most important educational book in Europe for two centuries. His dialogues showed students, through instruction and example, better and worse behavior. What should be avoided? What is the recipe for a harmonious and tranquil life? What are our obligations to other members of society? Erasmus explores these questions and many more.

For example, in one colloquy, Erasmus composed a conversation between a young man and a prostitute, something that would surely scandalize many parents today. This colloquy was a model for young men on self-control: how to resist self-indulgent temptations and decline the salacious propositions that they were sure to encounter in life. Erasmus wanted to prepare children for the world that was, and not shelter and patronize them. He wanted to give them stories and examples that taught them the art of social life, and how to engage with the world wisely and with grace.

Francesco Patrizi, a humanist and proponent of this model of education, was among the first Western thinkers to call for *all* citizens in a republic to have the opportunity to obtain an education. Patrizi argued that we possess by nature an *affectio generalis*, or a general affection, that is in tension with our tendency toward selfishness and evil. A proper education cultivates this affection: it trains our minds and hearts to love and show kindness toward all of humanity—especially those we do not know, those who are not like us, and those who cannot do anything for us in return—an idea we just explored in our chapter on hospitality.

Again, education in the humanities, according to the Renaissance humanists, is what helps us diminish our tendencies

toward cruelty and to better respect our fellow persons. It cultivates our *humanitas,* or civility or "love of humanity," and keeps
our *immanitas,* or "savagery" or "cruelty"—our *libido dominandi*
and inner Gilgamesh—at bay. This pro-human ideal is also embedded in our language: the opposite of the Greek word *polis* is
idiótes, which means "private" or "individual" and which gives
us our modern word "idiot."

Renaissance humanists, writes Harvard intellectual historian James Hankins, recognized that a free and noble man—an
ingenuus—loves his fellow human beings; only narrow and perverse individuals hate their own kind. As the opposite of *humanitas*
is *immanitas,* the opposite of *philanthropia* is *misanthropia,* which
means "hatred of mankind." Such sentiments are expressions of
our self-love at its under-cultivated worst. Being human means
being fit for life with others, which requires that we cultivate our
humaneness. Post-Renaissance thinkers have noted this too. For
example, Adam Smith argued that while beauty and kindness
to others can be subjective and context-dependent and can take
many different forms, cruelty and inhumanity to our fellow man
is objectively ugly and condemnable.

Civility, the Liberal Arts, and Civics Education

The relationship between the *humanites* and civics education is
largely underrecognized today. But in the past, these two ideas
were inextricably connected. In a way that echoes our chapter
on integrity, *paideia, philanthropia, humanitas,* and civility linked
private character with public conduct, and connected inner disposition to outer actions. The humanities was the education of
a citizen. To people in ancient Greece and Rome and in Renaissance Europe, these ideas were an essential part of building
and sustaining the early democratic and republican systems of

government. These eras also provided the basis and inspiration for modern forms of democracy. Reclaiming these older notions of civility can help preserve and sustain modern democracies and free and flourishing human communities today.

Older models of learning were premised on three core ideas: learning by formal instruction, by example, and by practice. They sought to cultivate "right belief" in students, and from that right belief instill habits of "right action." We explored this theme in our chapter on integrity as we discovered how our character and actions inform and form one another. Each of these three modes of learning reinforces the others. Bringing these modes of instruction together serves the overarching aim of countering our selfish natures. To better understand the modern application, let's turn to a modern example of education in *paideia, humanitas,* and civility in practice: Great Hearts Academies.

Great Hearts Academies

Great Hearts, a network of classical charter schools, operates within the public school system. They differ from most public schools in some important ways. Primarily, as classical schools, they seek to revive the humanizing elements of the classical Greco-Roman world and apply them to their educational model today. Great Hearts aims to reorder the loves, as St. Augustine would say, bringing about a fundamental reorientation of our priorities. We must counter our self-love by practicing the habit of putting others, our fellow humans, before ourselves. In other words, as we've just discussed, the network aims to revive *paideia, philanthropia, humanitas,* and civility.

The Great Hearts schools follow C. S. Lewis's formulation of education. Echoing Plato and Aristotle, Lewis argues that the aim of education is a well-formed soul, which is in balance when "the head rules the belly through the chest." The head, or wise part of the soul, must oversee the belly, or appetitive part, through the chest, or courageous part of the soul.

Great Hearts serves twenty-one thousand students from kindergarten through twelfth grade across three cities in Arizona and Texas. The fundamental premise of the curriculum is that, as human beings, we are born with a tension between our deeply social and self-interested natures. We yearn for love and friendship, and yet are born with the *libido dominandi* and inward curve upon the self that frequently foil relationships. The classical model of education is an important and time-tested means of helping students overcome their selfish natures by exposing them to, and helping them cultivate a love for, the goodness, beauty, and truth that can be found in literature, poetry, philosophy, and art. Such things help to soften the rougher edges of human nature. They help to humanize us, and in so doing, help us recognize and appreciate the humanity in others.

Great Hearts' curriculum instills virtue in students through practice and learning. For example, learning the precision of a mathematical proof helps students cultivate their reasoning abilities by perceiving the logic underneath any form of argumentation, while sketching the petals of a flower with constant attention to light, lines, and form helps a student "unself" by encountering beauty. For Great Hearts, a well-trained mind is one that has overcome the ego and learned to view the self in relation to the wider world.

Great Hearts encourages the development of virtues—habits of mind and body—that lead students to desire what is good. Yet the schools acknowledge that no education is guaranteed to make a student perfectly civil or humane. This is especially true given the examples we have seen throughout this book—those who enjoyed an education that gave them taste, culture, and erudition, but were ruthless.

Some of history's greatest teachers produced bad students. Socrates, one of the wisest men who ever lived, taught Alcibiades—a vain general who managed to fight on three sides of the same war. He betrayed his home of Athens, which led to them being subjugated under Spartan rule for decades. Seneca, a Roman Stoic and lover of virtue (though deeply flawed himself), was the teacher of Nero, a megalomaniacal Roman emperor who eventually forced Seneca to die by suicide.

Great Hearts is merely one example of an institution that is reviving and cultivating the concepts of *philanthropia* and *humanitas*—and with them, civility—by embedding them in the very core of their curriculum and style of teaching. Through such a well-rounded education, the baser and vicious elements of our nature can be mitigated, and the more noble and virtuous aspects of the human personality fostered.

Classical Learning as a Tool of Healing and Equity

Great Hearts is not the only group that believes that creating a more just, equitable, and unified future in America depends on the revival of the liberal arts—the arts that make us free—and the humanities—the studies that help us become not only *human*, but *humane*. Others have recognized and continue to recognize this possibility of classical and civic learning to help make us better citizens, and to help heal the deep divides in our nation. Two important twentieth-century American leaders—Dr. Martin Luther King, Jr., and Robert F. Kennedy—did so, too.

Dr. King's "Letter from Birmingham Jail" reveals his intimate familiarity with the liberal arts tradition. In arguing against the evils of racial segregation in America, he knew that he had historical allies to help make his case. For instance, Dr.

King cites Socrates no fewer than three times in his letter. He writes, "I would agree with St. Augustine that 'an unjust law is no law at all.'" He invokes Thomas Aquinas: "To put it in the terms of St. Thomas Aquinas: An unjust law is a human law that is not rooted in eternal law and natural law."

The humanities and liberal arts traditions draw strength by building on the past. Great thinkers—from Socrates, to Augustine, to Aquinas, to Martin Buber, to Dr. King—were all familiar with the ideas of those who came before them. Their work and thinking are clarified, refined, and strengthened by engaging big questions in life: What is justice? What does it mean to be human? What is the best way to live? Their familiarity with how wise people across history had answered these questions before them helped them answer these questions for themselves, and having formulated answers to these questions helped them develop a clarified vision of the good and the just.

> *Education does not mean teaching people to know what they do not know; it means teaching them to behave as they do not behave.*
>
> —John Ruskin, nineteenth-century English writer

The above quotes from Dr. King's letter represent merely a few examples of the many thinkers and ideas that Dr. King imbibed and was influenced by, and in turn invoked in his battle against the evils of racial segregation. We can learn from Dr. King, and harness the power of intellectual history and humanistic tradition to elevate our conversation and pursue justice and equality in our world today.

Robert F. Kennedy also offers an example. In the wake of his brother's assassination in 1963, Jacqueline Kennedy gave him a copy of Edith Hamilton's *The Greek Way*. He devoured that and many more of Hamilton's books, in which he found consolation in a time of crisis. He had so immersed himself in the classical world that he instinctively turned to its wisdom just a few years later, when he found himself confronting yet another assassination.

Five years after the death of his brother, on the evening of April 4, 1968, Kennedy was scheduled to speak to a predominately African American crowd in Indianapolis, Indiana. Shortly before he was set to offer his remarks, he learned that Dr. King had been assassinated. With little time to prepare, he took to the stage and gave a short but powerful speech of reflection and consolation—words that drew inspiration from thoughts offered by Greeks two millennia earlier. I encourage you to enjoy the whole speech for yourself, but a few words are worth repeating here. Kennedy said:

My favorite poet was Aeschylus. He wrote: "In our sleep, pain which cannot forget falls drop by drop upon the heart until, in our own despair, against our will, comes wisdom through the awful grace of God."

What we need in the United States is not division; what we need in the United States is not hatred; what we need in the United States is not violence or lawlessness; but love and wisdom, and compassion toward one another, and a feeling of justice toward those who still suffer within our country, whether they be white or they be black.

He concluded his remarks, "Let us dedicate ourselves to what the Greeks wrote so many years ago: to tame the savageness of man and make gentle the life of this world."

Kennedy's soothing words had a remarkable effect. While many cities across the country suffered violence as people mourned the loss of Dr. King, Indianapolis was spared—it appeared those who heard Kennedy's words went home in peace. We each have the opportunity to follow in Dr. King's and Kennedy's footsteps and to use our rich intellectual heritage to sow peace and healing in an era of hatred and division. We each have the chance to make life in this world a bit gentler, more humane, and more civil. We can do as they did and deploy the humanizing effects of the liberal educational tradition to create a more just, free, equal, and unified future.

The great secret of morals is love; or a going out of our own nature, and an identification of ourselves with the beautiful which exists in thought, action, or person, not our own. A man, to be greatly good, must imagine intensely and comprehensively; he must put himself in the place of another and of many others; the pains and pleasure of his species must become his own.

—Percy Bysshe Shelley, nineteenth-century English poet

Universals of Civility in Education

The liberating and humanizing ideas underlying the liberal arts can be found beyond the ancient Greeks and Romans. These ideas exist in other cultures too, because, as we've discovered, the principles of human flourishing tend to stay the same across the human experience. We've seen that there is a core of human wisdom—a number of timeless principles of civility—that people have come to independently across time and place.

The good school does not just offer what the student or the parent or the state desires, but it says something about what these three ought to desire. A school is fundamentally normative, not a utilitarian institution, governed by the wise, not by the many. It judges man as an end, not as a means; it cultivates the human spirit by presenting a complete vision of man as he lives and as he ought to live in all his domains—the individual, the social, and the religious. It teaches the student how to fulfill his obligations to himself, to his fellow man, and to God and his creation. Its understanding of man, therefore, is prescriptive—and its curriculum and organization allegorize the scope, the sequence, and the vision that all men must recognize and accept as fundamental if they hope to grow to their full human stature.

—David V. Hicks, contemporary American writer

As we discovered in Chapter 1, the oldest book in the world, written by the ancient Egyptian vizier Ptahhotep in 2350 BC, was an educational civility manual. And we have seen how Ptahhotep's wisdom was echoed by many thinkers and in cultural traditions throughout history, even cultures that had no familiarity with one another. The classical model of education—and its increasingly omni-cultural approach—is undergoing a revival in America right now, which is a hopeful trajectory for the future of civility in our nation. Great Hearts is cultivating a holistic view—one that David V. Hicks describes in the quote on this page—not only of personhood but of civility. These full visions of the human person and their role in the broader social fabric is one that more of our mainstream educational institutions can use.

Educating in Civility, Not Politeness

Educational options for training in the humanities and in civility are increasingly available to all. This is good news, because, as we've learned, the liberal arts tradition is essential to rebuilding civility. In our divided moment, we need civility—not politeness. Politeness, with its aim of smoothing over differences and helping us just "get along," can invoke control of others, encouraging them to fit a certain norm. Civility, by contrast, encourages truly respecting the personhood and autonomy of others, seeing our unified common humanity first and foremost, and recognizing that we still have duties to others even when our views and preferences might differ. In encouraging students to see the beauty and value in their fellow human beings, educators and parents have the chance to cultivate the tolerance of difference.

Educating in civility requires a motivational shift—one that prioritizes human dignity and respect for others, and changes how we treat and interact with others. And, as we learned in our chapter on integrity, right conduct reinforces right thinking. Educators must be conscious of the ways that their overt instruction is supported—or undermined—by their unspoken actions and behaviors. It's sometimes said that example is the best teacher. Instead of modeling performative politeness, we each have the chance to be educators in our own lives—within our own spheres of influence, and with the students and young people we interact with.

Educators can be tempted to focus on politeness at the expense of civility. It's easy to have the rules on posters on the wall, and to have students memorize lists of dos and don'ts. It's easier to enforce obedience to rules than it is to inculcate the unseen change in motivation and values that civility requires. Educators, however, must keep the goal of civility front of mind. The rules can be helpful in reinforcing certain basic norms of propriety, but, as we have seen, the rules alone are not enough: they can easily be manipulated by children and adults alike.

When our classrooms conflate civility with politeness—or when they focus on compliance with rules over cultivating the internal disposition of civility—students, especially the underprivileged, are harmed. Sociologist and professor at the Harvard Graduate School of Education Anthony Abraham Jack has documented the way that the rules actively divide and oppress disadvantaged students on college campuses today. Admittance and financial assistance are often not sufficient to ensure that a student from a disadvantaged background can both fit in socially and succeed academically. The rules on many college campuses are unspoken, yet these students must navigate them. Their privileged peers have lived with and breathed the rules since birth, and take them for granted.

Jack suggests that schools respond to this problem by being more transparent and welcoming and clear about expectations in social life—for example, by defining explicitly what office hours mean, and by providing social acclimation courses for freshmen. But it is far more important to simply place less emphasis on the rules in the first place. Schools must instead focus on fostering civility. The goal must be to cultivate a change in values and motivations so that students demonstrate respect for others, rather than simply give off an air of polish.

Education as Cultivation, and the Language of Civility

Throughout this book, we've explored the way that our language informs how we think about civility today. We've established that civility itself is the language of lived moral values. The idea that civility is a virtue to be cultivated—to be achieved through effort, practice, and education in order for one to live peacefully with others—is also embedded in our language. The words we use to describe "civil" and "uncivil" conduct follow a pattern: they evoke the imagery of taking raw materials and improving them with cultivation and effort. In this way, they mirror the process of education: taking the raw stuff of humanity and making it into something better, richer, and more fertile.

As we have seen, the word "civility" is related to the Latin word *civis,* the root of our words "citizen," "city," and "civilization." These ideas have an important trait in common: they are unnatural, they must be cultivated, and they must be maintained with effort. Education and civility are forms of cultivation and civilization. Both connote taking the raw state of humanity and pruning it to make it better. The opposite of civility and civilization, meanwhile, is barbarism—conduct that emerges from our baser nature, which has not undergone the process of refinement to make it fit for life with others, and which seeks to harm our fellow human beings instead of helping them.

The etymology of civility's synonyms—including "urbane," "refined," "suave," "sophisticated," and "courteous"—also capture the image of creating something better with concerted effort. Their opposites—words such as "mean," "vulgar," "brutish," "savage," "coarse," and "uncouth"—all describe states of being closer to nature, and suggest under-cultivation and under-education.

The word "politeness"—from the Latin word for "polish" or "make smooth"—follows this same pattern. Its inverse— "rudeness," which comes from the Latin *rudis,* meaning "raw" or "rough"—also connotes a lack of cultivation. Again, it invokes the image of taking raw material and polishing it to make it *appear* better. But, as we should be familiar with by now, polishing does not change the thing being polished: it's easy to follow the rules and still act viciously. An education in the humanities is important to reviving civility, because it fosters cultivation not just of a person's surface actions, but of their soul as well.

Creating Civil Ecosystems, Creating a More Civil World

My mother's core message to parents and teachers has always been that educating and influencing the next generations of citizens is a duty and a privilege we each bear. Each facet of influence in a child's life—parents, schools, teachers—has a part in this work, with each facet bolstering, or undermining, the others. Though my mother has reached millions of people with her work, her vision of change is fundamentally small-scale and localized. It's about creating little ecosystems that inculcate civility in new generations. Creating new cultures of civility often begins at home, with the moral norms of the family, as many ethical and cultural traditions have recognized. The cultural groundwork laid in the home is then reinforced and supported by a network of relationships that help children form sound habits of thought, practice, and ultimately character that sustain them for a lifetime.

> *When the family is destroyed, the eternal family laws are lost, and when the law is lost, lawlessness overwhelms the whole family.*
>
> —*Bhagavad Gita*

My home growing up—and my mother's home growing up with her mother, my grandmother—was filled with character-building interventions that were reinforced at every turn. My mother knew that once we stepped outside, we'd be subjected to any number of degrading influences. She understood that the home was the only part of our lives she could truly control. She flooded our home life with influences that filled our hearts and minds with uplifting and inspiring content. My mother taught these ideas—of civility, of its relationship to character, and of the duty of parents, teachers, and a child's broader community to foster it. But she also lived them in her own life, and practiced them with my brothers and me.

She knew that change starts small—at home, with the individual family, the individual child, and the little, steady practices, reminders, and habits that form a child's character. A child's character builds their life—and a single child's life can help direct the future of a nation and can change the world.

We each have a role to play in fostering civility in future generations. It begins with leading by example, and by upholding the timeless principles of civility grounded in human dignity. To continue the metaphor of civilization as a garden from Chapter 1, each person is a plot of fertile land within that garden. We each inherit a specific [agri]cultural context when we are born, and undergo a certain process of cultivation by means of the values, education, beliefs, and rituals of our society. This process of cultivation tills the rawness in our nature, and "brings forth" human possibility, as the etymology of the word "education" suggests. Each seed that is planted and cultivated in the soil of our soul is a value, habit, or ritual. After our first cultivation,

> *Manners are made up of trivialities of deportment which can easily be learned if one does not happen to know them. Manners . . . are the outward manifestation of one's inner character.*
>
> —Emily Post

we may look back and appreciate the wisdom of the seeds that were tended to. We may continue to nurture them and plant them in the lives of our children, in students, and in the people around us.

We may come to see other seeds as weeds—degrading norms, rituals of politeness that promote style over substance. These we can choose to uproot and change. We may sow new seeds altogether—better values, rituals, and habits—that are more aligned with the people we want to be, and with the society we want to produce. Above all, we realize that the garden of civilization of the past need not be the one of our present and future. Too often, people simply go through life without questioning, or even being aware of, the seeds in their gardens. When and if they have the chance to cultivate the fertile soil of new, younger lives, they merely plant the seeds that were planted in their own lives.

Whether or not we are mindful of it, we participate in an iterative, interconnected, interdependent process of cultivating our own gardens, and those of others, and the garden of civilization itself. We can, though, choose to uproot the invasive, toxic, barbaric weeds, such as the notion that some human life is of more value than others. We can elect to nourish the seeds and cultural values that bring us together, such as the value that all human life is intrinsically valuable, and that cruelty is not an option. Again, if such seeds don't exist, we can plant them, to the end of fortifying our relationships and our communities.

My mother's vision for a more humane and civil future is reminiscent of how Eleanor Roosevelt viewed a future with greater respect for human dignity and human rights. It is also a vision we can all adopt in our own lives, and on our own journeys to creating a more civil world for future generations. We must begin "in small places, close to home—so close and so small that they cannot be seen on any maps of the world," as Roosevelt said. Civility, personhood, and human dignity must be cultivated in small places, because it is not enough that they merely be *known*. They must also be *loved*, for it is only if they are loved that they will be *lived*.

How to create ecosystems of civility at home and in the classroom: a field guide for parents and teachers

1. Remember that the goal of education should be cultivating a love of our fellow persons, ordering our passions, and curbing our self-love so that our social natures might flourish. Remember the relationship between *paideia, philanthropia, humanitas*, and civility, and draw inspiration from this long-standing, comprehensive approach to student teaching and learning. Adopt a holistic view of education—one that cares about practical skills, but also about character and the disposition of the heart.

2. Model the disposition of civility for your children and students. They are always watching.

3. Help your children, from an early age, form habits of putting others first.

4. Instill the value that *being* good is always better than *appearing* good—and that civility is more important than mere politeness.

5. Remember that change starts close to home, and in the small places. A parent is a child's first and most important teacher. Almost everyone has little people in their lives over whom they have influence, and it's easy to overlook the great responsibility we have to the next generation. Don't take those moments of influence for granted. Make the most of those opportunities and use them to instill and model values of civility and love of others—not self-love or mere politeness. This is a way to practically love

and respect the little ones in your life—the calling of true civility—and to nurture future generations.

6. Have dinner at home together as a family. Teach children the prevailing customs of the day and of the culture you live in—for example, show them how to set the table and eat with a fork and knife, or with chopsticks, or with hands. But teach them to be humble and open when encountering people who have different norms, and to be skeptical of norms that degrade personhood. Remind them not to look down on others because of difference. Teach and model kindness toward our fellow human beings, the best education you can give the young.

12

Misplaced Meaning and Forgiveness

The Oscar-winning 1987 Danish film *Babette's Feast*, based on the 1958 novel by Isak Dinesen, is a story about love, beauty, and forgiveness—attributes we need more of in order to see ourselves through our divided moment, and into a more civil future.

An austere Protestant minister lives in a small town in Denmark with his two beautiful daughters in the late nineteenth century. He both models and imposes on them a life of self-denial. He denies them marriage by refusing their many suitors, and for one daughter, suppresses the opportunity to fulfill her creative dream as an opera singer in Paris. When the minister dies, the two daughters spend the remainder of their lives nurturing the small religious community he left behind. Over time, the community exchanges comity for bickering and bitterness toward one another for long-past offenses. The townspeople settle into a life of displaying outward acts of piety while internally nursing grudges and cursing the neighbors in the pews next to them. The sisters do not know how to respond.

One evening, a stranger named Babette arrives at the doorstep. Displaced from her home country of France in a time of civil unrest, during which she lost her husband and son, Babette requests refuge in exchange for serving as their housekeeper. They take her in. Though puzzled by the town's ascetic life, defined by rancid bacon, boiled fish, and stale bread, Babette is grateful for their friendship and hospitality in her time of need. One day, Babette receives a letter with some astonishing news: she has won ten thousand francs in the lottery, enough to enable her to live comfortably for the remainder of her days. She instead resolves to make a gift of her earnings to the sisters and the community, all of whom had showed her hospitality when she'd needed it most. Babette decides to prepare a special meal for them to thank them for their kindness. After some persuasion, they accept.

When the sisters and the townspeople see the exotic ingredients for the meal begin to arrive—a giant sea turtle, quails, and (heaven forbid!) wine—they agree to attend the meal out of respect for Babette. But in order to avoid temptation, they resolve not to enjoy it.

Babette invests weeks in preparing the meal. When the evening of the dinner arrives, an illustrious general, Lorens Löwenhielm, is in town. The townspeople sit down to eat, determined in their puritanical resolve. While they're at dinner, just

> *Mercy and truth, my friends, have met together. Righteousness and bliss shall kiss one another.*
>
> —General Lorens Löwenhielm, *Babette's Feast*

being together pricks long-standing wounds and grudges, and they begin to bicker, bringing up old grievances, gossip, and resentments against one another. But course after course, delicacy after delicacy—caviar, Veuve Clicquot champagne, turtle soup, and more—are prepared and served with great love, and the hardened hearts of the townspeople begin to soften.

Over the duration of the meal, their attachments—to grudges, resentments, hurts of the past—are displaced by a renewed love for their community. They surrender to the tenderness of old friendships, and to the joy of sharing a beautiful meal together. The townspeople leave the dinner table that evening changed. Being physically and emotionally filled enables them to forgive. The extravagant grace of the feast that Babette has prepared nourishes their bodies and their souls, giving them a renewed affection for one another. The evening of healing, unity, and harmony revives their strength and fortifies their motivation to participate in the tricky business of life together in community.

Babette's Feast reminds us of the theme that we began this book exploring: peaceful coexistence is challenging and fragile. It requires vigilant nurturing. This book began its examination of the soul of civility with the oldest story in the world and the oldest book in the world. The oldest story in the world, *The Epic of Gilgamesh*, described the timeless challenge to civility and to human community: the self-love and will to dominate others that is an indelible part of the human condition. The oldest book in the world, *The Teachings of Ptahhotep*, outlined the solution: the disposition of civility that requires us to sacrifice our desires for the sake of others.

Community and relationship are the highest end of the human experience, though they can easily devolve as our selfishness divides us, as the townspeople learned. But though civility is fragile and can be lost, *Babette's Feast* shows us how it can also be recovered.

Recovering Civility by Filling Our Emotional Reserves and Recovering Shared Loves

When the civic bonds of affection are strained—and when our relationships and communal life are defined by bickering and fixation on difference—we must cultivate rituals of personal rejuvenation outside of the divisions that define our world. We must rediscover shared passions beyond the battles that deplete and exhaust us. We must refresh our inner reserves, as the townspeople were refreshed by Babette's feast, so that we can reenter life together with strength and grace.

We've learned throughout this book that civility doesn't mean avoiding difficult conversations or ceasing to fight for our convictions. That's the stuff of politeness, which smooths over our differences as opposed to dealing with them head-on, and is never enough to meaningfully, sustainably resolve deep-seated conflict.

Civility requires us to keep the dignity and personhood of those we disagree with front of mind. Running from disagreement, or pretending differences don't exist, is not an option. Being overcome by the battles and chaos of the world is a recipe for despondency. Building habits of personal renewal involves recovering pursuits that nourish our souls. This is essential if we're to have sufficient emotional and personal stamina, fortitude, and mercy to do life together well, and to navigate the deep challenges of our day.

Our Divided Moment

Today, simple, everyday decisions—such as what newspapers we subscribe to; where we send our children to school; where, whether, and how we worship; what sporting teams we support; and where we get our coffee or buy our running shoes—have divisive, political valence.

In recent years, many high-minded people have made worthy efforts to help people be "nicer" to one another, and to promote "reaching across the divides." These initiatives are not enough to aid us in our challenging position. We need to recover pursuits and activities that have nothing at all to do with politics. We've "overdone" democracy, and the political project in general, by making them too central to our lives.[1] In overdoing democracy and the public sphere, we undermine them.

We've allowed too much of our daily lives and mental consciousness to become saturated with political content and activity. As traditional touchstones of meaning—church, family, community—have declined in recent decades, people are now turning to politics to derive their meaning in life. Because people are deriving their meaning from their own political views—as well as assessing the value of others based primarily on *their* politics—it is becoming impossible to talk rationally about issues in public life. It's time to put politics back in its proper place.

Instead, we can reclaim our mental territory with activities that give us life, and don't exhaust and deplete us. When we're emotionally exhausted, we're less likely to show grace, and more likely to see offense and infer malicious intent where it wasn't meant. People empty their emotional reserves by having hatred-laden arguments or by trying to change circumstances in the world around them that are beyond their control. Too many misplace their meaning in politics, which means disagreements are interpreted as threats that undermine their very existence. The result is that we are hypersensitive and less equipped with the forbearance to tolerate difference, and are left with a weakened ability to navigate disagreement with grace.

When politics is the primary lens through which we view the world—when our own political beliefs are the most important things in our lives—it makes it easier to dehumanize those who disagree with us, and to justify cutting people out of our lives and out of society. Civility doesn't require us to check our convictions at the door. It simply requires that we keep the personhood and equal moral worth of others front of mind—including that of those with whom we vehemently disagree.

The result of too much politics is our toxic modern public discourse, and a deteriorating public and private life. Friends are cutting off friends, and family members are cutting off one another over political differences. Companies take stances on every political issue, because "silence is violence." Customers either patronize or boycott companies for taking those stances. Every apolitical happening—including, for example, the tragic fire that badly damaged Notre-Dame Cathedral in Paris—becomes a Rorschach test. Media pundits and columnists overlay the story with a message that affirms their own political beliefs, and those of their audience.

What else does this craving, and this helplessness, proclaim but that there was once in man a true happiness, of which all that now remains is the empty print and trace? This he tries in vain to fill with everything around him, seeking in things that are not there the help he cannot find in those that are, though none can help, since this infinite abyss can be filled only with an infinite and immutable object; in other words, by God himself.

—Blaise Pascal, seventeenth-century French polymath

Overdoing politics has crowded out all other personal, civic, and communal good, and contributed to our public division and toxicity. Recovering politics requires recovering civility—an appreciation of personhood and our duties to one another. It also requires us to recover our love for things *other* than politics, and to put politics in its proper place. To do this, it's not enough to merely insist that we remove the influence of politics from our lives and minds. That's not possible, and there are important and just causes worth defending and fighting for. We must first desaturate our lives of politics, and then fill in life-giving, soul-enriching pursuits that will make civility, and our politics, both better and possible.

Nineteenth-century Scottish theologian, pastor, and philosopher Thomas Chalmers outlined an ecology of the human soul in his essay "The Expulsive Power of a New Affection." Human beings are built to *love*, he says. We have an inner emptiness, a soulish craving, that we seek to fill with our love of this or that. Sometimes, we fill our inner emptiness with loves that are harmful to us and others. If we desire to love something less, we cannot just empty the heart of the old love. We must replace it with something else. "Nature abhors a vacuum," he writes. "Such at least is the nature of the heart, that though the room which is in it may change one inmate for another, it cannot be left void without the pain of most intolerable suffering."

Chalmers argues that there are two ways to replace old affections with better ones. The first is to become disgusted by the old love and to withdraw from it. But this still leaves the problem of the vacuum—the empty hole in our soul and life. The second way—and the more powerful—is to confront the heart with something *more* beautiful, so that attachment to the old affection fades.

To his Christian audience, Chalmers advises displacing one's love of sin and of the earthly world with the beauty of the divine and transcendent, an entity "more worthy of attachment." Shifting our affection to something nobler, higher, and worthier of our love will prevent people from falling into bad habits with old, harmful affections. A person's "new affection"—for God or something else—will displace and expel the old, ignoble affection.

When it comes to our unhealthy love of politics—our misplaced meaning in public life—we can't just snap our fingers and make our harmful affection vanish. It won't stay vanished on its own. We must replace it with a more beautiful, life-giving

There are two ways in which a practical moralist may attempt to displace from the human heart its love of the world—either by a demonstration of the world's vanity, so as that the heart shall be prevailed upon simply to withdraw its regards from an object that is not worthy of it; or, by setting forth another object, even God, as more worthy of its attachment, so as that the heart shall be prevailed upon not to resign an old affection, which shall have nothing to succeed it, but to exchange an old affection for a new one.

—Thomas Chalmers, nineteenth-century Scottish theologian

love. We need an enduring *motivation* to keep the old, harmful love in its place and out of our lives. Our bonds to old habits and addictions can be permanently broken only when we have replaced them with better habits. We can replace them with better ones only when we have the vision of something more true, good, and beautiful to love and pursue.

Chalmers's prescription—to displace love of sin for love of God—is Christian in nature, but there are secular examples of this "theory of displacement." Atheist philosopher Auguste Comte believed in "literary hygiene," a sort of Gresham's law for books and ideas. Instead of the notion that "bad money drives out good," literary hygiene's mantra, similar to Chalmers's idea, suggests that "good loves drive out bad." Only a taste for good books and ideas will permanently supplant a taste for inferior ones.[2]

Chalmers and Comte make an important observation about human nature. It's not enough to simply eradicate a preexisting toxic affection such as an overfixation with politics. We must reclaim the territory that politics holds in our lives and fill it with something else.

But what?

As we depoliticize our lives, there are many more noble, life-giving pursuits that we can embrace instead. Intellectual curiosity, friendship, and a renewed appreciation for beauty are merely a few.

Civility is central to displacing our inordinate, unhealthy love of politics. As we've learned throughout this book, it helps us overcome our selfish natures so that our social natures can flourish. It reorients our priorities so that we care about our fellow human beings instead of political gains. Civility can also help us reclaim and recover other, better parts of our lives, to the end of greater personal fulfillment and, with luck, a restored civic life.

> *The heart must have something to cling to—and never, by its own voluntary consent, will it so denude itself of its attachments, that there shall not be one remaining object that can draw or solicit it. . . . The love of the world cannot be expunged by a mere demonstration of the world's worthlessness. But may it not be supplanted by the love of that which is more worthy than itself?*
>
> —Thomas Chalmers

Cultivating Curiosity

Curiosity has the power to help heal our divides.

"Nothing in life is humdrum," Arnold Bennett, author of *How to Live on 24 Hours a Day*, writes. *Everything* is interesting through curious eyes. Curiosity breeds curiosity, and curiosity fills our heart and nourishes our soul.

We learned this from Braver Angels, and from Great Hearts Academies, and from the many writers, thinkers, and philosophers quoted throughout this book, and from my mother: curiosity about the world around us displaces the self, and reduces the self-love that consistently destabilizes the human social project.

Curiosity is a disposition of fundamental wonderment about the world around us. It is a zealous interest in questions related to the human condition: Who are we? What is our purpose? What is our position amid the cosmos?

Curiosity requires the humility to recognize our natural limits as human beings, and to realize that we never have known, never can or will know all the answers to these and other important questions in life. More than that, it requires the modesty to respect that people will approach and answer these questions differently.

Curiosity begets curiosity. The more you know—about people, cultures, different ways of life—the more you *want* to know. "The appetite for knowledge grows by what it feeds on," as Arnold Bennett wrote.

The barriers to curiosity today are familiar and many: A toxic media culture that erases the nuance and complexity of life, reducing our world to one of good and evil, black and white. Public leaders who model moral certainty about matters that ought to be open to humble inquiry. Institutions with built-in biases toward maintaining the status quo instead of encouraging cultures that relentlessly ask questions. Even our biology—which prefers the comfort of certitude to the vulnerability of the unknown—seems to pose a challenge to the curious life.

The enemy of curiosity is certainty. We can cultivate curiosity by becoming comfortable with complexity. We can choose to reject easy answers. We can "unbundle" people and experiences, and choose to see the part in light of the whole. We can get a "daily dose of wonder"—an idea we'll return to later in this chapter—by encountering beauty and pondering the infinite mystery and complexity of the universe. Curiosity can help us get our eyes off ourselves and our small problems, and fill us with the humble recognition of the beauty of the world and others around us. It puts our small problems in perspective. It helps us recognize that we don't have all the answers, which can foster interest in the perspectives of people who hold different opinions than we do.

This is where civility and curiosity intersect. The more we stay mindful of all we do not know in life—the more we stay mindful of our own ignorance—the less likely we are to dismiss those we disagree with as ignorant or evil. We are empowered to see people as they really are: magnificent and complex yet fallible, simultaneously capable of both greatness and wretchedness. Curiosity endows us with the perspective that *everyone*—no matter their opinions, education level, or background—has something to teach us. The more we stay open to all that the world, and those around us, can teach us, the more likely we are to treat others with the decency and respect that they deserve.

Knowing something isn't enough. To know it with one's head isn't the same as loving it with one's heart. As Blaise Pascal said of the difference between head and heart knowledge in his *Pensées*, "The heart has reasons that reason cannot understand."

There are many self-help, civility, and etiquette books that tell you they have the secret to winning friends and influencing people. They promise to teach you ways to be more polished, likable, and interesting. But as my mother taught, the best way to be both likable and interesting is to be *curious*—to have a disposition of wonder and humility that earnestly believes that every situation and person has something to teach us.

The Transformative Power of Friendship

In our opening chapter, we learned how Enkidu's offer of friendship to Gilgamesh transformed the latter from a cruel tyrant into a magnanimous friend. Gilgamesh was motivated and inspired to be a better person because of Enkidu's invitation into relationship. After their reconciliation, *The Epic of Gilgamesh* follows their adventures together until, quite tragically and suddenly, Enkidu falls ill and dies.

Gilgamesh tried desperately to keep his friend alive, and was utterly destroyed when he finally died. Gilgamesh grieved for a full week, in denial over his friend's death until a maggot crawled from Enkidu's nose. Devastated, Gilgamesh is determined to defy his own mortality, and begins a journey to attain everlasting life. Along his

"My friend Enkidu, whom I loved so dear, who with me went through every danger, the doom of mortals overtook him.

"Six days I wept for him and seven nights: I did not surrender his body for burial until a maggot dropped from his nostril. Then I was afraid that I, too, would die. I grew fearful of death, so I wandered the wild.

How can I keep silent? How can I stay quiet? My friend, whom I loved, has turned to clay. My friend Enkidu, whom I loved, has turned to clay. Shall I not be like him and also lie down, never to rise again, through all eternity?

—Gilgamesh, mourning the loss of his friend Enkidu

journey, Gilgamesh realizes that his friendship with Enkidu was what gave his life joy, and that immortality without friendship isn't a happy prospect at all. Realizing that the fulfillment of his life in friendship with Enkidu cannot be replaced, Gilgamesh accepts his mortality, but still resolves to find meaning in the reminder of his finite days.

As it did for Gilgamesh, recovering friendship can transform both ourselves and our world. We've explored throughout this book the notion that recognizing the humanity and inherent dignity of those around us is the basis of civility and of a truly civilized society. It is a necessity to *survive* as a species. To *thrive*, however, we need something more. We need friendship.

"Friendship is unnecessary," C. S. Lewis wrote in *The Four Loves*. While it has no explicit *survival value*, it is instead something that

> *I have no duty to be anyone's friend and no man in the world has a duty to be mine. Friendship is unnecessary, like philosophy, like art, like the universe itself (for God did not need to create). It has no survival value; rather it is one of those things which give value to survival.*
>
> —C. S. Lewis, twentieth-century English literature professor and author

gives *value to survival*. Friendship, like art, can flourish only after our basic needs are met, when we are in a position of relative safety and stability instead of in a state of war against our fellow man, nature, or ourselves. Such goods are what constitute civilization.

Friendship, like curiosity, requires vulnerability, a trait our current culture abhors. In avoiding vulnerability, we avoid true friendship, but we also become less ourselves, less human.

In recent decades—as a survivalist, high-stakes, life-and-death perspective has dominated our discourse—friendship has suffered. As a result, our society has, too.

To love at all is to be vulnerable. Love anything, and your heart will certainly be wrung and possibly be broken. If you want to make sure of keeping it intact, you must give it to no one and nothing, not even an animal. You must carefully wrap it round with hobbies and little luxuries and routine and avoidances of entanglement, and then lock it up in the casket or coffin of your own selfishness. And this means that in the long run, the alternative to tragedy, or at least to the threat of tragedy, is damnation, for in that casket—safe, still, and unventilated in the darkness—it will go bad; not broken, but finally unbreakable, impenetrable, resistant to all good and joy. . . .

—C. S. Lewis

Friendship is a basic affection for others, a trust placed in them that allows us to fulfill our abiding need for community. As we've discovered throughout this book, human beings are self-loving yet social. We can only flourish as a species when we subvert our egos so that our social natures can flourish in community.

In recent decades many thoughtful people have been concerned about the deterioration of American civic life, and about the rise in loneliness, suicide, and "deaths of despair." Amid these compounding crises of loneliness, we can each use the power of friendship to be part of a better world—one more firmly grounded in empathy, compassion, and affection for our neighbors and fellow citizens. We're often too utilitarian in how we live our lives. We focus only on what we get out of a relationship, instead of what we can give—a recipe for unhappiness.

St. Augustine told us that curbing the *incurvatus in se,* the inward curve upon the self in our nature, and the *libido dominandi,* or the lust for domination that defines human nature, begins with reordering our loves—with combating the instinct we each have to meet our own needs before those of others.

Both the *incurvatus in se* and the *libido dominandi* are manifestations of humankind's fundamental self-love. Both help explain much of our modern psychological malaise, from the loneliness crisis, to the prevalence of incivility in our public life, to disastrous levels of political polarization, to the collapse of our national identity. They are the enemy of the sacrifice that leads to joyful and fulfilling lives through relationship and human community. We don't need more efforts to encourage people to be selfish with their time and more selective with their friendships. We do that naturally—and to our own detriment. Our personal fulfillment and happiness are not the end and purpose of friendship—nor of life in general.[3]

When we cut people out of our lives because we disagree with them or they no longer meet our needs, we feed our self-love. We instrumentalize others, reducing them to their "function" in our lives. We disregard the infinite complexity of the human person. Many of us likely have examples of friendships that have been strained due to differences of opinion. Maybe some of us have been cut off, or have been tempted to cut others off, as a result of these differences.

> *One of the most beautiful qualities of true friendship is to understand and to be understood.*
>
> —Lucius Annaeus Seneca, first-century Roman philosopher

It's easy to be tempted to oversimplify others—defining them by their worst traits, or by the things that bother us most—instead of staying mindful of the complex nature of humanity. We each come to our beliefs for many reasons. Civility requires us to see and respect the humanity and dignity of others—including people unlike us, those who can do nothing for us, and those we disagree with.

Our contemporary social divisions have caused many people to end friendships or family relationships over differences in belief. This happens because we don't make the distinction between people's *views* and the people they *are:* our childhood best friend, our beloved aunt, our father, our grandparent. Keeping the relationship in mind—the history we have, the trust we've built, the memories of days gone by—can help us put our disagreements into perspective.

We must remember to "unbundle" people—to separate the person from their harmful view or deed. We don't have to approve of every aspect of another person, or agree on every public policy issue, in order to be friends with them. Unbundling people means resisting the urge to essentialize and define others based on one aspect of who they are, and countering our tendency to see everything in terms of black and white, right or wrong, good and evil.

Instead, unbundling others allows us to embrace the diversity and beauty of the human personality. It means choosing to see the *part* of a person in light of the *whole*, or seeing the things that bother us or that we disagree with in light of the dignity they hold as persons. It can be challenging to think in these nuanced terms—to hold multiple things to be true at once, and to see the virtues in others alongside their vices. But a tolerant society, and flourishing friendships, depend on trying to do so with a bit more frequency.

As both Aristotle and Cicero noted—and as we discussed in our chapter on civility and hyper-partisanship—friendship, and basic mutual affection, are vital not only to the health of the *civis*, but to ourselves. Cicero notes that the Latin roots of the words for "friendship" and "love" are the same. "Friend" in Latin is *amicus*, and the "love" in Latin is *amare*. This relationship is true in Greek, too. The word *philos* means "friend" in Greek, and *phileō* means "I love."

Socrates—someone I've "unbundled" by separating his good views from his bad—can teach us this. The Stoic philosopher Epictetus said that the most important thing we can learn from Socrates is how to have a debate without it descending into a quarrel. Socrates was open to engaging anyone, anytime—no matter how outlandish or immoral he thought their views. If we choose to follow Socrates' path, we can learn from his method: gentle, persistent questioning. He did not fume, nor berate or condemn his interlocutors. We can learn from Socrates how to keep discussions of important ideas amicable, and how to prevent them from ending important relationships in our lives.

The Overview Effect and the Sublime

Have you ever dreamt of going into space? If so, you're in good company. The cosmos has riveted the imaginations of explorers, scientists, and writers across human history. Yet only a rarefied six hundred people have left our atmosphere and encountered our galaxy firsthand. When they have, they've uniformly had the same permanently life-changing experience of looking back at planet Earth and being humbled in awe and wonder at the magnificence of what they see.

This is called the Overview Effect, a term coined by author Frank White in 1987. When people encounter the Overview Effect, White says, they are overcome by the oneness of the human race, and the arbitrariness of our differences. From the perspective of the heavens, divides in borders, language, religion, race, ethnicity, and socioeconomic status fade. People are made aware of their own insignificance, and of the smallness of our earthly problems. Their mindset is elevated, and their lives are forever changed.

As *Star Trek* actor William Shatner reflected on his experience of the Overview Effect during his space expedition, "It can prompt an instant reevaluation of our shared harmony and a shift in focus to all the wonderful things we have in common instead of what makes us different. It reinforced tenfold my own view on the power of our beautiful, mysterious collective human entanglement, and eventually, it returned a feeling of hope to my heart. In this insignificance we share, we have one gift that other species perhaps do not: we are aware—not only of our insignificance, but the grandeur around us that makes us insignificant. That allows us perhaps a chance to rededicate ourselves to our planet, to each other, to life and love all around us. If we seize that chance."

> *There are no borders or boundaries on our planet except those that we create in our minds or through human behaviors. All the ideas and concepts that divide us when we are on the surface begin to fade from orbit and the moon. The result is a shift in worldview, and in identity.*
>
> —Author Frank White on the Overview Effect

We may not all have an opportunity to go into space, but we each have the chance to experience the Overview Effect—and doing so can help us create a more civil present. We can each experience the transcendent, the sublime, in our everyday experience, which can elevate our perspectives, heal our souls, and give us the inner strength and grace necessary to do life together.

Being civil with people we do not like, and having difficult conversations that respect friendship, can be exhausting. We must regularly refresh and renew our souls. Pursuing activities that connect us with the sublime and beautiful instills within us transcendence and awe and enlarges our hearts. Beauty, transcendence, and awe—the "daily dose of wonder" that we discussed in our discussion of curiosity—can help fill the deep well of our souls. They give us the equanimity necessary to do this joint project of society.

Anticipating the remarkable power of the Overview Effect, Edmund Burke explored the relationship between the sublime, beauty, transcendence, and awe in his 1757 treatise *A Philosophical Enquiry into the Origin of Our Ideas of the Sublime and Beautiful*. We often use the term "sublime" to refer to something very pretty, or something we enjoy a good deal. But for Burke, the sublime was more than that. For him, encountering the sublime is an experience that reminds us of our smallness and insignificance: observing a ferocious storm, looking up at the stars at night, gazing on the beauty of a mountain—or looking down on Earth from the cosmos.

When we observe and encounter the cruelty, violence, wildness, vastness, and power of nature—the force of waves crashing on rocks, trees overturned by the wind, or the vicious, anti-life environment of space that William Shatner noted—we are made to feel like nothing. We're reminded of our profound fragility. This reminder of our smallness checks our ego, and helps us maintain a healthy perspective about our role in the greater world around us.

Encountering the sublime helps us keep the annoying and irksome aspects of daily life in their proper place. The sublime ennobles our souls and shrinks our egos and self-interested desires. We're better able to navigate and maneuver the often-grating nature of life together. We become more tolerant of difference, more open to other ways of looking at the world, and less handcuffed by the myopia of our pride. The sublime helps us to take the high and long view of life.

To better equip us for life together, we must build habits of introducing the sublime into our daily lives. After a long day at the office or an afternoon spent in traffic, we can rejuvenate ourselves by looking up at the stars at night, or reading a poem, or listening to a song, or contemplating a work of art that enriches our interior life. Recent research recommends pursuing daily doses of awe in order to help us harness the benefits of the sublime, from lowering stress levels to increasing creativity and overall well-being.[4] There are personal benefits—both physical and emotional—to encountering the sublime and the beautiful, and there are social ones as well.

> *Let us dedicate ourselves to what the Greeks wrote so many years ago: to tame the savageness of man and make gentle the life of this world.*
>
> —Bobby Kennedy

In *On Beauty and Being Just*, Elaine Scarry makes the case that we should harness the power of beauty to help nourish our souls and create a better, more just world. Scarry's first argument about beauty is similar to Burke's on the sublime. She asserts that encountering beauty moves the viewer away from the center of things. As we surrender and give way to the effects of beauty on our soul, it shakes up and shatters our ego. As our self-centeredness is displaced, we are more willing and able to see and empathize with others.

Second, Scarry states that beauty compels us to act. When we encounter it, we yearn to hold on to it, and to create more of it. We photograph, sculpt, or paint something exquisite in nature. We write a poem to capture a profound emotion. Beauty begets beauty. As we share beauty, we enlarge and enrich our souls, and those of others.

Third, beauty beckons us to pay heightened attention to our surroundings. Continued exposure to beauty cultivates our eyes and heart to see beauty everywhere, even in the less obvious places. A snowstorm calls us to examine the intricate details of a single snowflake. As the obviously beautiful trains our minds to pay attention to the often-overlooked beauty around us, it can prompt us to act justly toward those people in our lives we might overlook, but who still deserve our care and attention. As we see and appreciate the details of the people we are surrounded by—the color of their hair, the texture of their skin, the softness of their smile—we see the fullness of their humanity. We appreciate that they are people with dignity who deserve to be celebrated, not pawns to be used.

Lastly, the balance, proportion, symmetry, and harmony of beauty sensitizes our minds and hearts to notions of fairness and justice. The ancients argued that there is a unity of beauty, justice, goodness, and truth. If that is the case, as Scarry contends, it makes sense that if we get more of one, we get more of the others.

> *The question of Beauty takes us out of surfaces, to thinking of the foundations of things.*
>
> —Ralph Waldo Emerson

Twentieth-century Irish philosopher Iris Murdoch makes a similar point about the imperative to "unself." Murdoch believed in the power of beauty and nature to displace ourselves from the center of our universe, and to see others and the world around us as they truly are.[5] She gives the example of sitting at home, wrapped up in resentment and self-love, lost in a rabbit hole of her own anxiety and problems, and "brooding perhaps on some damage done to [her] prestige." Then, the simple observation of a kestrel, a small falcon, changes everything. Murdoch writes, "The brooding self with its hurt vanity has disappeared. There is nothing now but kestrel. And when I return to thinking of the other matter it seems less important." The power of art, beauty, and nature can "clear our minds of selfish care." The unselfing process cannot be forced, but can only be achieved by losing oneself in the self-forgetful pleasure that dissolves our selfish obsessions.

Life together is vexing. We each have a role to play in the partnership of living well that comprises society. But if we go too long without tending to our interior lives, the frustrations of life with others can make us cruel and savage. Our public life today is led by people who have become miserly because they've gone too long without encountering the beautiful to fill their emotional and spiritual well. In our fraught and divided moment, the sublime and the beautiful, nature and art, have the possibility to fill us up, nourish our hearts and minds, and guide us toward the good, the true, and the just. The sublime can calm the selfish and ferocious aspects of our nature, and make us gentler, kinder, and more open to doing the hard work of coexisting with others.

Here are some practices of self-care and leisure time I've found helpful in restoring the soul, and in nurturing and cultivating a rich interior life that is prepared to endure the ebbs and flows and vexations of life with others.

1. From time to time, reflect on what a gift it is to be human. You are a miracle.
2. Be gentle and kind to yourself. As you better appreciate your own humanity, you will begin to more habitually appreciate that of others.
3. Cultivate gratitude. Gratitude is the antidote to the fear, deprivation, and anxiety from which much incivility and

discourteous conduct originates. Grateful people are more joyful people—more emotionally and practically generous, and braced to endure the slings and arrows of the day.

4. Take a break from people and connectivity to the outside world. Take a retreat and a "digital fast," even if just for half a day. Remember, we can only have rich, vibrant lives with others if we have the solitude to discover who we are.

5. Incorporate an encounter with the sublime into your daily routine. Get your daily dose of wonder to keep your "fat, relentless ego" in check.

Maximizing Every Human Interaction

Encountering the sublime helps us think of ourselves less, and of others more—a lesson I learned from my Grandma Margaret. If scientists had set out to create the world's best Mary Kay saleswoman, they would have created my grandmother, Margaret Loughrin Johnston. On the one hand, growing up it felt as if my grandmother was always selling *something*. It didn't matter if she was retailing heathy chocolate or skin care in pink jars. She was always eager to share her hope in new products, or her Christian faith. On the other hand, I learned that for Grandma, it wasn't about the bottom line. It was about people.

Grandma's true passion was creating friendship and building community wherever she went. My mother and Joanna Taft are the same way. They taught me the value of making the most out of every interaction, that there is no such thing as an ordinary, casual human encounter. To my grandmother, no meeting with another person was neutral. Every exchange was an opportunity for her to bless others, and for her to share her hope and joy for life with them. She maximized every moment she had with others.

Grandma, always socially fearless, had no qualms about approaching a complete stranger. She treated everyone she met with the same dignity, kindness, and grace. Sometimes, people were taken aback by her extroversion. Who strikes up a conversation with a stranger at a coffee shop? Some people might even call that intruding into someone's personal oasis, a very *impolite* thing to do.

> *Wherever there is a human being there is a chance for kindness.*
>
> —Seneca

> *That kindness is invincible, provided it's sincere—not ironic or an act. What can even the most vicious person do if you keep treating him with kindness and gently set him straight—if you get the chance—correcting him cheerfully at the exact moment that he's trying to do you harm.*
>
> —Marcus Aurelius, *Meditations*

While she surprised some, Grandma Margaret's kindness brightened the days of countless others over the course of her lifetime. She saw life with others for the gift that it was, and never took a moment of it for granted. In a world plagued by darkness, loneliness, and a lack of hope, the intentionality that my grandmother brought to every exchange, and her fervor for cultivating friendships, undoubtedly made the world a brighter, more connected place.

The Mellifluous Echo of the Magnanimous Soul

We are all familiar—either personally, or through reading the news, histories, or memoirs—with the potential of a single individual, especially a parent, to make decisions that have unfortunate reverberations in the lives of those around them, often affecting generations. Generational trauma is often the cause of the tragic headlines we are greeted with each day.

Less frequently do we hear stories of the inverse: tales describing how one incredible, extraordinary human being, one magnanimous soul, produces positive consequences that reverberate across time. Such people have tremendous strength of character and raw determination. They act as their family's social glue and foundation. Through their lifestyle and cumulative decisions, they influence those around them—and the generations after them—for the better. These magnanimous souls, people of great personal strength and benevolence, live out a beautiful song—a song that produces a mellifluous echo in successive generations. They initiate a virtuous cycle that begins by building into the lives of those they meet, who in turn build into the lives of yet more individuals. My grandmother epitomized this type of life.

> *Every deed and every new beginning falls into an already existing web, where it nevertheless somehow starts a new process that will affect many others even beyond those with whom the agent comes into direct contact. . . . The smallest act in the most limited circumstances bears the seed of the same boundlessness and unpredictability; one deed, one gesture, one word may suffice to change every constellation. In acting, in contradistinction to working, it is indeed true that we can really never know what we are doing.*
>
> —Hannah Arendt

We each have the chance to make investments of our time

into relationships that can pay dividends for generations to come. When we consider the people who exerted the greatest positive influence on our lives, it's worth reflecting: Who influenced *them*? Who invested in them and helped them become who they are? No one exists in a vacuum. We do not become who we are in isolation. We come to our personality and identity because of the tragedies and the blessings in our lives. We can create legacies of beauty and grace—a mellifluous echo— that will reverberate across time and place, as my grandmother and mother did, and as I hope to do. We can each harness our capacity to infuse light and life into our every interaction by reclaiming our own spheres of influence, and strengthening our relationships and society one act of civility at a time.

The Hidden Reason Behind Incivility Now

My grandmother had an exquisite ability to see beyond someone's world-weary, calloused exterior, and to see them as a person first—someone who likely was in need of a word or act of kindness that day. Even if people brushed her off, she didn't take it personally: she knew it was more likely about them than a reflection on her. She appreciated an oft-forgotten truth: much aggression, hostility, and incivility that defines our contemporary culture originates from people's failure to see themselves as they really are—as beings with inherent, irreducible dignity and objective worth. Self-loathing and struggles with self-acceptance can often contribute to outbursts of anger, frustration, and other manifestations of incivility among people. An insufficiently robust appreciation of the dignity of the human person—an insufficiently high view of the beauty of one's own humanity—often expresses itself in frustration toward others. When people devalue themselves, they often devalue and disrespect the personhood and dignity of others. My grandmother had the uncommon ability to see past gruff, angry exteriors and to show kindness in response.

We also underestimate how much it means to others when we reach out to them.[6] This, combined with our instinctive negative response to hostility and rejection, means we often miss opportunities to foster friendship and community. We don't fully appreciate how receptive people are going to be to our bids for friendship. We undervalue how much our outreach means to people, and often fail to see how fulfilling a small positive interaction with others can be.

Adopting Grandma Margaret's approach, and her noble, compassionate view of others, takes work. Lashing out at people who lash out at us is the easy thing to do—but is often the least productive response. What kind of world could we create if only a few of us, in response to hostility, chose to see the wounded people beneath the hardened, uncivil exterior—and chose to repay cruelty with compassion and grace?

Unoffendability: The Superpower of the Twenty-First Century

In addition to being able to see the human beyond the gruff exterior, Grandma Margaret had a superpower, perhaps the most important of the twenty-first century: unoffendability. Grandma was utterly unflappable. It didn't matter how unkind someone was—she never retaliated. In our hypersensitive and polarized days, where people's emotional reserves are frequently depleted, we're constantly on alert, ready to detonate at a moment's notice. Often, hearing something we don't like can be the small trigger that puts us over the edge. As we've learned, civility demands that we tell others things they may not want to hear. That's what true respect means. Civility also requires that *we* accept things *we* don't want to hear.

It's easy to misconstrue people's words and actions as offensive—again, especially when we're running on empty. We interpret a thoughtless action as a malicious one, which puts us into fight-or-flight mode. Social rejection affects the brain in a way tantamount to physical pain, a response that has evolutionary roots: being expelled from the tribe meant almost certain death.

In addition to filling our emotional reserves so that we're less likely to take offense where it wasn't intended, there's something else we can do.

We can cultivate a superpower uniquely suited to our current moment.

We can choose to be *unoffendable*.

Instead of allowing a thoughtless or insensitive remark to cause us to lash out, we can choose to rise above it. Instead of letting social rejection cause us to be less willing to reach out to others in the future—or allowing that hurt to metastasize into anger and a source of further division—we can elect to keep giving and reaching out long after others would have given up. We can choose to keep making bids for friendship, and sowing seeds of civility and trust and community wherever we go.

> *Someone despises me. That's their problem. Mine: not to do or say anything despicable. Someone hates me. Their problem. Mine: to be patient and cheerful with everyone, including them.*
>
> —Marcus Aurelius

We can cultivate social resilience. When we allow ourselves to be hurt and offended by the words and actions of others, we give away our power. We can follow in the footsteps of the Stoics, such as Marcus Aurelius and Epictetus, who taught that we can choose not to be offended by the actions of others. We reclaim our power and autonomy when we respond to snubs or malice with kindness. We can each choose to be unoffendable, and to make the world a better, brighter, warmer, and more civil place.

How to Be Civil in a World That Values Politeness

As we've learned throughout this book, politeness is a technique. It's spectacle. It's content having the appearance of goodness without the substance of it. Civility, on the other hand, is means-oriented. It's a disposition of the heart. It sees people for who they are, not how they look. It's substance over style.

Civility is necessary for friendship, freedom, and flourishing. The world values politeness because it's useful for transient ends such as closing a deal, getting a job, or winning a date.

But if we want real and lasting and fruitful relationships—if we want harmony of the soul and society—we need civility.

How to Be Civil in an Uncivil World

Civility, as we've learned, is the basic respect we are owed by virtue of our shared dignity and equal moral worth as human beings. We owe this to others regardless of who they are, what they look like, where they are from, whether or not we like them, and whether or not they can do anything for us.

How can people committed to civility—and to the principles of decency, courteousness, and treating others with basic respect—succeed in a world of people who reject these ideals?

We've all encountered people who are willing to do whatever

it takes in order to get the upper hand. After those interactions, I've often thought: Was my commitment to civility in the face of incivility a handicap? Won't the person who is willing to go low—to throw off the shackles of decency and civility—always win out?

"How to be civil in an uncivil world" is a variation on an important question that people have been considering for a long, long time: How can a good person succeed in a world of evil?

Niccolò Machiavelli observed that in history, those who appear to have morals publicly, but privately dispense with values the moment they get in the way, tend to gain and maintain power. Machiavelli argued that the person who wants power must be willing to dispense with the moral bonds of civility if the need arises. While the civil person is constrained by their commitment to civility, the uncivil person can do whatever is necessary to win.

> *Politics have no relation to morals.*
>
> —Niccolò Machiavelli, sixteenth-century Italian political philosopher

Socrates took a different view. As we learned in our chapter on tolerance, Socrates said that justice and virtue are the health of the soul. If a person gets the better end of a business deal, wins an argument, or comes out on top of a political battle, but does so by cutting corners and being dishonest, he hasn't really "won" anything. His soul is unhealthy and sick. Socrates believed that anyone who acts with injustice does so out of ignorance—after all, who would willingly make themselves sick? Who would knowingly choose sickness of the soul?

Socrates argued that a just person has an excellent and healthy soul, and that the function of a just soul and person is to seek the same for others. People committed to civility today will respond to incivility by seeing the good in the uncivil. Those who dehumanize or debase others, and do whatever it takes to succeed, are hurting themselves most. But we can have compassion for these

Living well and living rightly are the same thing.

—Socrates

people and show kindness to them, knowing that, despite external appearances, they are suffering, whether they realize it or not.

Socrates and Machiavelli remind us of why we are civil in the first place. The reason to be civil isn't instrumental. Civility isn't merely a tool of success. Civility is instead a disposition, an outgrowth of seeing people as they really are: as beings with irreducible moral worth and deserving of respect. This is worthy for its own sake, even if it means we don't gain the upper hand in every business dealing.

Being uncivil is poisonous to the soul. When we treat people as means to our ends, it hurts and degrades them, and ourselves as well.

Machiavelli is famous for the amoral aphorism that "the end justifies the means."

Socrates would respond, "But what is your end?"

No earthly battle is worth compromising the health and life of our soul.

At the end of the day, we cannot control the civility or incivility of others. We can only control ourselves. Speaking to Professor Pangloss, the naïve Candide of Voltaire's novella offered a cogent response to the problem of evil in the world. It applies to how we might respond to incivility, too: *Il faut cultiver notre jardin.*

We must cultivate our garden.

Our duties to making the world better start at home, in how we live every day. We don't know what effect our efforts to elevate our own conduct today might have in the lives of others tomorrow. We cannot tell how the seeds of civility we sow in the lives of others now might grow and yield fruit years after we are gone. To cultivate any garden requires belief in and hope for tomorrow. It requires faith in things unseen—beneath the surface of the soul of our lives. Our faith can seem futile and misplaced—especially when all we see grow are the pernicious weeds that we must uproot daily. But just when we think all is lost, we see the resilient life of a small shoot puncture the surface of the soul, and are affirmed that our efforts are worthwhile.

Rediscovering the Power of Forgiveness

There are many serious and important topics in our era that demand action. To effectively have the conversations and create the plans to remedy the important issues of our day, we must reclaim civility, and the fundamental respect for others it commands, despite deep and profound differences. Civility requires respecting others by telling hard truths and engaging in robust debate. But we'll be able to have reasoned, productive, and robust debates only if we enjoy activities outside of politics that nurture our interior lives, and give us the inner strength to engage in the battle of ideas and public life with grace. We must reclaim pursuits and values—things such as curiosity, friendship, humor, and beauty— that bring us joy and give our lives meaning beyond politics. Our democracy, our freedom, and human flourishing depend on this.

Of course, this is easier said than done. There remain many open wounds from political battles in history, both recent and distant. How can they be healed? Even if a moment of healing and forgiveness occurs, what happens when grudges persist? William Blake tells us in his powerful poem "A Poison Tree" that wounds unattended to—spiritual, emotional, and psychological needs unmet for too long—fester and grow. Bitterness is herbicide for the garden of civilization. It attacks and corrodes the root of our souls, depleting us and leaving us nothing to give others.

Bitterness metastasizes hearts and minds, and emotions surface in harmful ways that may surprise us. We need the fertilizer of forgiveness to nourish us, and to allow us to nourish others, and to sustain the joint project of cultivating the garden of civilization. In helping us reclaim a high view of the humanity in both ourselves and others, civility equips us to have the candid, honest conversations that are necessary for healing. It's the water that enables the fertilizer of forgiveness to help grow and nurture our souls. Civility gives us a way to constructively communicate and

I was angry with my friend;
I told my wrath, my wrath did
*   end.*
I was angry with my foe:
I told it not, my wrath did grow.
And I watered it in fears,
Night and morning with my
*   tears:*
And I sunned it with smiles,
And with soft deceitful wiles.
And it grew both day and night.
Till it bore an apple bright.
And my foe beheld it shine,
And he knew that it was mine.
And into my garden stole,
When the night had veiled the
*   pole;*
In the morning glad I see;
My foe outstretched beneath the
*   tree.*

—William Blake, nineteenth-century English poet and painter, in his poem "A Poison Tree"

navigate our disagreements. Politeness, which papers over differences, is a breeding ground for resentment and bitterness.

This partnership of civilization requires us to show grace to one another—a thousand times in a thousand ways each day. It requires forgiveness.

After conflict, the human soul longs for reconciliation, heal-ing, and wholeness. Two people are needed for reconciliation, but sometimes both parties in a conflict aren't prepared for rapprochement. Thankfully, only one person is needed for forgiveness—a place of much freedom and joy.

One barrier to forgive-ness is feeling as if our short-comings are small compared to the wrongs done against us. Jesus Christ tells a par-able of a servant's huge debt forgiven by his king—only for the servant to turn around and call in another, far smaller debt owed to him, even throwing the debtor in prison for being unable to pay. The gracelessness of the ungrateful servant reveals that he did not allow the forgiveness of his big debt to penetrate his heart.

> *Hatred and anger are the greatest poison to the happiness of a good mind. There is, in the very feeling of those passions, something harsh, jarring, and convulsive, something that tears and distracts the breast, and is altogether destructive to that composure and tranquillity of mind which is so necessary to happiness, and which is best promoted by the contrary passions of gratitude and love.*
>
> —Adam Smith

This story shows that it is easier to forgive others when we remember the times when we've been forgiven. When we've been forgiven for misdeeds—and our innate self-love means we've all fallen short and hurt those around us—we have a duty to forgive others. Staying mindful of our own mistakes—and the forgiveness that we've been given—fills us with gratitude, and enables us to in turn forgive more freely.

Forgiveness doesn't mean forgetting. It doesn't mean allow-ing the same people to repeatedly harm us. Nor does forgiveness mean sweeping grievances under the rug, failing to confront the hurt in our own souls, or confronting others with the hurt they've done to us. Forgiveness requires accountability, personal responsibility. It sometimes means respecting ourselves and others enough to be honest with them about the harm they may have caused.

Often people may not know the grief they've caused. Others may know and not care. But at least we'll know that we've done all we can to respect ourselves and others. Our efforts to reconcile help us heal, forgive, and move forward in wholeness and with greater inner strength. We are freed from the bitterness that is the poison, the herbicide, to the tender soil of our soul.

We may think that anger gives us power. But in fact it drains us of it, because we are trying to change the behavior of others through harboring a lethal emotion. Maybe it's the Irish in my blood, but I have a long memory and sometimes find it difficult to forgive quickly—and to let past grievances stay forgiven. For some reason, it seems safer—and makes me feel less vulnerable—to stay angry instead of letting go. Often, hurts and frustrations I've endured manifest in unhealthy ways. At other times, I've found many life-giving outlets for the frustration—journaling, kickboxing, talk therapy—that have been helpful. But I've found that forgiving eradicates the root cause of the hurt, and is the ultimate solution.

Too often, it seems that people use woundedness as an excuse to lash out at others. They use their wounds to fuel their righteous anger, and justify harming anyone who gets in their way. People forget that violence—verbal, emotional, or physical—hurts themselves as much as it does others. It debases them. Harming others makes them less human. Our hurts are never an excuse to hurt others, and hurting others will never make the world a better place.

I fall short of the ideals of both civility and of quick forgiveness daily, and it often has negative consequences for how I interact with others. Without creating a fresh slate each day, it's easy to operate in the world hobbled, wounded and bumping into other wounded people without the grace and emotional wealth required for life with others. I continue to remind myself of these lessons, and have found encouragement in the words of the apostle Paul, who wrote "As far as it depends on you, live at peace with everyone."

As far as it depends on you. We are more in control of our emotions—and of our responses to our emotions—than we realize. When we fill our souls with endeavors that give us life, such as curiosity, friendship, and beauty—we are less likely to be litigious about the small things in life. We are less likely to walk through our every day running into and up against others—our self-love is less likely to bump up against the self-love of others. We are not on our own. We are not monads, and we don't live in a vacuum. Adopting a reverence for life in all of its forms, choosing to be kind to all living things, ennobles us and the world around us.

Conversely, when we harm others, even in the name of pursuing a greater justice, we, too, are also hurt. When we are hurt by others, as William Blake noted, we hurt ourselves if we choose to drink the bitter poison of resentment—when we let our anger fester—and fail to forgive. This is how Erasmus defined civility in his handbook for young people five hundred years ago. This principle of good living together in community, alongside the many others that we have explored in this book, is remarkably timeless.

Together, as we've discovered throughout this book, they comprise the soul of civility.

A Thank-you Gift

Gracious reader,

Your time is your most valuable possession, and as a thank-you for your investment in reading this book, I'd like to gift you with a two-month subscription to Wondrium, a platform that will foster your quest to make the world a better and brighter place, both now and for future generations.

Human beings live at the intersection of prediction and surprise. Our brains love predictability and take shortcuts to help us understand ourselves and the world around us. These assumptions are often useful, but sometimes wrong.

Learning new and surprising things helps us to break out of the mental models that tempt us to box in, essentialize, and label those around us. Intellectual exploration helps us change and grow, and by becoming new people ourselves, we appreciate the newness and greatness in those around us.

Enter Wondrium, which is a media streaming platform for the incurably curious, lifelong learners. Home of The Great Courses, it is a place where I have long nourished my mind, broadened my intellectual horizons, grown, and emerged out of my periods of excessive self-love and stagnancy to engage better with those around me.

I'm thrilled to give you TWO FREE months to enjoy Wondrium content. On Wondrium's platform, you can explore content from thousands of experts on virtually any topic under the sun that you've ever wanted to learn about. There, you can also try out my own televisual series, called *Storytelling and the Human Condition,* a globe-spanning, time-jumping, media-traversing tour of the human narrative tradition that helps us understand who we are and our place in the world. I was finishing the book and creating the series at the same time, which means that both projects harness the power of storytelling to help us appreciate the gift of being human, the role of storytelling and civility to humanize us and make us more humane, and also how both can help bridge our social, cultural, and political divides.

If you would like to infuse your life, friendships, and conversations with greater freshness and fun—if you want to get beyond the façade, the veneer, and the polish and enjoy authentic relationships with others—go to alexandraohudson.com/civilitygift to claim this gift.*

Go ahead and "Stuff your eyes with wonder," as Ray Bradbury memorably wrote.

You won't regret it. Happy learning!

—*Lexi*

*This offer is available as of the first printing of this book in 2023 and for the foreseeable future, but if you are reading this in some distant future era and are having difficulty claiming it, please reach out to the customer service team at The Great Courses/Wondrium at https://www.thegreatcourses.com/support/contact-us, and tell them Lexi sent you!

Thank you again for being here.

Acknowledgments

This book is the product of ideas that I have been reflecting on and grappling with my entire life, and was written over a period of nearly ten years. I became a different person over the course of creating this book, and I'm thankful to so many people who formed, taught, corrected, and encouraged me along the way.

Thank you to those who took the time to speak with me about these ideas, who read my work and offered feedback that helped make me a better thinker and writer—and who made this book stronger. Thank you to the people I have met, who have written to me, who disagreed with me, or who directed me to new writers, texts, and resources. You helped me change my mind, brought me closer to truth, and made this book richer, and more textured and nuanced.

To George Witte, for believing in this project when the rest of the world didn't, and for bringing out the very best of these ideas so that this book could be a useful tool for cultural healing and human flourishing. Thank you for your vision of what this project could be—a meditation on the timeless principles of civility. Thank you for allowing me the ample time and space to get all my thoughts on one (very long) piece of paper, and for your patience as I chiseled and refined my ideas so that they were in a form most likely to help readers think more clearly about civility in our world today. I'm grateful to have had the chance to work with an editor who is so caring, thoughtful, and wise.

Thanks to my agent, Mark Gottlieb, whose knowledge of and passion for the writing biz and support for my work is always a great help.

I am grateful to the design team at St. Martin's Press, especially the talented Young Lim, for helping create a cover for this book that brought to life its ideas.

To Emily and Charlie Dameron and Gabby and Sherif Girgis: thank you for your much-needed early encouragement with this project—reading and choosing to find and affirm the merit in the early pages of my often-incoherent, cobbled-together ideas. Thank you for the many conversations about first principles and the nature of the good life, and for being ever-present reminders of the high promise of friendship and life in relationship with others.

Thanks to Erik Satie and Antonín Dvořák for your creative genius, which provided tranquil and inspiring compositions that fostered my thinking, reading, and writing.

Thank you to the friends, mentors, and intellectual influences who encouraged me along the way with conversations, kind words, advice, and even reading and critiquing portions of my work: AJ Jacobs, Caroline Breashears, Les Lenkowsky, James Hankins, Francis Fukuyama, Eric Adler, John Kasson, Richard Boyd, Madeleine Will, and so many wonderful others.

My friend Tyler Cowen tried many times to persuade me against writing this book. "Only write a book if you feel like you have a disease and writing the book is the cure," he said. He is correct: creating a book is tough stuff, and his wise advice on this and many other aspects of my life and writing have been helpful. He helped me think critically about the purpose behind my writing the book, reminded me that I literally couldn't not write it, and was a great encouragement along the way. I'm thankful to him.

To Sherry Turkle: thank you for your generous criticism. You read an early draft of this manuscript in record time, and put civility into practice by telling me hard truths about where the book required improvement. You honored me by reading it, and honored both the project and the craft of writing by making this book better. As Dana Gioia said, "For a [writer], writing criticism is an act of generosity, a gift to the art itself."

Speaking of Dana: thank you for always pushing me toward excellence. You always remind me to keep my standards high, and my work ethic even higher. You forbid me from getting complacent. Thank you for reminding me to write the book I want—not the book that the market will bear. Thanks also for introducing me to Rainer Maria Rilke, Cyril Connolly, and countless other creators I'd never have discovered on my own. Learning from them and from you keeps me sharp. As Connolly said, "Better to write for yourself and have no public, than to write for the public and have no self." And "Art is made by the alone for the alone. . . . The reward of art is not fame or success but intoxication. . . ." Your encouragement to create for its own sake, to revel in the madness of art, keeps me honest and leaves me grateful.

To my wonderful friends Laura Morris, Hannah Stickney, Miranda Metah, Una Osili, Jeanne Reusche, and Joanna Taft— thank you for being constant reminders that life in friendship is worth the effort, and the richest life there is.

I'm thankful to my intellectual communities. The wonderful team at Braver Angels has for so long supported this project and my work, especially April Lawson, John Wood, and Mónica Guzmán. My friends at Young Voices helped give flight to my many, often heady ideas, and challenged me to communicate them in new ways to a mainstream audience. Thanks especially to Casey

Given and Stephen Kent for that. To my friends at the Liberty Fund, including Steve Ealy, Peter Mentzel, Hans Eicholz, Pat Lynch, and Leonidas Zelmanovitz, who invited me to conferences that exposed me to great thinkers, and to ideas I never would have encountered on my own, many of which ended up in this book. Over lunch one day, Steve, Peter, and Hans also graciously helped me make sense of a scrambled array of words and thoughts I had scribbled on a piece of paper—thoughts that I knew had some connection to one another, and which formed the body of this book. Thank you to each of you for your wonderful conversation, encouragement, ideas, and friendship.

Thank you to Wondrium, and the wonderful team at The Teaching Company, for creating content and a platform that helped me cover novel intellectual territory for this book—and for inviting me to create my course for you, *Storytelling and the Human Condition*, while also writing this book. Doing so encouraged me to harness the exceptional power of stories throughout this book, which I hope was a service to my readers.

Thank you to Tim Keller, whom I've never had the pleasure of meeting, but whose sermons have provided endless clarity and hope in a world and era of ambiguity and despair.

Thank you to Amir Pasic and Patrick Rooney at Indiana University's Lilly Family School of Philanthropy. I'm thankful for your inviting me into an institutional home with library credentials (!) and for your continued support of my work.

Thank you to other institutions that supported my research and work, such as the Achelis & Bodman Foundation. Thanks also to the Fund for American Studies, for selecting me to be a Novak Fellow, and especially to Roger and Mary Kay Ream for your friendship.

To Tim Swarens, my editor at *USA Today*, who allowed me to explore many ideas related to this book in my columns—and for always making my writing and thinking better.

To my father, for first introducing me to the beautiful, the good, and the true. Thank you for showing me the power of storytelling, as well as modeling for us the importance of solitude and the richness of the interior life and the life of the mind. In this vein, thank you to other great teachers and professors in my life—Dr. Yorguson, for teaching the International Baccalaureate higher-level history class that initiated a lifelong love affair with the wisdom of history. To Calvin Townsend and Darren Provost, for showing me examples of the thinkers and ideas that built our world. Like my father, you all taught me why it is important to love the beauty and truth in history and storytelling, you showed me where to find it, and you helped me understand how to embody and create it in the world around me.

To my mother, for giving me an impossible standard of grace, love, and forgiveness—the forgotten cornerstones of the human social project—to aspire to. Thank you for showing me what dauntless, courageous sacrifice for relationship is.

To Zuri and Sam, for being great brothers, and for reminding me to not take myself or my work too seriously.

To Kian, my first reader, collaborator, and encourager, my best friend, my beloved, and my favorite intellectual sparring partner—thank you for believing in me and this project. Thank you for the constant encouragement, the willing ear to listen to my ideas, and the critical eye that helped make my writing better. Nietzsche was wrong about many things, but he was right when he said that marriage is a long conversation. Creating this book is as much your success as mine, Kian; our constant dialogue about all subjects under the sun makes it difficult to know where your ideas end and mine begin. Thank you for always being up for hearing me verbalize a new connection, insight, thought, or idea—and for telling me honestly when it's crazy. Thank you for co-creating this work of art that is our life, marriage, and family.

To Percival James and Sophia Margaux, to whom I dedicate this book: I became a mother over the course of writing this book. Becoming a mother made me painfully aware of the preciousness and fleeting nature of time. The costs associated with writing and finishing this project—cherished moments away from my children—were high. They likely won't remember the time away from me, but I'll remember the time away from them. I am grateful to them for endowing me with the reason to start this project—to make the world a more tolerable and joyful place to live—and with the motivation to finish it. I hope it proves a worthy investment and helps improve the world that you grow up in.

And to the Civic Renaissance community, for offering feedback on many of the ideas that ended up in this book, for learning and covering new intellectual territory alongside me, and for your constant encouragement. This community of curious, lifelong learners eager to heal our world with the wisdom of the past, beauty, goodness, and truth will change the world, and I'm thankful to be on this journey with them.

Notes

Introduction

1. First names and an interest in etiquette aren't the only things that unite these Judiths. Incidentally, each of them also has ties to the state of Massachusetts. Judith Bowman's Protocol Consultants International is based in Boston. Judith Ré taught celebrated manners classes at the Ritz-Carlton Hotel in Boston. Judith Martin attended Wellesley College, and my mother began teaching her manners classes out of our home in Quincy, Massachusetts.

2. "Civility," Dictionary.com, accessed September 20, 2022, https://www.dictionary.com/browse/civility.

3. "Politeness," Dictionary.com, accessed September 20, 2022, https://www.dictionary.com/browse/politeness.

4. "Politeness," Johnson's Dictionary Online, accessed September 20, 2022, https://johnsonsdictionaryonline.com/views/search.php?term=politeness.

5. "Greatness, wretchedness. The more enlightened we are the more greatness and vileness we discover in man," Pascal wrote in fragment 443 of his *Pensées*. "Man's greatness comes from knowing he is wretched: a tree does not know it is wretched. Thus, it is wretched to know that one is wretched, but there is greatness in knowing one is wretched." (397)

1. A Timeless Problem

1. St. Augustine, *The City of God*, Preface. For a thoughtful discussion on Augustine's *libido dominandi*, see this blog post by teacher and historian Paul Kause: https://minervawisdom.com/2019/03/29/augustines-city-of-god-xi-understanding-the-libido-dominandi/.

2. Norbert Elias, *The History of Manners*, 120.

3. See *The Origins of Courtliness: Civilizing Trends and the Formation of*

Courtly Ideals, 939–1210 by C. Stephen Jaeger for more commentary on Elias's sources and oversights.

4. Rod Aya, "Norbert Elias and 'The Civilizing Process,'" *Theory and Society* 5, no. 2 (1978), 219–28, http://www.jstor.org/stable/656697.

5. Joseph W. Kane and Adie Tomer, "Parks Make Great Places, but Not Enough Americans Can Reach Them," Brookings Institution (August 21, 2019), https://www.brookings.edu/blog/the-avenue/2019/08/21/parks -make-great-places-but-not-enough-americans-can-reach-them/.

6. "Woodrow Wilson Foundation Finds Only One State Can Pass U.S. Citizenship Exam," Woodrow Wilson National Fellowship Foundation (February 15, 2019), https://woodrow.org/news/one-state-pass-us -citizenship-exam/.

2. A Timeless Solution

1. For more on *The Teachings of Ptahhotep*, see *The Literature of Ancient Egypt: An Anthology of Stories, Instructions, and Poetry* by William Kelly Simpson et al. (Yale University Press: 2003).

2. Asa G. Hilliard et al., *The Teachings of Ptahhotep: The Oldest Book in the World* (Blackwood Press: 2012).

3. Neelakanta Maharaaj, *The Art of Success Derived from Hindu Scriptures* (January 2020), https://books.google.com/books/about/The_Art_of _Success_derived_from_Hindu_Sc.html?id=vrNoEAAAQBAJn.

4. Terry L. Papillon, translator, *Isocrates II*. (University of Texas Press: 2004).

5. Isocrates praised Egyptian customs, laws, and ways of life, suggesting that Greeks who followed their example would be wise. See *Isocrates with an English Translation in Three Volumes* by George Norlin (Harvard University Press: 1980).

6. George Norlin, *Isocrates with an English Translation in Three Volumes* (Harvard University Press: 1980).

7. Amy Olberding, *The Wrong of Rudeness: Learning Modern Civility from Ancient Chinese Philosophy* (Oxford University Press: 2019), 28.

8. Petrus Alfonsi, *Disciplina Clericalis*, 5.

9. Ibid 42.

10. Ibid 104.

11. Ibid 111.

12. I appreciate this quip from John Gillingham's masterful essay "From Civilitas to Civility: Codes of Manners in Medieval and Early Modern England," 2002, Transactions of the Royal Historical Society, Sixth Series, https://www.academia.edu/36985633/From_Civilitas

_to_Civility_Codes_of_Manners_in_Medieval_and_Early_Modern _England.

13. For an excellent reflection on *Urbanus Magnus* by Daniel of Beccles, see *The Making of Manners and Morals in Twelfth-Century England: The Book of the Civilised Man*, Routledge 2017.

14. Thomasin von Zirclaria, *Der Wälsche Gast (The Italian Guest)*, trans. Marion Gibbs and Winder McConnell (Western Michigan University: 2009).

15. Fraser James Dallachy, "A Study of the Manuscript Contexts of Benedict Burgh's Middle English 'Distichs of Cato,'" (2013), http://theses.gla.ac .uk/4179/1/2013dallachyphd.pdf.
    Richard Hazelton, "Chaucer and Cato," *Speculum* 35, no. 3 (July 1960), 357–380, https://www.jstor.org/stable/2849730.

16. http://sites.fas.harvard.edu/~chaucer/special/authors/cato/cat-fran.html.

17. https://founders.archives.gov/documents/Franklin/01–02–02–0017.

18. John Gillingham, "From Civilitas to Civility," *Transactions of the Royal Historical Society* (2002), https://www.academia.edu/36985633/From _Civilitas_to_Civility_Codes_of_Manners_in_Medieval_and_Early _Modern_England.

19. Norbert Elias, *History of Manners*, 79.

3. Integrity

1. For more on the delightful Shaftesbury, see "Shaftesbury on politeness, honesty, and virtue" by Michael B. Gill, accessed May 4, 2023: https:// michaelbgill.faculty.arizona.edu/sites/michaelbgill.faculty.arizona.edu /files/Shaftesbury%20on%20Politeness,%20Honesty,%20Virtue.pdf

2. For Anna Delvey's fuller story, see Jessica Pressler's longform reported article "How Anna Delvey Tricked New York's Party People," The Cut (May 2018), https://www.thecut.com/article/how-anna-delvey-tricked-new-york.html.

3. "Announcing Fyre Festival," YouTube.com (January 12, 2017), https:// www.youtube.com/watch?v=mz5kY3RsmKo.

4. Ibid.

5. Eric Levenson and Deborah Bloom, "Fyre Festival: When a $12,000 Luxury Festival in Paradise Turns into Chaos," CNN (April 29, 2017), https: //www.cnn.com/2017/04/28/entertainment/fyre-festival-disaster-trnd/.

6. Lydia Ramsey Pflanzer, "How Elizabeth Holmes Convinced Powerful Men like Henry Kissinger, James Mattis, and George Shultz to Sit on the Board of Now Disgraced Blood-Testing Startup Theranos," *Business Insider* (March 19, 2019), https://www.businessinsider.com/theranos -former-board-members-henry-kissinger-george-shultz-james-mattis -2019–3.

7. Bobby Allyn, "Former Theranos CEO Elizabeth Holmes to Be Sentenced on Sept. 26," NPR (January 12, 2022), https://www.npr.org/2022/01/12/1072612059/former-theranos-ceo-elizabeth-holmes-to-be-sentenced-on-sept-26.

8. Thanks to Stephen Covey and his classic work, *The Seven Habits of Highly Effective People,* for this example, framework, and vocabulary.

9. G. A. Johnston, "Morals and Manners," *International Journal of Ethics* 26, no. 2 (January 1916), 201.

10. Werner Jaeger, *Paideia: The Ideals of Greek Culture*, trans. Gilbert Highet (New York: Oxford University Press: 1945), 13.

11. Amy Olberding, *The Wrong of Rudeness: Learning Modern Civility from Ancient Chinese Philosophy* (Oxford University Press: 2019).

12. Thoughtful people from Adam Smith to della Casa and others have agreed on this point about the objective ugliness of human cruelty.

13. John Kasson recounts this dynamic in his wonderful book *Rudeness & Civility: Manners in Nineteenth-Century Urban America* (Hill and Wang Publishers: 1990).

14. Ibid.

15. For an extended discussion on this problem, see John Kasson's remarkable work *Rudeness & Civility*.

16. Wing-tsit Chan, *A Source Book in Chinese Philosophy* (Princeton University Press: 1963), 790.

17. Luke 6:9.

18. Matthew 23:23–34.

4. Freedom, Democracy, and Human Flourishing

1. Winnie Hu, "New York Leads Politeness Trend? Get Outta Here!" *The New York Times* (April 16, 2006), https://www.nytimes.com/2006/04/16/nyregion/new-york-leads-politeness-trend-get-outta-here.html.

2. Ibid.

3. Ibid.

4. Matthew Tempest, "Blair Launches 'Respect' Action Plan," *The Guardian* (January 10, 2006), https://www.theguardian.com/politics/2006/jan/10/immigrationpolicy.ukcrime.

5. Dominic Casciani, "Q&A: Respect Agenda," BBC News (January 11, 2006), http://news.bbc.co.uk/2/hi/uk_news/4597378.stm.

6. "Top 5 Most Visited Countries in the World," Hudson's Global Residence Index, accessed September 20, 2022, https://globalresidenceindex.com/top-5-most-visited-country-in-the-world/#:~:text=%231%20France,country%20a%20must%20for%20travelers.

7. "Shock Horreur: Finance Minister Tells Cash-Strapped (and Perennially Rude) French to Be Nice to Tourists," *Daily Mail* (June 20, 2014), https://www.dailymail.co.uk/travel/article-2663673/France-told-nicer -visitors-boost-tourism.html.

8. Feargus O'Sullivan, "Paris Metro System Forced to Admit Parisians Act Like Jerks," Bloomberg (August 7, 2012), https://www.bloomberg .com/news/articles/2012–08–07/paris-metro-system-forced-to-admit -parisians-act-like-jerks.

9. Peter Allen, "French Admit They ARE Rude as Paris Metro Bosses Launch Poster Campaign of Hilarious Anti-social Animals Encourage 'la Civilité,'" *Daily Mail* (July 26, 2012), https://www.dailymail.co.uk /news/article-2179450/French-admit-ARE-rude-stroppy-Paris-public -transport-bosses-launch-campaign-civility.html.

10. Natalie Huet, "Parisian Official Start Politeness Campaign," Reuters (2013), https://rec.travel.europe.narkive.com/g3xmfCXG/parisian -official-start-politeness-campaign.

11. Henry Grabar, "A New Ad Campaign Asks Parisians to Be Nice to Tourists," Bloomberg (June 20, 2013), https://www.bloomberg.com/news/articles /2013–06–20/a-new-ad-campaign-asks-parisians-to-be-nice-to-tourists.

12. Ibid.

13. Peter Allen, "French Admit They ARE Rude."

14. Keith Thomas, *In Pursuit of Civility*.

15. Roger Scruton, "Real Men Have Manners," *City Journal* (Winter 2000), https://www.city-journal.org/html/real-men-have-manners-11832.html.

16. I'm indebted to Lynn Truss's *Talk to the Hand*, published by Gotham Books in 2005, for inspiring this discussion.

17. Erasmus of Rotterdam, *A Handbook on Good Manners for Children* (Preface Publishing: 2008), Introduction, 7.

18. Nathan Tarcov, *Locke's Education for Liberty* (University of Chicago Press: 1984), 137–41, 181.

19. Erasmus of Rotterdam, *A Handbook on Good Manners for Children* (Preface Publishing: 2008), 81.

20. Roger Scruton, *Beauty: A Very Short Introduction* (Oxford University Press: 2011), 81.

21. Visser, *The Rituals of Dinner*.

5. Civil Society

1. For more on the "third place" see Ray Oldenburg's 1989 book *The Great Good Place*. See also Eric Kleinenberg's *Palaces for the People*, wherein he outlines the importance of shared spaces—such as libraries—that, like

the porch, help to heal our societal divisions by fostering relationship, trust, and friendship at the individual level.

2. See John Rae's biography of Adam Smith, *Life of Adam Smith*, 1965.

3. Ronald Hamowy, "Adam Smith, Adam Ferguson, and the Division of Labour," *Economica* 35, no. 139 (August 1968), 249–259, https://www.jstor.org/stable/2552301.

4. Tunisian historian and professor Moḥammed Talbi defines *aṣabiyah* as "at one and the same time the cohesive force of the group, the conscience that it has of its own specificity and collective aspirations, and the tension that animates it and impels it ineluctably to seek power through conquest." Moḥammed Talbi, *Ibn Khaldûn: Sa Vie—Son Oeuvre* (Maison Tunisienne de l'Edition: 1973), 44.

5. Ibid.

6. Ibn Khaldun, *The Muqaddimah: An Introduction to History,* trans. Franz Rosenthal (Princeton University Press: 2015), https://ia903106.us.archive.org/22/items/etaoin/The%20Muqaddimah%20–%20An%20Introduction%20to%20History%20by%20Ibn%20Khaldun.pdf.

7. Adam Ferguson, "An Essay on the History of Civil Society," (1767), accessed September 20, 2022, https://oll.libertyfund.org/title/ferguson-an-essay-on-the-history-of-civil-society.

8. Stjepan G. Meštrović and Hélène M. Brown, "Durkheim's Concept of Anomie as Dérèglement," *Social Problems* 33, no. 2 (December 1985), 81–99, https://www-jstor-org.proxy.ulib.uits.iu.edu/stable/800554?seq=2.

9. For more on this theme, see Robert Wuthnow's 2002 book, *Loose Connections: Joining Together in America's Fragmented Communities.*

10. Students of public health find that life expectancy is highest and people are more trustful in communities. Researchers of public health have found that life expectancy is higher and more trustful in communities, but they're also more efficient. As Robert D. Putnam writes in *Bowling Alone*, "A society of a generalized reciprocity is more efficient than distrustful societies for the same reason that money is more efficient than barter."

11. Francis Fukuyama, "Social Capital, Civil Society, and Development," *Third World Quarterly* 22, no. 1 (February 2001), https://www.researchgate.net/publication/44828808_Social_capital_civil_society_and_development.

12. See Stanford sociologist Mark Granovetter's famous 1973 article "The Strength of Weak Ties" for more on this theme.

13. See Robert Putnam, *Bowling Alone* (Touchstone Books: 2001) for more on this idea.

14. See Ernst Gellner, *Conditions of Liberty: Civil Society and Its Rivals* (Penguin: 1994).

6. Equality

1. Tom Wolfe, "Pell-Mell," *The Atlantic* (November 2007), https://www
   .theatlantic.com/magazine/archive/2007/11/pell-mell/306312/.

2. See Founder's Archives: https://founders.archives.gov/documents/Jefferson
   /01–42–02–0143–0004

3. Tom Wolfe, "Pell-Mell."

4. Anthony Merry, "Merry to Hawkesbury, 6 December 1803," December
   6, 1803, F.0.-5, 41: 54–56, Great Britain, Foreign Office, https://dds-crl
   -edu.proxy01.its.virginia.edu/item/423407.

5. Benjamin Ogle Tayloe, *In Memoriam: Benjamin Ogle Tayloe* (Sherman &
   Company: 1872), 137, https://tinyurl.com/mu6k8zay.

6. Thomas Jefferson, "II. Canons of Etiquette, 12 January 1804," accessed
   September 20, 2022, https://founders.archives.gov/documents/Jefferson
   /01–42–02–0143–0003.

7. Tocqueville, *Democracy in America*, 997.

8. Nathan Robinson, "The Class System," *Current Affairs* (March 31, 2018),
   https://www.currentaffairs.org/2018/03/the-class-system/.

9. Tamar Adler, "A Manners Manifesto," *The New York Times* (March 11,
   2015), https://www.nytimes.com/2015/03/15/magazine/a-manners
   -manifesto.html.

10. For more on this, see Bee Wilson's delightful book, *Consider the Fork*.

11. "Though the truth was, I saw him not when he did it. I will suppose he
    had killed me. . . ."

12. De Benneville Randolph Keim, *Hand-book of Official and Social Etiquette
    and Public Ceremonials at Washington* (1889), 11, https://books.google
    .com/books/about/Hand_book_of_Official_and_Social_Etiquet.html
    ?id=Iag9AAAAYAAJ.

13. Ibid, 9.

7. Civil Disobedience

1. Thomas Jefferson, "Equality," *Notes on the State of Virginia* (1784), 137–43,
   162–63, https://press-pubs.uchicago.edu/founders/documents/v1ch15s28
   .html.

2. Edward Coles to Thomas Jefferson, September 26, 1814, E. Coles Papers, Princeton University Library.

3. Thomas Jefferson, probably trying to quote this famous line from memory, references Aeneid 2.508–510, but misquotes it. Virgil's lines are
   "Trementibus aeuo circumdat nequiquam umeris et inutile ferrum cingitur."

4. For more on this idea, see Burton Zwiebach's *Civility and Disobedience*
   (Cambridge University Press: 1975), 153.

5. John Stuart Mill, *On Liberty*, 131.

6. *On Liberty*: "The human faculties of perception, judgment, discriminative feeling, mental activity, and even moral preference, are exercised only in making a choice. He who does anything because it is the custom, makes no choice."

7. M. K. Gandhi, *Satyagraha in South Africa* (Desai Navajivan Publishing House: 1968), 109–10.

8. Mahatma Gandhi, *All Men Are Brothers* (Desai Navajivan Publishing House: 1958).

9. Martin Luther King, Jr., *The Autobiography of Martin Luther King, Jr.*, ed. Clayborne Carson (Warner Books: 1998), 23–24.

10. "Letter from Birmingham Jail," African Studies Center, University of Pennsylvania, accessed September 20, 2022, https://www.africa.upenn .edu/Articles_Gen/Letter_Birmingham.html.

11. "John Brown's Raid on Harpers Ferry," History.com, accessed September 20, 2022, https://www.history.com/this-day-in-history/john -browns-raid-on-harpers-ferry.

12. Willis Mason West, *American History and Government* (Allyn & Bacon: 1913), 539, https://books.google.com/books?id=W3FHAAAAIAAJ &pg=PA539&lpg=PA539&dq=I+will+be+as+harsh+as+truth,+and+as+ uncompromising+as+justice&source=bl&ots=ZO9iKb-ITJ&sig=Dmlo fdTQK-xq_-oCK5zHRQwsxa4&hl=en&sa=X&ved=0ahUKEwiv4rT 6rPrbAhWJ5oMKHX9bCkc4FBDoAQgzMAI#v=onepage&q=I%20 will%20be%20as%20harsh%20as%20truth%2C%20and%20as%20un- compromising%20as%20justice&f=false.

13. "(1857) Frederick Douglass," BlackPast (January 27, 2005), https:// www.blackpast.org/african-american-history/1857-frederick-douglass -if-there-no-struggle-there-no-progress/.

14. David Geggus, ed. trans., *The Haitian Revolution: A Documentary History* (Hackett Publishing Company: 2014).

15. Even with all he accomplished in Illinois, Coles never stopped working to end slavery in his home state of Virginia. In one instance, later in their lives, Coles visited Madison and left thinking he had persuaded Madison to free his slaves upon his death. He was disappointed to learn that Madison had instead left them to Dolley. George Washington was the only president to free all his slaves upon death, though during his lifetime he determinedly maintained possession.

8. Polarization and Tolerance

1. I viewed many hours of C-SPAN footage from before and after the series of civility summits for this narrative: "Bipartisan Congressional Retreat Preview," C-SPAN (February 11, 1997), https://www.c-span.org/video /?78783–1/bipartisan-congressional-retreat-preview; and after the 1997 retreat: "Bipartisan Congressional Retreat," C-SPAN (March 11, 1997), https://www.c-span.org/video/?79562–1/bipartisan-congressional-retreat.

2. David S. Broder, "The Rediscovery of Civility," *The Washington Post* (March 30, 1997), https://www.washingtonpost.com/archive/opinions/1997/03/30 /the-rediscovery-of-civility/357e8eb7–8398–430b-b1bb-003524366855/.

3. For a more in-depth analysis of the effects of these civility initiatives in Congress, see Kathleen Hall Jamieson's report, accessed here: https: //cdn.annenbergpublicpolicycenter.org/Downloads/Civility/Old%20re-ports/Civility%20report%20March%201998.pdf.

4. Braver Angels was originally named *Better* Angels, a nod to Abraham Lincoln's First Inaugural Address, but changed their name to Braver Angels in 2019 after The Better Angels Society—which is associated with Ken Burns's documentary films—threatened legal action if they did not change their name.

5. For a deeper exploration of the underlying ideas of Braver Angels Debates, written by Braver Angels Debates creator April Lawson, see "Building Trust Across the Political Divide: The Surprising Bridge of Conflict," Comment Magazine (January 21, 2021), https://www.cardus .ca/comment/article/building-trust-across-the-political-divide/.

6. Juliet Eilperin, "Frayed House Prepares for its Civility Camp," *The Washington Post* (February 25, 1999), https://www.washingtonpost .com/archive/politics/1999/02/25/frayed-house-prepares-for-its-civility -camp/d036ab87–63a0–4001-b598-c9d98e1dfc54/.

7. For the press conference given before the 1999 civility summit, see the C-SPAN archive: "Bipartisan Congressional Retreat," C-SPAN (February 24, 1999), https://www.c-span.org/video/?120921–1/bipartisan -congressional-retreat.

8. "Charles Kincaid Trial: 1891," Encyclopedia.com, accessed September 20, 2022, https://www.encyclopedia.com/law/law-magazines/charles -kincaid-trial-1891.

9. Aristotle discusses the virtues of friendship throughout his work, but for extended explorations of friendship, see his *Nicomachean Ethics*, Book VIII, and Book VII of his *Ethics*.

10. For more on the role of institutions in a free society, see Yuval Levin's 2020 book, *A Time to Build: From Family and Community to Congress and the Campus, How Recommitting to Our Institutions Can Revive the American Dream.*

9. Citizenship in a Digital Age

1. H. Beverley, *Report on the Census of Bengal* (Bengal Secretariat Press: 1872), 160.

   David Livingstone, *Missionary Travels and Researches in South Africa* (Harper & Brothers: 1858), 567.

2. For more on this idea, see Cheshire Calhoun's "The Virtue of Civility," *Philosophy and Public Affairs* 29, no. 3 (2000).

3. For more on this topic, see *The Squeaky Wheel* by Guy Winch (Walker and Company: 2011).

10. Hospitality

1. Fiona Whelan, *The Making of Manners and Morals in Twelfth-Century England: The Book of the Civilised Man* (Routledge, 2017.)

11. Education

1. See Cicero's *De re Publica (On the Republic)* for a primary source on *humanitas*.

2. James Hankins, "The Forgotten Virtue," *First Things* (December 2018). ("The humanist theory of civility and *humanitas* linked civil conduct tightly with character.")

12. Misplaced Meaning and Forgiveness

1. For more on this thesis see Robert Talisse's book *Overdoing Democracy: Why We Must Put Politics in its Place* (Oxford University Press: 2019). Here, he explains why aiming for "better" politics will never be a viable or permanent solution because politics is the problem in the first place.

2. Alex Beam, *A Great Idea at the Time* (PublicAffairs: 2008), 196.

3. C. S. Lewis observed this phenomenon, affirming that aiming for happiness alone as an end is insufficient. Echoing Christ's words found in the New Testament book of Matt. 6:33—"But seek ye first the kingdom of God, and his righteousness; and all these things shall be added unto you"—Lewis wrote in his *Mere Christianity*, "Aim at Heaven and you will get Earth 'thrown in': aim at Earth and you will get neither."

4. Dacher Keltner, "Why Do We Feel Awe?," *Greater Good Magazine* (May 10, 2016), https://greatergood.berkeley.edu/article/item/why_do_we_feel_awe.

5. For more on Murdoch's idea of unselfing, see her book *The Sovereignty of Good* (Routledge: 2001).

6. Nicholas Epley, "The Surprising Power of the Social Outreach," *Scientific American* (May 15, 2020), https://blogs.scientificamerican.com /observations/the-surprising-power-of-social-outreach/.

Index